Understand the Middle East (since 1945)

Stewart Ross

For UK order enquiries: please contact Bookpoint Ltd, 130 Milton Park, Abingdon, Oxon OX14 4SB. *Telephone:* +44 (0) 1235 827720. Fax: +44 (0) 1235 400454. Lines are open 09.00–17.00, Monday to Saturday, with a 24-hour message answering service. Details about our titles and how to order are available at www.teachyourself.com

For USA order enquiries: please contact McGraw-Hill Customer Services, PO Box 545, Blacklick, OH 43004-0545, USA. Telephone: 1-800-722-4726. Fax: 1-614-755-5645.

For Canada order enquiries: please contact McGraw-Hill Ryerson Ltd, 300 Water St, Whitby, Ontario L1N 9B6, Canada. Telephone: 905 430 5000. Fax: 905 430 5020.

Long renowned as the authoritative source for self-guided learning – with more than 50 million copies sold worldwide – the **Teach Yourself** series includes over 500 titles in the fields of languages, crafts, hobbies, business, computing and education.

British Library Cataloguing in Publication Data: a catalogue record for this title is available from the British Library.

Library of Congress Catalog Card Number: on file.

First published in UK 2004 by Hodder Education, part of Hachette UK, 338 Euston Road, London NW1 3BH.

First published in US 2004 by The McGraw-Hill Companies, Inc.

This edition published 2010.

Previously published as *Teach Yourself the Middle East since 1945*

The **Teach Yourself** name is a registered trade mark of Hodder Headline.

Typeset by MPS Limited, a Macmillan Company.

Printed in Great Britain for Hodder Education, an Hachette UK Company, 338 Euston Road, London NW1 3BH, by CPI Cox & Wyman, Reading, Berkshire RG1 8EX.

The publisher has used its best endeavours to ensure that the URLs for external websites referred to in this book are correct and active at the time of going to press. However, the publisher and the author have no responsibility for the websites and can make no guarantee that a site will remain live or that the content will remain relevant, decent or appropriate.

Hachette UK's policy is to use papers that are natural, renewable and recyclable products and made from wood grown in sustainable forests. The logging and manufacturing processes are expected to conform to the environmental regulations of the country of origin.

Impression number   10 9 8 7 6 5 4 3 2
Year   2014 2013 2012 2011

Acknowledgements

The author would like to express his sincere thanks to Dr Ghazwan S. Boutros, Piers Wilkinson and Mohammed Abdelhadi for their most useful help and advice during the writing of the various editions of this book.

Credits

Front cover: © Judith Collins/Alamy

Back cover: © Jakub Semeniuk/iStockphoto.com, © Royalty-Free/Corbis, © agencyby/iStockphoto.com, © Andy Cook/iStockphoto.com, © Christopher Ewing/iStockphoto.com, © zebicho–Fotolia.com, © Geoffrey Holman/iStockphoto.com, © Photodisc/Getty Images, © James C. Pruitt/iStockphoto.com, © Mohamed Saber–Fotolia.com

Contents

Meet the author

Welcome to *Understand the Middle East (since 1945)*!

While a number of friends said I was mad to attempt a short
summary of the complex recent history of so controversial a region
as the Middle East, sufficient readers made kind comments about
the first two editions of this book for me to believe that the taxing
task was worthwhile. My aim in this third edition, as in the previous
ones, is to provide the student and general reader with a clear,
unbiased, up-to-date and readable account of events in what has
perhaps been the most important region of the world over the last
60 or so years. I hope that once readers have finished this book, the
daily news they hear or read will make just a little more sense and,
if they are students, they will be in a better position to move on
to further studies.

Inevitably, much of what follows is current affairs rather than
history. Many topics are highly controversial, evoking strong
passions and, on occasion, raw and painful memories. I have done
my level best to be objective on all issues, consulting widely
and refraining from ill-considered judgement. Nevertheless,
my interpretations will not always please everyone: no comment
on the Middle East ever does. Please accept, though, that I write
simply to inform. Opinion I leave to the reader.

Stewart Ross, 2010

Only got a minute?

Recently, the Middle East has rarely been out of the headlines. The strategically invaluable but troubled region has faced massive challenges both internally and externally generated.

Population increase and urbanization brought unprecedented social and economic upheaval. Water supply became a major issue and tensions arose between the fabulously wealthy oil- and gas-producing nations of the Gulf and states less blessed with natural resources. People were torn between an espousal of modernity, in the form of Western liberal capitalism, and maintaining their heritage, often expressed through a resurgent Islam.

Political problems further unsettled the region. Difficulties included the establishment of the new state of Israel in Palestine, and nation-building following the withdrawal of Britain and France. Inherited and imposed constitutions generally gave way to authoritarian rule. In Iraq, this produced the tyranny of Saddam Hussein and the horrific Iran–Iraq War (1980–8). By 2000, elements of democracy and respect for human rights were taking root across the region. The remarkable survival of a form of representative government in Lebanon, despite a debilitating civil war, was an inspiration to others seeking fairer regimes.

Because of their vital supplies of oil and gas, and the West's determination to maintain the State of Israel, the states of the Middle East were subjected to a range of outside influences. These included wooing (through aid and arms supply) by both sides in the Cold War, clandestine interference in domestic government, and armed intervention. While maintaining military bases and training local forces, Western powers also conducted overt, post-colonial operations in Egypt, Lebanon, Kuwait, Iraq, Yemen and Iran.

Four major wars were also fought between Israel and her Palestinian-backing Arab neighbours in 1948–9, 1956, 1967 and 1973. Despite Israeli victories, they did nothing to solve the problems arising from the unilateral establishment of Israel in 1948.

5 Only got five minutes?

Few regions of the world have undergone greater change since the end of the Second World War than the Middle East. Rarely out of the headlines, it has struggled to cope with huge demographic, social and economic change as well as a fierce resurgence of Islam.

These developments took place within territories that, in most cases, were simultaneously crystallizing into modern nation states. Many of these had been dreamed up by European colonial powers, and one – Israel – was imposed on the region against the wishes of the majority of inhabitants. The situation was further complicated by external intervention, especially during the Cold War (1947–90). Old conurbations like Cairo swelled to gigantic proportions, while tiny settlements such as Riyadh and Dubai expanded into gleaming new cities. Water supply became a major issue, notably around Lake Tiberias and the Jordan Valley. Tensions also arose between the fabulously wealthy oil- and gas-producing nations of the Gulf (e.g. Saudi Arabia and Kuwait) and states not so blessed with natural resources (e.g. Yemen and Syria). Patterns of life that had remained little changed for centuries were suddenly broken, threatening the traditional solidarity of families, clans, sects and regions.

The peoples of the Middle East were torn between an espousal of modernity, in the form of Western liberal capitalism and its glittering manifestations, and holding fast to their ancient heritage. The result was sometimes bizarre – Dior beneath the burka – and occasionally, as when it fed the blind rage of Islamist terrorism, terrifying.

Democracy developed slowly, although by the twenty-first century many administrations were becoming more representative of the people. Versions of democracy survived in Israel and in Lebanon despite a fearful civil war (1975–90). Iran developed a form of Islamic representation from 1979 onwards and the US established elected government in Iraq after conquering the country in 2003–4. Elsewhere, as in Kuwait and even in Saudi Arabia, there was an increased willingness to allow elected consultative assemblies, although executive power normally remained in the hands of hereditary monarchs or self-appointed dictators.

War scarred much of the history of the Middle East after 1945. The establishment of Israel in 1948 was followed by the First Arab–Israeli War. A second followed in 1956, Britain and France fought with Israel, and a third and fourth in 1967 and 1973. All demonstrated the overwhelming superiority of the Israeli military; its rapid victory in the Six Day War of 1967 was one of the most remarkable campaigns of modern times. Israeli forces also made large-scale incursions into Lebanon in 1978, 1982 and 2006.

By far the bloodiest and bitterest war was fought between Iran and Iraq, 1980–8, ostensibly over disputed territory at the head of the Persian Gulf. Iraq was involved in two other large-scale conflicts. In 1990–1 Iraqi forces invaded Kuwait and were driven out by a UN-backed coalition. The second and much more controversial war began in 2003 with a US-led invasion of Iraq. The reasons for this campaign appeared to stem somewhat tendentiously from the USA's response to the suicide attacks by Middle Eastern extremists on New York and Washington in 2001.

A great deal of the region's instability arose from the foundation of Israel in the former mandate of Palestine in 1948, and subsequent Israeli expansion through conquest. The Palestinians, deprived of the country planned for them by the United Nations, became a stateless people. Their grievances found expression in the formation of the Palestine Liberation Organization and in many acts of violence against Israel. The Israelis invariably responded with disproportionate force. By the 1980s, the Palestinian cause had been espoused by Islamists, often with Iranian backing. The most remarkable manifestations of Palestinian misery were two anti-occupation uprisings, the Intifadas (1987–93 and 2000–4). Small steps forward were taken too; the establishment of an elected Palestinian Authority (1994), peace treaties with Israel and Egypt (1978) and Jordan (1994), and Israeli withdrawal from Gaza (2005). Nevertheless, the Israeli–Palestinian impasse is hardly nearer settlement in 2010 than 50 years previously.

10 Only got ten minutes?

There is no agreed definition of the term 'Middle East', that rich, volatile, highly important region where three continents meet and where the old and the new lie so starkly side by side. This brief summary focuses on the Arabian peninsula, Iran, Kuwait, Iraq, Syria, Lebanon, Jordan, Israel-Palestine and Egypt.

For most of the states of the Middle East, the period following the Second World War was one of swift and dramatic transformation in demography, politics, society and economics. Rarely out of the headlines, almost all governments struggled to cope with the challenges they faced. Latterly, the resurgence of militant Islam added a new level of passionate complexity to the situation.

These developments took place within territories that, in most cases, were simultaneously crystallizing into modern nation states. Many had been dreamed up by European colonial powers. The French, for example, had created Syria and Lebanon out of regions of the defunct Ottoman Empire; Britain had done the same with Iraq, Jordan and Palestine. The latter was then thrown into chaos by the emergence of the State of Israel, imposed on the area by the UN against the wishes of many inhabitants.

The situation in the region was further complicated by external intervention, especially during the era of the East–West Cold War (1947–90). The US and wealthy European states, for instance, supported Israel as a bastion against the influence of Soviet communism. There was evidence, too, of governments being toppled with the clandestine aid of Western secret services.

Old cities like Cairo swelled into gigantic conurbations, while tiny settlements such as Riyadh and Dubai expanded into gleaming new cities. Water supply became a major issue, notably around Lake Tiberias and the Jordan Valley where Israel became dependent upon water collected in regions it had occupied by force.

Tensions also arose between the fabulously wealthy oil- and gas-producing nations of the Gulf and states not so blessed, like Yemen and Syria. Fighting along the border between Saudi Arabia and Yemen was a good example. Patterns of life little changed for centuries were suddenly broken, threatening the traditional solidarity of families, clans, sects and regions. In desert areas, the nomadic way of life was disappearing fast.

Faced with such stresses, the peoples of the Middle East were torn between an espousal of modernity, in the form of Western liberal capitalism and its thousand and one glittering manifestations, and holding fast to their ancient heritage. The result was sometimes bizarre – Dior beneath the burka – and occasionally, as when it fed the blind rage of Islamist terrorism, terrifying.

From the 1960s onwards, it was Middle Eastern terrorism that most forcibly brought the region to people's attention. First it was the hijackings, bombings and assassinations of Palestinian groups, notably the attack on the Munich Olympics (1972); then came the wave of Islamist incidents, culminating in the Al Qaeda bombings of New York and other cities in the early years of the twenty-first century.

The Western-style democracies set up by Britain and France were in most cases short-lived. Dictatorships of varying degrees of harshness appeared in Egypt, Syria and Iraq. Elsewhere, absolutist monarchy was normally the form of government. In Jordan and some Gulf states, regimes were generally relatively benevolent.

In such difficult circumstances, democracy developed slowly. Nevertheless, by the twenty-first century many administrations had became more representative of the people. Versions of democracy survived in Israel and, despite a fearful civil war that came close to tearing the country apart (1975–90), in Lebanon.

After the people had overthrown the highly unpopular and absolutist Shah Pahlavi in 1979, Iran developed an Islamic republic that incorporated some carefully controlled elected representation.

The USA worked with the newly created Iraqi government to establish elected government from 2004 onwards. Elsewhere, as in Kuwait and even Saudi Arabia, there was an increase in willingness to allow elected consultative assemblies, although executive power normally remained in the hands of hereditary monarchs or self-appointed dictators.

War scarred much of the history of the Middle East after 1945. The First Arab–Israeli War (1948–9) followed the establishment of the State of Israel and resulted in the carving up of the proposed Palestinian state. A second Arab–Israeli War (1956) saw Israel, fighting against Egypt in a bizarre neo-colonial alliance with Britain and France, conquer the Sinai peninsula, although it was later obliged to return gains. This was not the case in the Six Day War (1967). In one of the most remarkable campaigns of modern times, Israel defeated Egypt, Syria and Jordan, and retained control over the Golan Heights on its frontier with Syria, the Gaza Strip along the Mediterranean coast, the Sinai, and the West Bank of the River Jordan.

A fourth Arab–Israeli War (1973) confirmed Israel's overwhelming military superiority, although initial reverses led to it agreeing a peace deal with Egypt (Camp David, 1978). Other Israeli military operations, notably its large-scale incursions into Lebanon in 1978, 1982 and 2006, and into Gaza in 2008–9, won more disapproval than respect because by now the country was regarded worldwide as the regional bully rather than the target of hostile neighbours. Israel, itself a nuclear power, secretly attacked nuclear installations within Iraq and Syria.

By far the bloodiest and bitterest war was fought between Iran and Iraq in 1980–8, ostensibly over disputed territory at the head of the Persian Gulf. The conflict once again demonstrated the influence of the US: under the incompetent overall command of the dictator Saddam Hussein, the Iraqi armed forces would probably have collapsed before the fanatical assaults of Islamist Iran if the US had not provided invaluable aid and strategic surveillance information. The war cost 1 million lives.

Iraq was involved in two other large-scale conflicts. The first occurred in 1990–1 when its forces invaded Kuwait and were driven out by a UN-backed coalition in which the US was the major partner. The victors stopped short of toppling Saddam Hussein.

The second and much more controversial war began in 2003 with another US-led invasion of Iraq. This time there was no holding back and Hussein's regime fell. The reasons for the campaign appeared to stem – albeit somewhat tendentiously – from the USA's response to the suicide attacks by Middle Eastern extremists on New York and Washington in 2001. Tragically, the US had prepared far more assiduously for the war than for post-war reconstruction of the ruined, leaderless country. Years of 'insurgency' followed in which hundreds of thousands died and millions fled. By 2010, however, as US troops finally prepared to leave Iraq, there was a chance that they might have left a working democracy.

A great deal of the region's instability arose out of the foundation of Israel in the former mandate of Palestine, and subsequent Israeli expansion through conquest that left the Palestinians stateless. Their grievances found expression in the formation of the Palestine Liberation Organization and many acts of violence against Israel and its allies. The Israelis invariably responded with disproportionate force. Throughout much of this period, the volatile, charismatic Yasser Arafat, head of Fatah, was the undisputed leader of the Palestinian people.

By the 1980s, the Palestinian cause had been espoused by Islamists, often with Iranian and Syrian backing. The new influence manifested itself in two groups, the Palestinian Hamas and the Lebanese Hezbollah. Both professed an unwillingness to compromise with Israel, a stance that latterly put them at odds with Fatah.

The most remarkable manifestations of Palestinian misery were two anti-occupation uprisings, known as the Intifadas (1987–93 and 2000–4). The first was very much a spontaneous anti-Israeli outburst; the second was more orchestrated, and more bloody.

Despite the ongoing violence, small steps were taken to reconcile the Israeli and Palestinian positions. Jordan followed Egypt's example and made a formal treaty with Israel in 1994. The same year saw the Oslo Accords pave the way towards an independent Palestine with the creation of an elected Palestinian National Authority. Eleven years later, Israel withdrew from its settlements in Gaza. It retained the Golan and much of the West Bank, however, and by 2010 the Israeli–Palestinian impasse seemed hardly any nearer settlement than it had been 50 years previously.

1

The crossroads of the world

This chapter will cover:
- *definitions of the Middle East*
- *the region's physical geography*
- *its diverse racial and social mix*
- *the religions of the Middle East.*

What is the Middle East?

Mick Jackson's award-winning film for television *Threads* (BBC, 1984), exploring the effects of nuclear war on Western civilization, was criticized in some circles as overly fanciful. One of the film's principal assumptions, however, was never challenged: the Third World War would be sparked by events in the Middle East. Jackson's assertion is as alarmingly valid today as it was two-and-a-half decades ago.

Why?

The roots of today's conflict and instability in the Middle East twist deep into the soil of history, far beyond the compass of this book, to Biblical times. One may even speculate whether they lie deeper still, in the prehistoric millennia when the great continents were formed. For the Middle East is the only region on earth where three continents meet. Here, in a gigantic crossroads between Europe, Asia and Africa, peoples from East, West, North and South have come together over the centuries to trade, exchange views, worship – and make war.

Before going further, we need to be clear about our terms. Defining the 'Middle East' is fraught with difficulty because, at the simplest level, 'east' and 'west' are relative to one's vantage point: speaking literally, India is Egypt's 'middle east', and so on. The US State department and some United Nations bodies, sticking to an older, more logical and geographically precise stance than most, prefer 'Near East' for the region lying between the Mediterranean Sea and the Indian Ocean. But this does not avoid another problem.

As many scholars have pointed out, to English speakers 'the East' remains a value-laden expression. Australians, inhabitants of the East but European-American in culture, are traditionally made honorary Westerners. 'Middle East' is a European phrase whose current usage comes from the Second World War command structure of the British Army. It is far from ideal to persevere with a label which, to some minds, still carries imperialist overtones. There is, however, no widely accepted alternative.

Finally, commentators rarely agree on a precise geographical definition of the Middle East. This book takes in Lebanon, Palestine/Israel and Egypt along the eastern seaboard of the Mediterranean, Syria and Jordan further inland, Iraq and Iran bordering the Persian Gulf, and the Arabian peninsular states of Saudi Arabia, Yemen, Oman, the United Arab Emirates (UAE) and Kuwait. A broader approach might embrace Greece, all the Arab states of North Africa, the Sudan, Afghanistan, Cyprus and Turkey. Our narrower definition excludes – with one exception – all states that play in the Union European Football Association (UEFA) Champion's League football competition or who participate in the Eurovision Song Contest. The exception is Israel. But as we will see, Israel is often the odd one out in Middle Eastern affairs.

The geography of the Middle East

SEAWAYS

Seen from space, the Middle East is largely a patchwork of browns and yellows within blue borders. This simplified view reveals basic truths about the region's history. The prevalent dun colour of the land reminds us that much of it is barren and inhospitable, making the few fertile areas – the splashes of green amid the swathes of beige – all the more valuable and sought after. A great deal of Middle Eastern turmoil since the ending of the Second World War has been about who controls this favoured terrain.

The blue areas are, of course, the sea. Here again simple geography teaches a vital lesson. The multiplicity and complexity of the region's seaways emphasize their importance to world trade. In 1945 they were perhaps even more important than today. The reason was the Suez Canal, the 163 km (101 mile) link between the Mediterranean and the Red Sea constructed with great difficulty almost 150 years ago by the remarkable French engineer Ferdinand de Lesseps. Ever since its completion in November 1869, the canal has offered virtually all vessels a fuel- and time-saving short cut on the journey between Europe and Asia. It was in the interest of all nations with ambitions of world influence to see that such a vital waterway, described by the British Prime Minister Anthony Eden as 'Britain's windpipe', remained safe and open to all.

....
Insight
As the maximum permitted draft for vessels using the Suez Canal is 19 m (62 ft), some supertankers offload part of their cargo for passage through the canal and then reload at the other end. Operations are in hand (2010) to deepen the canal to make it accessible to virtually all shipping.
....

At the northern end of the Suez Canal lies the Mediterranean, the sea that joins the Middle East to Europe, the Atlantic and the Americas. This alone gives it key strategic importance. At the close of the Second World War this importance was paramount because the eastern Mediterranean, via the Dardanelles and the Black Sea, was the Soviet Union's only southerly link with the world's oceans.

Leaving the Suez Canal at its southern end, the great majority of ships sail down the Gulf of Suez, through the steamy Red Sea and into the Indian Ocean. From here they have access to any number of destinations in the eastern hemisphere. One or two, however, may take an altogether different course, turning north-east after leaving the Suez gulf and entering the narrower Gulf of Aqaba through the Strait of Tiran. At its northern end lie two towns, Aqaba and Eilat. In 1945 this was also the meeting point of three frontiers, making it a likely trouble spot.

Another such unstable area was encountered by ships that chose to bear to port (left) after passing the British base at Aden and followed the Arabian coastline until a seaway appeared in the north-west. This is the Arabian (or Persian, depending on one's politics or education) Gulf, a strip of sea dividing Arabia from Iran and giving the states along its shores access to the wider world. Today, as they have done for nigh on a century, tanker after tanker passes through its narrow neck at the Straits of Hormuz laden with oil and gas for the world's vehicles, industries and homes.

For its seaways alone, in 1945 the Middle East was a region of supreme strategic importance.

RIVERS AND LAKES

The Middle East is arid. Rainfall is generally slight and erratic; in the inland desert areas it rarely exceeds 80 mm (5 inches) a year. The entire Arabian peninsula contains only one river that flows all the year round. Throughout the region life-sustaining water is found mostly underground, emerging on the surface only in oases or through bore holes. The exceptions – and they are mighty exceptions – are three river systems. These are the Nile in North Africa, the River Jordan (including the Sea of Galilee, also known as Lake Galilee and Lake Tiberias) running parallel to the eastern shore of the Mediterranean, and the Tigris-Euphrates. This last rises in Turkey and flows through Syria and Iraq to the head of the Persian Gulf.

Many millennia ago these broad rivers were the umbilical cords of our human civilization. Beside their waters first appeared the most significant of all human achievements: farming, cities, law, the wheel and writing – the rest, one might say, has been mere footnotes. Be that as it may, the cords were cut long ago and the footnotes are now our major concern.

The magnificent heritage of the river civilizations of Mesopotamia and ancient Egypt serves as an important reminder to those raised in other cultures never to underestimate or take for granted the peoples of this fertile crescent. They may not be at the forefront of today's technology, but they are acutely aware that they were planting crops and erecting awe-inspiring palaces when the rest of the world was eking out a living by scavenging and hunting. Furthermore, as we shall see (pages 12–17), these people gave the world the three great monotheistic religious faiths whose tenets underpin much of the morality of the modern world. It is a heritage of which the region is justly proud, and its people do not take kindly to outsiders telling them – or even directing them – how to manage their own affairs.

Politically speaking, a river is either a uniting force or a boundary. In the case of the Nile and the Tigris-Euphrates it is the former, the very lifeblood and *raison d'être* of both Egypt and Iraq. Now, as in 1945, the Jordan is somewhat different. It had not always been so. Like the Nile, in Biblical times the Jordan had been a unifying artery through a dry land. Dreamers and idealists hope that one day it will serve the same purpose again.

The Jordan is also geographically unlike the region's other two great waterways in that it does not reach the open sea. Indeed, it is the furthest below sea level (400 m/1,300 feet at its southern end) of any river in the world. It rises on the slopes of Mount Hermon

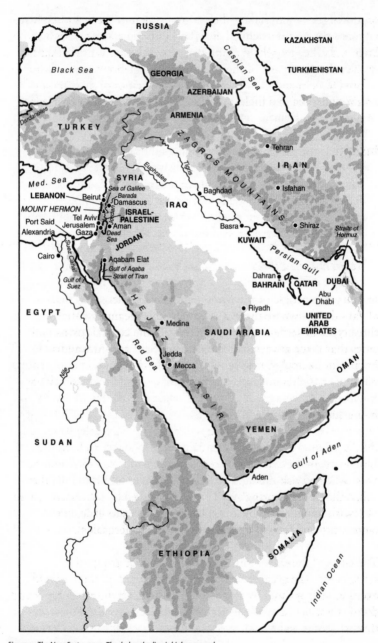

Figure 1.1 The Near East c. 2010. The darker shading is higher ground.

on the borders of Syria and Lebanon, flows into the Sea of Galilee, where it pauses for a while before meandering south through a huge rift valley to perish, along with any fish that venture that far, in the salty graveyard of the Dead Sea. The Hebrew author who located Sodom and Gomorrah, the biblical cities of infertile sin, on the shores of this lifeless expanse was not without a grim sense of humour.

Insight

As knowledge of the common Jewish-Christian-Islamic heritage is essential for understanding today's Middle East, readers are advised to develop at least a nodding acquaintance with the traditional tales found in the Old Testament and the Koran.

TOWNS AND CITIES

In 1945, the people of the Middle East lived where they had always done – where there was water. This meant essentially three types of settlement. First there were the coastal towns and cities that made money from trade (Port Said and Alexandria in Egypt, for example), fishing (Gaza in Palestine) and, in a few cases, pilgrimage (Jedda in Saudi Arabia). Many were small, somewhat run down and hampered by poor transport links inland. An interesting exception was the historic Palestinian port of Jaffa, at one time or another governed by ancient Egyptians, the Israelites, the Assyrians, Alexander the Great, the Turks and Richard the Lionheart. In the early twentieth century, its history took another twist when Jewish immigrants founded a new suburb which they called the 'Hill of Spring', or Tel Aviv. Swelled by successive waves of Jewish immigrants, by 1945 Tel Aviv-Jaffa was Palestine's largest city and second in importance only to Jerusalem.

The cities of the rivers formed another distinct group of settlements. The greatest were Cairo and Baghdad, thriving and exciting metropolises by any standards, with all the advantages and disadvantages of city life. Perhaps we should also add Damascus to this list as it draws water from the River Barada before the stream disappears again into the desert. The Syrian capital is probably the world's oldest continuously inhabited settlement.

The river cities of Iran included several in the west athwart waters that flowed into the Persian Gulf, and three ancient capitals. These were Shiraz, famous for its wine, gardens and poets, Isfahan, the city of azure mosques, and Tehran, where the 'Big Three' of Stalin, Roosevelt and Churchill gathered in the latter stages of the Second World War to hammer out a post-war division of the spoils.

The third group of settlements was the oases. Into this category came some of the great cities of the early twenty-first century, particularly the Saudi capital of Riyadh and the Jordanian capital of Aman (the 'royal David's city' of the Christmas carol). In 1945, both were pale shadows of what they were to become. Riyadh, in particular, was little more than a straggle of mudbrick houses, mosques and tatty, ramshackle palaces set about a confluence of stony wadis (dry river beds that run only occasionally). Far more important were the Muslim holy cities of Mecca and Medina, both a fair distance from the Red Sea and some height above sea level.

Peoples and societies

ARAB NATIONALISM

The Middle East is widely associated with the word 'Arab'. This, unfortunately, adds little to our understanding of the region. Before the emergence of Islam almost 1,400 years ago, an Arab was someone, almost certainly a nomad, who lived on the Arabian peninsula. Around them dwelt such varied Semitic peoples as Syrians, Persians, Egyptians, Jews, Babylonians and so forth, all speaking their own languages. With Islam the situation became more complex because Arabic, the language of the Arabian peninsula and now the Koran, became the formal language of much of the Middle East. This has left us with only one reasonably coherent definition of an Arab: someone who speaks the Arabic language.

In the second half of the nineteenth century, nationalism burned bright across Europe. As well as forging the German and Italian nations, it rattled the British in Ireland and helped create a host of small but fiercely patriotic states in the Balkans. The reverberations were felt in the Middle East, too, where from the 1860s onwards, Arab intellectuals began to talk of an Arab nation. The romantic concept rested on three legs – two historical, one linguistic. The first was the shared past of the people who had spread Islam; the second the common heritage of an empire (the Caliphate) that at its height had been larger than that of the Romans; and the third a common language. The Arab 'awakening' found its first voices in literary and scientific societies. One of its earliest focal points was the Syrian Protestant College of Beirut, later to become the American University of that city. As we shall see in the next chapter, during the First World War, Arab nationalism moved into the political sphere when Arabs helped the Allies dismantle the empire of the Ottoman Turks which had previously encompassed all Arab lands.

By the 1920s, Arab nationalism was going nowhere. It was increasingly in competition with the individual nationalisms of the Egyptians, Iraqis, Syrians, Jordanians, Lebanese, Saudis and others. Politicians and poets of the time – like the Iraqi dictator Saddam Hussein in more recent years – liked to talk of Pan-Arabism, a coming together of all Arabic-speaking peoples, but no individual or group emerged as a focal point around which they might coalesce. The concept was still there in 1945, but it was no nearer realization than it had been at the beginning of the century.

DIVERSITY

Anyone who has travelled across the Middle East will be instantly aware why Arab nationalism has made so little headway. The majority of people might understand the same holy Koranic language, but the local variations used in everyday life by Arabic speakers are as numerous today as they were 50 years ago. Even something simple like the numbers one to ten sound very different in the mouths of, say, Lebanese, Saudis and Egyptians. It is not just a matter of accent, either. Common words and phrases also vary widely. Not only that, but each speaker normally insists that their dialect is closest to the Koranic original. Consequently, to adapt a phrase often used about the Americans and the British, the Arabs are a people divided by a common language.

Insight

Just one simple example of how Arabic can vary from place to place: in Arabia the number three (3) is pronounced 'thalatha', while the Lebanese use 'tlété'. Arab friends assure me that they can tell where Arabic speakers are from the moment they open their mouths!

Shared ethnic ancestry is not an essential component of nationalism, but it might help. Here again Arab nationalism ran into problems. Although the majority of the peoples of the Middle East were originally Semitic, over the millennia any vestige of racial exclusivity – an unpleasant concept at the best of times – had totally disappeared. This is backed up by a glance at the figurative art of the ancient Egyptians: their land was evidently populated by a broad racial mix thousands of years ago.

The situation at the close of the Second World War was further complicated by the existence of numerous Middle Eastern groups who did not regard themselves as Arab. The largest in number were the Farsi-speaking Iranians, heirs to a very different culture from much of the rest of the region. Even within Iran itself there was a host of separate tribes, languages and dialects. Iraq, with its sizeable population of Kurds, was similarly diverse. In 1914, Baghdad had the largest concentration of Jews in the entire Middle East. Other cultural and linguistic minorities scattered across the region included Armenians, Turks, Nubians and Greeks. Claiming the right to establish a separate state of their own, by far the most troublesome minority were the Jews of Palestine.

Diversity was as much social as racial and linguistic. In many parts of the region, structures of society that had lasted for centuries were still largely intact. With some exceptions, at the basic level it took the form of the traditional family headed by the father-husband. This patriarchal pattern was repeated in the tribe, clan, or extended family, giving society a semi-feudal structure of small, highly independent units. One feature of this fragmented and very personal arrangement was that local loyalty was usually stronger than loyalty to the state or its government. Indeed, as we shall see in Chapter 2, in several areas the concept of the nation state was only just beginning to take hold. Even in the twenty-first century, it was still competing with more traditional allegiances. For example, the Iraqi regime of Saddam Hussein relied heavily on members of his clan, the Bejat, and their tribal allies around the town of Tikrit.

The division between town and countryside – house dwellers and tent dwellers – had long been another pronounced feature of the region. During the twentieth century, it tended to accentuate as the gap between lifestyles changed. Western influences – cars, dress, social customs, liberal education and a different attitude towards women – were increasingly noticeable in the big cities, the ports of the Mediterranean seaboard and areas where a few families were growing rich on the income provided by oil. In such places public pronouncements on the traditional lifestyle were often divided, swinging between singing its praises when challenged by the West, to mocking it as primitive and backward in the company of urban compatriots. Since at least the end of the First World War, in some Arab-speaking lands the term 'Bedu' – a traditional nomadic tribesman – was being used as a term of abuse.

Nowhere was the divide in the Arab world clearer than between Egypt and the rest of the Arabic-speaking areas. Subject to prolonged Western influence for well over a century, and with a population larger than those of Arabia, Syria, Lebanon, Palestine and Transjordan (see page 35) combined, flourishing industry, an established bureaucracy and a sophisticated banking system, Egypt was an anathema among its traditional-minded neighbours. It would have taken a minor miracle to persuade it to combine with them into anything resembling an Arab nation state.

Religion

No picture of the Middle East in 1945, or at any time, is complete without more than a passing reference to religion. The region is, after all, the birthplace of Judaism, Christianity and Islam (in chronological order of inception). The spiritual heart of all three remains in the lands where they originated. It is, of course, too simplistic to say that the turmoil that has wracked the area in recent years is purely or even largely religious in origin – no more were the medieval Crusades, those ultimately unsuccessful attempts by Western Christians to conquer and hold the Muslim-controlled holy places of the Bible. Nevertheless, as well as inspiring and supporting believers, religion invariably spiced the rhetoric of Middle Eastern conflict. We cannot go any further, therefore, until the complex vocabulary and background of the three faiths involved are understood.

JUDAISM

Judaism, the religion of the Jews, was the only one of the three major Middle Eastern religions linked to a specific people. (Islam was tied to a language, Arabic, but not to a race.) At its heart lay the belief that the one God – creator of the universe and the embodiment of divine love and divine justice – had chosen the Jews to be the vehicle of His way: 'For you are a people consecrated to the Lord your God: of all the peoples on earth the Lord your God chose you to be His treasured people' (*Book of Deuteronomy*). The Jews' very personal God had made a pact (covenant) with them: in return for being His chosen people they were to obey His pattern and structure of life set out in His teaching (the Torah). As long as they did this, one day all other people would recognize God's ways and follow them too. Then the whole earth would bear witness to the love, peace and justice of God.

Another part of God's covenant involved giving His people a specific land. This was Israel. With its sacred capital of Jerusalem, at its largest (known as 'Greater Israel' in the twentieth century) it had once stretched beyond the east bank of the River Jordan. However, for a series of complex reasons, by late Roman times very few Jews actually lived in the promised land. They had been dispersed (the Diaspora) and lived in small, mostly urban communities around Europe and, to a lesser extent, the Middle East. A few went back to Israel – the Holy Land – on pilgrimage, and a tiny number still lived there. For the great majority, however, the idea of returning to Israel was not a practical concept but a religious one. Going back to the promised land was equated with the establishment of perfect peace and harmony on earth.

At least that is how it was seen until the later nineteenth century.

Christian Europe had rarely treated the Jews well or even fairly. As a distinctive minority, they were an obvious target for racial hatred, a tendency reinforced by the Roman Catholic Church when it condemned them as the people who had killed Jesus Christ. Even more unjustly, in the nineteenth century an unholy alliance of the political right, the Roman Catholics, and the Orthodox Church blamed the Jews for conspiring to bring about the excesses of the French Revolution.

Insight

For many centuries the liturgies of both the Orthodox and Roman Catholic Christian churches contained disparaging references to the Jews. Phrases used included 'an impious and law-breaking people' (Orthodox) and 'the swarm of deicides [god-killers]' (Roman Catholic).

At different times during the century, Russia, France, Syria, Hungary and several other states witnessed outbreaks of cruel anti-Semitism. The nineteenth century was also the age of nationalism. Understandably, therefore, a number of Jews began to link the ancient concept of a return to the promised land (Israel) with modern nationalism. In other words, if the Germans, Italians, Serbs, and so forth could have their own state, why not the Jews? The name adopted by the new movement was 'Zionism'. It derived from 'Zion', a poetic name for Israel.

Zionism was never a single, clear-cut movement. There were some for whom it represented a religious ideal, while others saw it as a political expedient to provide the Jews with a safe haven. Whatever the motives, since the obvious place for the establishment of a Jewish homeland was where it had been in Biblical times, by 1945 the turmoil that Zionism was causing in Palestine was beginning to impact upon the entire region (see Chapter 3).

CHRISTIANITY

The Jewish faith spoke of a redeemer who would reconcile humankind to God. Christians believed that in Jesus Christ they had found this redeemer. Born in Bethlehem to humble parents, Jesus had been crucified outside Jerusalem by the Romans (with the connivance of the Jewish authorities), and had then supposedly come back to life for a while. According to accounts written shortly afterwards – the New Testament of the Bible – he had also proclaimed himself to be the long-expected redeemer: none other than the Son of God. He was reported to have performed miracles that bore out his supernatural powers.

Eventually adopted by the Roman Empire, Christianity spread far more widely than Judaism had ever done. Although it accepted aspects of its Jewish heritage, such as God's Ten Commandments (laws) for living a righteous life, it was a much less specific, more metaphysical faith than Judaism. According to the New Testament, unlike Judaism and, later, Islam, Jesus did not set down a practical code for holy living, nor did he exclude any people or race from becoming Christian. His two basic tenets were to love God and love your neighbour as yourself. God Himself was perceived less as a human-type being and more of an embodiment of love.

A faith based upon such abstract foundations was open to widely differing interpretations. These manifested themselves in dramatic schisms within the 'Church', as the body of Christians was known. Very simply, those following the leadership of the Pope in Rome separated from the Orthodox Church centred on Constantinople (Istanbul). Then the Orthodox Church split between Greek and Russian varieties, and the Roman Church into Catholics and

Protestants. There were also all kinds of lesser divisions, such as the Coptic Christians of Abyssinia (Ethiopia) and the Maronites of Syria, not to mention the myriad divisions within Protestantism.

One thing all these various Christian Churches had in common was a shared history with the Jews and a veneration for the places in Palestine where Jesus had lived, taught and died. In spite of this, Christians amounted to less than five per cent of the population of the Middle East in 1945.

ISLAM

Islam, which means literally 'surrender' (to God or 'Allah'), was the historical successor to Judaism and Christianity. Inheriting aspects of both, it accepted the Biblical figures of Noah, Moses and Jesus as true prophets. It reserved the position of last and greatest prophet for Mohammed, a seventh-century inhabitant of the Arabian town of Medina who, Muslims believe, received God's word. As it was delivered to him via the Angel Gabriel, Mohammed had it written down in the Koran. Hence the basic Muslim profession of faith: 'There is no god but God; Mohammed is the prophet of God.'

The Koran, backed up by early traditions set out in the Hadith, forms the basis of the Muslim faith. Indeed, compared with Christianity, it was rather more than a faith: it was also a set of specified religious practices and, more widely, a whole way of life. These closely linked Islam to politics and gave rise to the concept of the Islamic state. Before the twentieth century, the idea of an Islamic country having a non-sectarian government was an anathema. This way of thinking was revived in the later twentieth century when states such as Iran attempted to return to a unified Islamic government, law (Sharia law, based on the Koran and the sayings of the prophet) and culture.

Insight

The extent to which the Koran should be interpreted literally or metaphorically is the subject of intense and often bitter debate. Non-theologians are advised to steer well clear.

Islam's strengths were many and real. Its blunt simplicity gave believers certainty and self-confidence: they had accepted the right way and so were destined for a heaven redolent with physical (according to some theologians) as well as spiritual delights. The unwavering rituals of prayer five times a day, the annual fast and the once-in-a-lifetime pilgrimage to Mecca settled the lives of believers within a secure and reassuring framework. The faith's emphasis on community – the essential equality of all believers and the need for the wealthy and fortunate to support those less well positioned than themselves – helped give the faith a mass following.

From the beginning, Islam displayed undertones of violence that distressed adherents of more pacific beliefs and philosophies. Much of the faith's early expansion was carried out by a holy war ('jihad') that established a Muslim empire, or Caliphate, stretching from India to Spain. The conquered were presented with the unenviable choice between conversion to Islam or taxation (Jews and Christians), or death (pagans). From time to time since then, more extreme Muslim groups have resurrected the concept of jihad to justify armed resistance to perceived oppression.

The contest for the position of caliph – head of the Muslim political-religious state – was sometimes accompanied by astonishing cruelty. The first caliph of the Abbasid dynasty, for instance, broadcast his ruthlessness by taking the name as-Saffah or 'Blood-shedder'. Violence also manifested itself in brutal punishments handed down in some fundamentalist societies. Nevertheless, it may be argued that these, like the veiling of women, were based on tribal custom and not Islam.

Despite the precise nature of many of its teachings, Islam, like other faiths, has had its fair share of schism and split. The largest and most enduring began as a dispute over the leadership of the movement and went on to acquire distinctly separate theological positions. The majority, comprising mostly Arab Muslims, were the Sunni. The minority, based originally in Iran (Persia), were the Shia.

Other sects include the Isma'ili, the Ahmadiyah and, perhaps, the Druze, although there is some dispute whether the latter are really Muslims at all.

Unfortunately for the peace of the Middle East, the Muslims, just like the Jews and Christians, regard Jerusalem as a holy city. It was the direction in which Muslims originally faced when praying and, according to tradition, was the place from which Mohammed once physically ascended into heaven. In short, a place well worth fighting for.

Summary

This is the colourful stage on which our tragic drama is set. In some ways, the Middle East in 1945 was little different from what it had been 500 years previously. It was still a largely barren region where water sources and fertile land were jealously guarded. Despite the widespread and uniting prevalence of the Arabic language and the Muslim faith, there remained startling differences between city and desert, interior and coast, Africa and Asia, rich and poor. In other words, it was as mysterious, proud, fragmented, diverse and unquestionably important as ever.

Nevertheless, the previous 50 years had seen crucial changes. First, the developed world's thirst for oil was making the region, where the largest deposits of the liquid gold were to be found, among the most strategically vital on earth. Second, at the end of the First World War the Middle East's dominant power, the Turkish Ottoman Empire, had collapsed. In its place had sprung up an unstable patchwork of uneasily independent states and territories governed by imperial European powers. Finally, the traditional settlement pattern was threatened by a determined attempt to establish in the region the entirely new state of Israel.

The story of these developments, completing the picture of the Middle East in 1945, is the subject of the next chapter.

THINGS TO REMEMBER

1 *The Western phrase 'Middle East' is no more than a term of convenience for a region with no specific or agreed boundaries.*

2 *However it is defined, the Middle East – the only region on earth where three continents meet – is of undeniable strategic importance.*

3 *Over the last century and a half, the construction of the Suez Canal and the exploitation of the Middle East's oil and gas resources have enormously added to the region's importance.*

4 *Rapidly growing populations have put the region's relatively scarce water resources under mounting pressure.*

5 *The earliest recorded human civilizations originated in the Middle East, affording the region a history of unparalleled richness.*

6 *The great cities of the Middle East are largely situated on the coast, on a river or around an oasis.*

7 *The majority – but by no means all – of the Middle East's populations are Arab, a term that means little more than a speaker of Arabic.*

8 *In a region in which the nation state is a relatively new introduction, the family and the clan are often the strongest social bonds.*

9 *The three great monotheistic faiths – Judaism, Christianity and Islam – all originated in the Middle East.*

10 *Judaism, Christianity and Islam are umbrella terms that cover a wide range of distinct groupings and sects.*

2

States and mandates: Middle Eastern politics to the end of the Second World War

This chapter will cover:
- *the collapse of the Ottoman Empire*
- *Allied plans for the Middle East made during the First World War*
- *the emergence of new independent states by 1945*
- *the continuation of British and French power in the region.*

Ottoman collapse

At the beginning of the twentieth century, the governments of the Great Powers of Europe showed no special interest in the Middle East, and that of the United States even less. As long as shipping passed through its waters uninterrupted, pilgrims made their way unmolested to its holy places, and a growing volume of oil flowed from its wells in the Gulf, they were by and large content. The prevailing masters – the relatively easy-going Ottoman and Persian Empires – were permitted to run their own shows without undue interference. For what was on offer, the cost and political danger of large-scale intervention was simply not worth it.

The Turkish Ottoman Empire, with its ancient capital of Constantinople (Istanbul), had dominated the Middle East for

400 years. For about half this period – at least since the emergence of Russia as a major power – Ottoman authority had commonly been regarded as 'in decline'. However, unlike the British Empire, which in the twentieth-century world would suffer a political heart attack and pass away almost overnight, its Turkish counterpart took a remarkably long time to pass away. It was still breathing in 1900, although it had lost almost all its possessions in Europe. Elsewhere, Western imperial powers had helped themselves to bits they wanted: the Russians in the Caucasus, the French in Algeria and Tunisia, and the British in Cyprus, Egypt and some grubby coaling stations and sandy ports around the fringe of the Arabian peninsula. Finally, after a fresh wave of depredations shortly before the First World War, the Ottomans were left with the rump of an empire that embraced, roughly speaking, the modern states of Turkey, Iraq, Saudi Arabia, Syria, Lebanon, Jordan, and Israel-Palestine.

Insight

Such was the paralysis within the later nineteenth-century Ottoman administration that almost the entire imperial navy, the third largest in the world, remained rotting in port for nigh on 30 years.

The eventual demise of the Ottoman Empire was brought about by its decision to join the First World War on the side of the Central Powers (Germany, Austria-Hungary and Bulgaria). Turkish armies, fighting throughout the Middle East, tied down many Allied troops and inflicted notable reverses upon them in Mesopotamia (modern Iraq), on the Gallipoli peninsula and in the Caucasus. In the end, though, single successes did not add up to an overall victory, and on 30 October 1918 the demoralized and near-bankrupt Ottomans signed an armistice.

Three agreements

For some while the Allies had been discussing what to do with Ottoman possessions when the First World War ended.

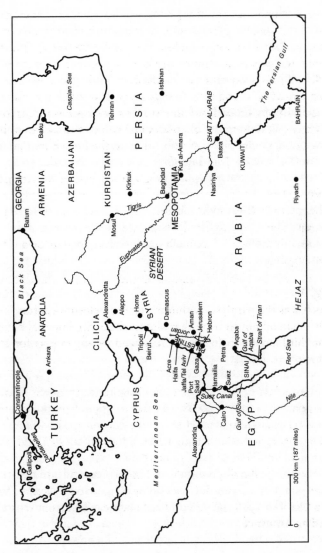

Figure 2.1 The Middle East around the time of the First World War.

Before Russia succumbed to a communist revolution, the British and French had even suggested that the tsar might like to take Istanbul and control of the Dardanelles as part of the spoils of a victorious war. It is anyone's guess whether they meant to honour such generous terms. Of several other wartime agreements concerning Ottoman possessions, at least three were equally contentious.

THE MCMAHON–HUSSEIN CORRESPONDENCE

The first may be found amid the lengthy correspondence between Sir Henry McMahon, the British Consul-General in Egypt, and Hussein, the Grand Sharif or Emir (in reality a sort of hereditary governor) of Mecca. McMahon headed one of the 20 or so British government departments with a finger in the Middle Eastern pie. Hussein was a clever if enigmatic figure. As head of the respected Hashemites, a tribe (blood-related 'clan' might be more accurate) descended from the Prophet Mohammed, and guardian of the Muslim holy cities of Mecca and Medina, he had as good a claim as anyone to speak for the Islamic Arab 'nation'. Because the emir's allegiance to the Ottomans was shaky, McMahon took it upon himself to persuade Hussein, by correspondence, to come over to the Allied side.

From a British point of view, the correspondence course was a great success. The Arabs, led by Hussein's son Faisal and assisted and perhaps even inspired by the able and eccentric self-publicist T. E. Lawrence 'of Arabia', rose up in the Hejaz (western Arabia) and drove north to link up with British forces in Palestine. This was all very gallant and dramatic, but what precisely had these dashing, robe-clad Arab irregulars been fighting for?

The Arabs believed McMahon had offered independence to all Arab lands excepting certain 'portions of Syria lying to the west of the districts of Damascus' (Sir Henry McMahon, 24 October 1914). Apart from the fact that the British government – whatever their man in Cairo said – had little intention of surrendering control over so vast a region to unknown forces, the wording of the agreement itself is unclear. Part of the problem lies in the translation between English, a fairly specific language, and the more poetic Arabic. Unjustly and probably in a fit of frustrated pique, one European specialist wrote a few years later that each word of Arabic had five meanings: the original one, the opposite, a literary meaning unconnected to the first two, something to do with a camel, and something obscene. The nature of the 'districts of Damascus' and the precise 'portions' of territory have been hotly disputed. Did the latter, for instance, include Palestine? And if they did, what were the boundaries of that inexact area?

THE SYKES–PICOT AGREEMENT

From a practical point of view, the McMahon–Hussein agreement was rendered largely irrelevant by a secret understanding negotiated by the vigorous British diplomat Sir Mark Sykes and his French counterpart François Georges–Picot. In simple terms, to keep the Russians out of the region, the Sykes–Picot Agreement divided the Middle East into five parts. Britain and France were each to have an area they controlled directly and another that lay within their 'sphere of influence'. The huge British sphere contained a rather vague 'Independent Arab State'. The fifth area was the 'international sphere' of Palestine.

THE BALFOUR DECLARATION

The third Middle Eastern agreement was more of a one-sided announcement. In November 1917, the intellectual British Foreign Secretary, Arthur James Balfour, declared that, 'His Majesty's Government viewed with favour the establishment in Palestine of a national home for the Jewish people'. Although many reasons have been suggested for Britain's willingness at this point to back the idea of a Jewish homeland in the Middle East, none of them is entirely convincing. In the end, though, the motive was irrelevant. What did matter was that the world's foremost imperial power had given its blessing to the idea of a homeland in the Middle East for a specific racial group. Moreover, they had done so without consulting either those already living there or someone – perhaps the Emir Hussein? – who might speak on their behalf.

These three examples of imperial diplomacy proved crucial to the way the Middle East would develop after the dissolution of the Turkish Empire. The next step, therefore, is to examine how this wartime chicanery impacted upon the region in the post-Ottoman era.

The Arabian peninsula

SAUDI ARABIA

The British might have backed the Grand Sharif Hussein of Mecca as the principal power in the region of Arabia, but at least one of his neighbours believed the choice to be wrong. This was the virile and intelligent Abdulaziz Al Saud, a shortened version of a name which, in full, reads like an exercise in Old Testament genealogy. In the early twentieth century, Abdulaziz had captured the oasis town of Riyadh and established it as the capital of his desert state.

This vigorous princedom combined Bedouin toughness with the puritan fanaticism of a fundamentalist Islamic sect known as the Wahabites. Nominally loyal to the Ottomans before the First World War, during the conflict Abdulaziz received British subsidies. Afterwards the man the West knew as simply Al Saud ('The Saud') allowed his aggressive followers to expand his domain in several directions, most notably into Hussein's territory of the Hejaz. For a time Abdulaziz ruled as King of the Hejaz and Sultan of the Najd (Arabia's barren interior) before establishing himself as the absolute and independent King of Saudi Arabia (1932).

The new state's status rose sharply during the Second World War, when its vast oil reserves began to be exploited energetically by Aramco (the Arabian American Oil Company). Foreign workers appeared, as did more welcome foreign money. To a people whose way of life had in many respects altered little since the days of the Prophet himself, it was often confusing, sometimes alarming.

YEMEN

In Roman times, because of its comparatively fertile climate and superb position as a commercial entrepôt, Yemen was known as 'Arabia Felix' ('Fortunate Arabia'). Sadly, like a woman exploited for her beauty, Yemen's natural bounty brought it an unfortunate history. In the nineteenth century, it was divided between the Ottoman-held north and the British-held south. With the collapse of Ottoman power, North Yemen became independent while the South remained British.

The North's government passed into the hands of a somewhat ferocious imam (an Islamic leader – see insight box) by the name of Yahya Ibn Mohammed. After squabbling with his British and Saudi neighbours, by the end of the Second World War, Imam Yahya's very personal rule was attracting substantial internal dissatisfaction.

Insight

While in Shia communities the imam is both a cleric and a community leader, sometimes believed be divinely appointed, within Sunni communities an imam may simply be a prayer leader, teacher or scholar.

A STRING OF PROTECTORATES

Oman, Yemen's equally well-positioned neighbour along the south-eastern coast of Arabia, had once been the most powerful state on the peninsula. By 1945, such glory was a faded dream. The fractured state was the private possession of the reactionary Sultan Said Bin Taimur, whose authority rested on British protection.

Equally dependent upon Britain at this time was the cluster of sheikhdoms known today as the United Arab Emirates (UAE). Then styled the Trucial States, this loose tribal association had accepted British protection in the nineteenth century in return for agreeing to forego war, piracy and slavery. Like its neighbour Oman, its oil reserves had yet to be exploited. Once this began to happen, it transformed itself into the UAE, with Abu Dhabi as its capital (1971).

Qatar, Bahrain and Kuwait were the last three beads on the string of British protectorates decorating the north-east coast of the Arabian peninsula. Having long since signed agreements similar to those pertaining in Oman and the Trucial States, in 1945 all three were still under the protection of the British crown. Only Kuwait had begun widely to exploit its oilfields. Significantly, this had led Iraq, its powerful northern neighbour, to dig up old and somewhat fanciful claims to ownership of tiny Kuwait. While Britain retained a presence in the region, Iraq's claims remained purely rhetorical. At the end of the century, however, long after Britain's withdrawal, the Iraq of Saddam Hussein would try again, this time backing rhetoric with steel (see Chapter 11).

Iran

Excepting Turkey, which lies outside the scope of this book, Iran is the Middle East's only major non-Arab state. Its official language, Farsi (or Persian), is Indo-European. The country's adherence to Shia Islam also contrasts with the largely Sunni Islam of most Arabs, and it is justly proud of the glorious and independent heritage of its Persian past, reaching back to Classical times and beyond. Not surprisingly, tension between Arab and Iranian has always played a significant part in the history of the Middle East.

Like the Mediterranean Arab states, Persia (the name by which it was known at the time) received serious interest from the European imperial powers from the late eighteenth century onwards. The chief would-be predators were Russia, contemplating expansion from the north, and Britain, hopeful of securing the south for its oil and because of its strategic importance in relation to India.

The first generous foreign oil concessions were granted to British firms (the forerunners of British Petroleum BP) in 1901. Six years later, Britain and Russia, paying scant heed to Persian wishes, settled their differences by each taking a sizeable chunk of the country into their respective spheres of influence. Before and during the First World War, Persia was beset by famine, inflation and extreme political instability exacerbated by foreign intervention. The chaos continued after the war until Reza Khan, an army officer of ambition and ability, seized control first of the army, then of the government and finally, in 1925, of the throne.

Styling himself Reza Shah Pahlavi, the new shah changed the name of the country to Iran (derived from Aryan, originally meaning 'noble') and set about trying to modernize it and free it from foreign influence. This left him hated by conservatives at home and mistrusted abroad. Pro-Nazi sympathies alienated him still further and, when an Anglo-Soviet force invaded during the Second World War to keep open the route from the Gulf to the Soviet border, he abdicated and fled the country.

The new shah, Reza's son Mohammed Reza, was eager for support against Soviet-backed separatist movements in the north, and sided with the Americans. However, religious conservatives, hostile to all foreigners, remained very influential. The ending of the Second World War found the 26-year-old Shah Mohammed Reza, like his father, balancing precariously between past and present, tradition and modernization, Islam and secularism. It was an unenviable position he shared with several other of the region's governors.

Egypt

Of all the lands of the Middle East, it is perhaps Egypt, with its awe-inspiring pyramids and sphinx, that is the most alluring.

Yet for centuries, the wider world's knowledge of this increasingly peripheral feature of the Ottoman sphere was minimal. All this changed at the end of the eighteenth century when Napoleon I invaded the country in an attempt to disrupt British communications with India. The French emperor was accompanied by scholars, scientists and soldiers whose impact made Egypt the most Western-orientated state in the Middle East.

After Napoleon's defeat, Egypt's fortunes waxed and waned under a succession of rulers owing nominal allegiance to Constantinople. The opening of the Suez Canal (see page 3), together with bankruptcy and political instability, ensured that Western scrutiny of the country remained tight. Finally, in 1882, a British force occupied Cairo to guard their country's interests. Although announced as a temporary measure, the occupation lasted 40 years in theory, and in reality a lot longer.

Until the outbreak of the First World War, the government of Egypt took the form of a triple bluff. As the country was still within the Ottoman Empire, ultimate authority theoretically rested with the Sultan in Constantinople. For years, however, Egypt had paid little heed to its Turkish overlords. The country was run in the name of its 'khedive' (vice-sultan), his ministers and the advisory Assembly of Delegates. In practice, real power rested with neither the Ottomans nor the Egyptians but with a succession of British consuls. With a poetic touch of oriental romanticism, the system was known as the 'veiled protectorate'.

The veil was rudely ripped off when Britain went to war with the Ottomans in 1914. The British gave Egypt a sultan of its own, then promptly took away his authority by declaring the country a full protectorate under a high commissioner. (One of these, Sir Henry McMahon, we have already met – see page 22.) Military rule kept the country relatively quiet during the war. But immediately it ended, Egyptian nationalists, furious that independence was being offered to the 'unbreeched barbarians' of the Hejaz but denied to themselves, demanded immediate British withdrawal. When the British hesitated, a wave of strikes brought the country to a standstill. Protesters flooded the streets and violence against the occupiers and those associated with them mounted rapidly. The situation was not helped by an imperial official declaring that an Englishman could extinguish an Egyptian flare-up merely by spitting on it.

The British had little option but to accept Egypt's independence, although they reserved various powers to themselves pending a full treaty. They demanded control of 'imperial communications' – i.e. the Suez Canal – a guiding hand in foreign policy, security for foreign interests and minorities, and sole control over the Sudan, a land they and the Egyptians had conquered at the end of the previous century. Such a formidable list illustrates clearly that the newly independent Egypt remained very much within the British sphere of influence.

The country's constitution – a form of constitutional monarchy based, surprisingly, on that of Belgium – proved as insubstantial as its independence. The ball of power bounced elusively between three walls: the king (Fuad I, followed in 1936 by his son Farouk), the nationalist Wafd Party, and the British. Amid the chaos, two key developments emerged. One was a militant Islamic, anti-Western movement, the Muslim Brotherhood (1928). The second was a spirit of fellowship with other Arabs, particularly those also perceived to be suffering at the hands of imperialist Europeans. Nowhere was such suffering deemed to be more painful than in the troubled land of Palestine.

In 1936, Britain finally got the treaty it demanded of the Egyptian government, maintaining a strong British presence in the country. This swelled considerably during the Second World War, when the Egyptians gave reluctant support to the Allies in their struggle against fascism. The ending of the war found Egypt in a radical mood. Anti-British feelings were on the increase, fanned by nationalists demanding that the 1936 treaty be revised and all British forces withdrawn. The militant Muslim Brotherhood had grown into a mass movement.

During the war, Egypt had played a key role in forming the Arab League with Iraq, Lebanon, Saudi Arabia, Syria, Transjordan and North Yemen. The League's aim was to promote Arab unity and co-operation, and present a united front on common political issues. Foremost among these were events in Palestine.

Iraq

One of the principal reasons for the instability of the Middle East in recent times has been the painful process of defining and creating nation states in a region to which the concept was largely alien. Iraq is a classic example. Like Palestine, Saudi Arabia and other Middle Eastern countries of modern origin, at the beginning of the twentieth century a state named Iraq did not exist. Roughly speaking, the region that now carries the name comprised the three Mesopotamian provinces of the Ottoman Empire based around the cities of Mosul in the north, Baghdad in the east-centre and Basra in the south. As Mesopotamia, the region boasted a rich and glorious history, and Baghdad could justifiably claim to have once been one of the great cities of the world. Now, having been fought over by Ottomans and Persians (and at one time governed from Shiraz), all that remained of former splendours were shattered stones and proud stories.

It was the British who brought Mesopotamia out of the shadows. Having already established diplomatic and commercial links, during the First World War they invaded it from the head of the Gulf. After initial setbacks, imperial forces took Baghdad and by the time of the armistice were in occupation of all three

Mesopotamian provinces. Back in Britain, civil servants and politicians scratched their heads and wondered what to do with their new acquisition.

Their hand was forced by events. As we saw earlier (page 22), the Arabs felt betrayed by the Allied failure to honour agreements made with Hussein, the Hashemite Grand Sharif of Mecca, to grant them independence after the defeat of the Ottomans. One of Hussein's sons, Faisal, a close friend of T. E. Lawrence, had made a name for himself as leader of the wartime Arab revolt. Immediately after the war, he had been chosen as king of an independent Syria that was to include the region of Palestine. The Mesopotamian Arabs, not to be outdone and determined to create an independent state of their own, chose Faisal's brother Abdullah as their king. Within two years of the end of the war, the greater part of Mesopotamia was in armed revolt against the British, who were perceived as denying them nationhood.

The French inadvertently offered a solution to the problem by driving Faisal from Syria. The British then invited him to London and, in a stroke of extraordinary imperial hauteur, offered him the throne of Mesopotamia. The condition was that he shared control with Britain, which had no intention of letting go of an area that was looking as if it might contain significant oilfields. Faisal agreed to a binding treaty with Britain, his bemused people accepted him in a plebiscite and, on 23 August 1921, he was crowned king of the newly created country of Iraq. Meanwhile, the British had found alternative employment for his brother Abdullah (see page 35).

The Anglo-Iraqi attempt to produce a workable constitution for Iraq in the 1920s makes an interesting comparison with the American-Iraqi effort of the present century. Unlike the US-inspired republicanism of 2005, the former opted for a democratic scheme loosely based on the British constitutional monarchy. Not surprisingly, since the concepts of nation and democracy are slow-growing plants, its history was somewhat chequered. By the time of its collapse in 1958, Iraqis had been subjected to the rule of no fewer than 50 cabinets.

A common wish for full independence from Britain united the bulk of Iraqi politicians. However, once this goal had been achieved in the 1930s, any vestige of stability melted away. The many ethnic, religious, social and political differences within the manufactured state were almost impossible to reconcile. The massacre of Christian Assyrians by Iraqi troops shortly after independence is a striking example of the sort of lawless behaviour that threatened to become endemic. Faisal, an alien and politically inexperienced king imposed by a colonial power, was unable to control the situation. King Ghazi, his equally inexperienced son, made matters worse by involving the military in politics. His early death in a sports car crash brought his infant son Faisal II to the throne, with his uncle Abdullah acting as regent.

By the outbreak of the Second World War, the army was the principal force in Iraqi politics. Following the fall of France, a group of commanding officers decided that the cause of Arab nationalism might be better served by an alliance with the Axis powers rather than with the beleaguered Britain. This provoked a swift and successful British invasion, the removal of the army from politics and a declaration of war on the side of the Allies. When the fighting ended in 1945, the fledgling state of Iraq found itself in a familiar position: under the sway of the British and unsure how best to tackle an uncertain future.

Syria, Lebanon and Transjordan

SYRIA

At the end of the nineteenth century, Syria was another famous Middle Eastern region whose illustrious past contrasted unhappily with an unsure present. Long since absorbed into the Ottoman Empire, it was a vast, fuzzy-frontiered area that included all of modern Syria, Lebanon, Jordan and Israel-Palestine. Like Egypt, for many years it had been subjected to the direct influence of Europeans (and, unusually, Americans, whose missionaries had established a Christian college in Beirut). In this case, however, it was the French and not the British who had been the major players. They had built the country's railways and on one occasion had even sent in an expeditionary force to quell fighting between a Druze–Muslim alliance and the Maronites. In the cities, Western influence was clearly visible in the dress and lifestyle of the wealthier classes, not to mention in splendid Franco-Arab cuisine.

The First World War split Syrians three ways. The majority, for whom Islam was of paramount importance, tended to support the old empire as a bastion of their faith. Minorities, especially the Jews and Christians, looked favourably on the Allies. The third group were the Arab nationalists. Inspired by the words of Sharif Hussein and the actions of his son Faisal, they too looked to the Allies for salvation.

Modern Syria came into being after the war. The British remained in Palestine, the French in Lebanon, and, as we have seen, Faisal was declared king of a smaller but independent Syria. The French would have none of this, and the League of Nations – precursor to the UN and then little more than an Anglo-French club – agreed that Syria should become a French mandate on terms similar to those of the British presence in Palestine.

In many ways Syria prospered under the French. Indeed, it is unlikely that so diverse a country could have held together without the dominating hand of a colonial power. Nevertheless, it became increasingly clear that the French had little intention of handing over power to the Syrians, at least not in the immediate future. By the late 1930s, Syria had a constitution, an elected government and its first president, but in the face of a resolute French 'non' the entire apparatus of independence remained addled.

The deadlock was broken by the Second World War. The French Vichy regime, which had made a pact with the Nazis after the defeat of France in 1940, maintained its hold over Syria and allowed it to be used as a German air base. This drew an Allied invasion, spearheaded by the British who witnessed the unhappy spectacle of Frenchmen (Vichy supporters) fighting Frenchmen (the Free French led by General Charles de Gaulle). Prompted by Britain, the Free French agreed to Syria's independence and another president, Shukri al-Kuwatli, was elected in 1943.

It was not until 1946 that the French finally left Syria – again with British prompting – allowing the country onto the world stage as an independent founder member of the Arab League and the United Nations.

LEBANON

Lebanon was unusual among the states of the Middle East. First, separated from the hinterland by the spine of Mount Lebanon, this beautiful and balmy land tended to look west more than most other Arab states. Its links with the rest of the Mediterranean were reinforced by a commercial tradition that went back to the time of the pharaohs. For much of its recent history its core was the prosperous silk trade.

Lebanon's second unusual feature was the make-up of its population. Some 50 per cent of Lebanese were Christian: Maronites, Orthodox Roman Catholics and Protestants. The first two traditionally received French support, the third had strong links with the USA. The other half of the population comprised both Sunni and Shia Muslims, Druze (a secret, exclusive and sometimes British-backed monotheist sect generally recognized as closer to Islam than anything else) and Jews.

Such diversity, spiced with centuries of mistrust that had burst into fighting from time to time, was not an ideal recipe for harmonious living. It was hardly surprising, therefore, that when in the late twentieth century trouble flared to the south of Lebanon, it spread north over the border with hideous consequences (see Chapter 7). The situation was encapsulated in a traditional Arab joke: God laughed when He created the Sudan and wasn't thinking when He created Arabia; so what were You doing, asked the bemused Lebanese, when You created our beautiful land of cedar trees, blue seas and cool breezes? Ah, God smiled, just wait until you see who I've given you as neighbours.

Lebanese history between the World Wars followed a pattern similar to Syria's. Occupied by the Allies in 1918, it was made a French mandate. Arab nationalists resented the way Syria had been carved up and among certain sections of the Lebanese population pro-Syrian sentiments remained strong. Such feelings persisted after 1945 and are important to an understanding of events in more recent times.

Under a generally beneficent French supervision the tradition of a balanced government emerged. The post of president traditionally went to a Maronite, and that of prime minister to a Sunni Muslim, with the speaker of the chamber of deputies being a Shia. As in neighbouring Syria, the French – pre-war, Vichy and Free – were reluctant to hand over full authority to the locals. They were eventually forced to do so by British pressure at the end of the Second World War. The new, fully independent Lebanese Republic emerged as a member of the Arab League and United Nations in 1946.

TRANSJORDAN

Sharif Hussein of Mecca, it will be remembered, had two prominent sons. One, Faisal, had led the Arab revolt and had been installed by the British as King of Iraq. The second, Abdullah, had used British money and arms to tie down the large Turkish garrison in Medina during the Arab revolt. When the war ended he had diverted his forces to more personal aims, attempting to get the better of Ibn Saud. After an ignominious defeat, which had obliged the portly prince to flee across the desert in his nightshirt, he led what was left of his forces to attack the French in Syria.

The route from the Hejaz to Damascus took Abdullah, his 2,000 followers and their six machine guns across the British mandate of Palestine. This sprawling territory extended from the Mediterranean, across the River Jordan and expanses of barren desert, to an uncertain border with the territory of Ibn Saud. While Abdullah was resting in the village of Aman and casting about for local Bedouin support (never too difficult to obtain when there was prospect of booty), the Liberal British Colonial Secretary, Winston Churchill, was holding a conference in Cairo on the future of the Middle East.

The last thing Churchill wanted was Abdullah stirring up trouble with the French. To divert him, the British cut their Palestinian mandate into two. It was an extraordinary piece of state-making. The British retained the more fertile and more politically sensitive area to the west of the River Jordan, keeping for it the name Palestine. The rest – an impoverished and rocky desert with no towns, no rivers and scarcely any inhabitants (a total of about 200,000 was estimated, most of them Bedouin nomads) – they handed to Abdullah as the Emirate of Transjordan. The new emir seemed pleased enough with his windfall which, in area, amounted to almost three-quarters of British Palestine.

A treaty gave Transjordan a nominal independence, leaving financial, military and foreign affairs in British hands. Funded and protected by his British benefactors, who also provided him with one of the best fighting forces in the region (the Arab Legion), Abdullah survived to win full independence for his country after the Second World War. In 1949, he changed its name to the one it still bears today: the Hashemite Kingdom of Jordan.

By then, however, the outlook of the entire region had changed dramatically. To find out how and why, we now need to focus on the remaining quarter of Britain's Middle Eastern mandate: Palestine.

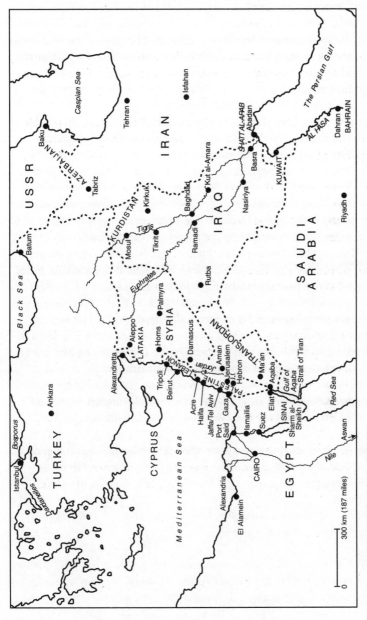

Figure 2.2 The central Middle East after the Second World War.

THINGS TO REMEMBER

1 *From the sixteenth century onwards, the bulk of the Middle East was incorporated within the Turkish Ottoman Empire.*

2 *In decline for some two centuries, the Ottoman Empire finally broke up during the First World War.*

3 *During the First World War, Britain sided with the 'Arab Revolt' against Ottoman rule.*

4 *Three controversial (and often contradictory) agreements – the McMahon–Hussein correspondence, the Sykes–Picot Agreement and the Balfour Declaration – attempted to determine the nature of the post-war Middle East.*

5 *After the First World War, Britain and France extended their influence over the Middle East when the League of Nations granted them 'mandates' – vast swathes of territory to be guided towards independent nationhood.*

6 *By 1945, the Arabian peninsula was dominated by the newly created (1932), oil-rich state of Saudi Arabia.*

7 *Britain retained its influence in the small states fringing the Persian Gulf long after the end of the Second World War.*

8 *A centre of rivalry between the USSR (Russia) and the West, Iran struggled for stability in the first half of the twentieth century.*

9 *While nominally independent, Egypt retained a strong British presence until the 1950s.*

10 *Between the wars, the mandates of Iraq, Palestine (sub-divided into Palestine and Transjordan), Syria and Lebanon moved with varying degrees of success towards independence.*

3

The promised land

This chapter will cover:
- *Palestine before the First World War*
- *British attempts to govern their Palestinian mandate between the wars*
- *the effect of the Second World War and the Holocaust on the Palestinian situation*
- *increasing violence within Palestine leading to the declaration of the State of Israel in 1948.*

Palestine

Palestine enjoyed its last few years of Ottoman rule. Recent reforms had made the region more prosperous and stable. Pilgrims, including the Emperor of Germany, came in ever increasing numbers to its holy places and major powers considered it sufficiently important to set up consulates in Jerusalem as well as in the regional capital, Damascus.

Palestine was also attracting Europeans as both temporary residents and permanent immigrants. Among the latter were small numbers of Jews fleeing poverty, prejudice and persecution in Eastern Europe. These usually poor and dispirited people were at first no more than a trickle. Over time, though, their number rose to a steady stream that carried with it long years of fear, mistrust, hatred and, eventually, the horror and suffering of war.

This chapter traces that story. It starts with the rise of Zionism and Arab–Jewish animosity to 1918, then covers the inter-war years when an increasingly divided Palestine was in British hands. The third part deals with the effect of the Second World War on the situation, leading to civil war and the foundation of the State of Israel.

Zion

'OUR COUNTRY'

As we saw in Chapter 1, there had always been Jews living in Palestine. Indeed, one estimate says that at the start of the nineteenth century, the majority of the population of Jerusalem were Jews. As might be expected, there were sporadic outbreaks of racial and religious friction, but by and large Jews and Arabs and their Turkish master rubbed along reasonably amicably.

Zionism changed the situation irrevocably. Following violent attacks on Jewish communities in Russia, in 1882 a group of Jewish exiles met in Constantinople. They named themselves the 'Lovers of Zion' and called for 'a home in our country. It was given to us by the mercy of God; it is ours as registered in the archives of history.' The 'our country' they spoke of was Palestine.

THE JEWISH STATE

The next important step in the Zionist movement came some ten years later. An Austrian Jew named Theodore Herzl, journalist and playwright, was asked by his newspaper to cover an anti-Semitic (anti-Jewish) scandal in France. His reporting convinced him that there was a 'Jewish problem' that could be solved only by the creation of a Jewish nation state. He set out his ideas in a highly influential little book, *The Jewish State* (1896). Interestingly, he did not specifically plump for Palestine as the place where this state might be established. A sparsely populated area of Argentina was one option – how different might the history of the last half-century have been had the suggestion caught on!

The year after Herzl's publication saw the first meeting, in Basle, Switzerland, of the World Zionist Organization. Here the mood was far more positively pro-Palestine and a mission was sent out to explore the ground. Its reply encapsulates with poetic precision what would become the tragedy of Palestine: 'The bride is beautiful but she is married to another man.' In other words, the region was well-suited to settlement but was already inhabited.

Undaunted, Jewish leaders set about furthering their programme of raising national awareness, winning international support and encouraging immigration into Palestine. In his quest for backing by a major power, Herzl first tried Constantinople. This was the obvious choice because Palestine still lay within the Ottoman Empire. The Sultan was unwilling to welcome more Jewish immigrants into a region where they were already attracting criticism as unwanted outsiders.

Herzl then turned to Britain, still the world's wealthiest and most influential nation and certainly the leading imperial power. Here he received a more favourable reception (as well as a suggestion that part of East Africa might make a less controversial national home for the Jews than Palestine). Although Britain did not formally agree to back Zionism, foundations were laid for a relationship that became official with the Balfour Declaration (see page 23).

SUPREMACY AND IMMIGRATION

An intellectual link had also been established between Zionism and imperialism. The principal motive for Britain's acquisition of an empire was commercial. It was justified on less materialistic grounds: Europeans were more politically, technologically and perhaps even morally advanced than the peoples they governed so it was their duty – 'the white man's burden' – to civilize them.

After the First World War the British Colonial Secretary, Winston Churchill, an enthusiastic supporter of empire, spelled out the link between Zionism and British imperialism when he declared that a 'National Home' for the Jews in Palestine would be 'good for the world, good for the Jews and good for the British Empire'. Zionists supported such sentiments by arguing that an influx of European Jews, bearing European culture and values, could only benefit the region. They were sure that Palestinian Arabs, perhaps hostile at first, would soon be won over when they saw the economic and political advantages that Jewish immigration brought.

The lower esteem in which many Jews held the Arabs is reflected in the extraordinary Zionist slogan: 'A land without people for a people without land'. No one disputed the second half of the catchphrase, but to dismiss the 535,000 Muslims (mostly Arabs) and 70,000 Christians living in Palestine in 1914 as non-existent was extraordinarily dangerous arrogance.

Insight

It is one of the supreme ironies of history that the Jews, who had been subjected to more racial intolerance than almost any other people, should themselves have displayed such open racist arrogance towards Arabs.

Prominent members of the European and American Jewish community helped establish banks and funds to assist Jewish immigration into Palestine. The most prominent individual benefactor was the French philanthropist Baron Edmond de Rothschild. Precise figures are impossible to come by, but perhaps 35,000 Jews entered Palestine in the 30 years before the outbreak of the First World War. By the same date, Jews may have owned two per cent of Palestinian land.

The proportion of Palestinian land held by the Jews in relation to their numbers was far less than that held by Arabs. Furthermore, the number of Jews entering Palestine was as nothing compared with the estimated 2 million who went to live in the United States over the same period. Here they formed an economic and political community whose influence would impact powerfully on the Middle East in the latter half of the century.

SEEDS OF CONFLICT

The arrival of perhaps 1,000 Jewish immigrants per annum in a region where their co-religionists had lived in comparative harmony with their neighbours for centuries need not in itself have caused problems. Difficulties arose not over numbers but attitudes.

Many Jewish immigrants had absorbed Zionist propaganda about their supremacy to the local people and about the land being theirs by moral (and even religious) right. Moreover, the new arrivals were often separatist. The original Palestinian Jews had been city dwellers, integrating within the communities of Gaza, Hebron, Jaffa, Jerusalem and elsewhere. As we saw with the foundation of Tel Aviv (see page 7), the immigrants planted exclusive colonies within Palestine, 47 of them by the end of the First World War.

The perceived threat of Zionism to the Arab way of life produced an understandable reaction. Palestinian Arabs, at least the educated section of their community, began to think in terms of a Palestinian nation. They went as representatives of Palestine to the Turkish Parliament in Constantinople and several exclusively Palestinian Arabic newspapers voiced the new nationalism.

Insight

The date of the birth of Palestinian nationalism is hotly contested. While some Palestinian scholars suggest the 1830s, many Israelis opt for the 1960s. As with many such controversies, the answer may lie somewhere between the two extremes.

Arab leaders took political action, too. They petitioned Constantinople to halt Jewish immigration, and when this failed they set up anti-Zionist societies in Palestine, Beirut and Constantinople. Finally, starting as early as 1886, Arabs occasionally took matters into their own hands and attacked the unwanted intruders. Although these outbreaks were small scale, they began a cycle of violence that endures to this day.

The British mandate

As we saw in Chapter 2, during the First World War Britain had raised both Arab and Jewish hopes. The correspondence between Sir Henry McMahon and Emir Hussein of Mecca had left the latter with the impression that the bulk of the Ottoman district of Syria would become an independent state. The Balfour Declaration of the following year, masterminded by the Russian-born Anglo-Jewish academic Chaim Weizmann, had offered formal British support for a Jewish homeland in Palestine. Given the mounting tension between Arabs and Jews in Palestine before the war broke out, these apparently contradictory agreements could do nothing but increase inter-communal strains.

THE POST-WAR SETTLEMENT

Because it would play such a major role in the Middle East from the Second World War onwards, it is worth noting here the American position regarding the Balfour Declaration and the future of the provinces of the former Ottoman Empire. Briefly, President Wilson's position was that the Arab peoples should have 'absolutely unmolested opportunity of autonomous development'. At the same time, he supported the idea of a national home for the Jews in Palestine.

Recognizing the possible contradictions in his policy, Wilson then appointed the King–Crane Commission to examine the situation in Palestine. It reported that the extreme Zionist position – that all Palestine (including lands east of the River Jordan) ought to become a Jewish state – was both wrong and impossible to achieve.

The answer lay in some sort of compromise. Since a Jewish homeland within or adjacent to an Arab state would need to be organized and refereed by a third party, Wilson came round to accepting the status quo. Britain, having seized Palestine during the war, continued in possession of what became known as a League of Nations mandate.

Before this came about, the Palestinian Arabs saw their hopes of independence finally dashed. Emir Faisal, briefly King of Syria, had included Palestine within his kingdom. When he was obliged to swap Syria for Iraq, the British kept control of Palestine while the French moved into what remained of Syria. Shortly afterwards the British separated off the eastern part of Palestine, beyond the River Jordan, as an emirate for Faisal's brother Abdullah. Palestinian Arabs were to refer to 1920, the year when all this happened, as 'the year of catastrophe'.

The Allies, largely ignoring the wishes of the people whose future they were determining, agreed the details above at a conference in San Remo. The mandate status of Palestine was later confirmed by the League of Nations. It meant that Britain's position there was strictly temporary – its task was to administer the territory while preparing it for democratic independence. However, the mandate also included the principles of the Balfour Declaration – the establishment of a Jewish national home in Palestine – and a Jewish Agency was to be set up to assist the British in this task. The only part of the settlement that angered some extreme Zionists was the total exclusion of Abdullah's Transjordanian fief from the homeland territory.

BRITAIN'S HEADACHE

The Arabs rejected the idea of a British mandate from the start. As far as they were concerned, its only positive feature was the recognition of Palestine as a separate political entity. The rest they abhorred. What right had foreigners either to divide their land or force them to accept a state within a state? What they wanted, quite reasonably, was a fully democratic Palestine that embraced all peoples living there. Some moderate Arab leaders suggested a compromise whereby the US would replace Britain as the supervising power. As the mandate was responsible to the League of Nations, a body that the US Congress had rejected, the idea was a non-starter.

The intensity of Britain's headache becomes clear when we understand why the Palestinian Jews rejected a single democratic Palestine. Not only would it mean abandoning the concept of the Jewish homeland, but it would also make them a small and disliked minority (perhaps ten per cent) in a predominantly Arab-Muslim state. In such a situation, they feared, their rights and perhaps even their livelihoods would be imperilled.

British administrators carried out the logistical side of their mandated duties with laudable efficiency. Their efforts to improve life in Palestine attracted some 50,000 Arab immigrants as well as many more Jews. They modernized transport by expanding the rail network and building roads; they built schools and sewage treatment plants, laid water pipelines and increased the provision of electricity. All the while, though, their task was made harder and harder by the background of inter-communal violence.

As far as the second part of Britain's mandated duties was concerned – preparing Palestine for democratic self-government while also honouring the Balfour Declaration – most far-seeing administrators soon realized it was impossible. Caught between two irreconcilable communities, they came to see the mandate as a sort of curse. Consequently, because no time limit had been set on it, observers began to wonder whether they would ever leave.

Such rumours were reinforced by activity at the eccentric Sodom and Gomorrah Golfing Society, where the élite of the occupying power, under armed escort, perspired around a brown and barren course beside the Dead Sea. The trophy for which they competed was a statue of Lot's wife. The original had been carved with Biblical correctness from a block of salt. When it wore away, the club committee replaced it with a more lasting version in durable marble. The symbolism was clear: the British were there for the duration.

1920s

It is estimated that the Jewish population of Palestine doubled in the ten years after the First World War. Immigrants did not arrive in a steady flow. After an initial rush, the British, worried by the Arab reaction, imposed limits. At the same time, Jewish land purchases continued apace. These were sometimes made from absentee Arab landlords. On a number of occasions such acquisitions led to Arab peasants being turned off land they and their ancestors had farmed for years. Tensions ran understandably high and the British declaration that it was not their intention to turn Palestine into a Jewish state cut little ice with disaffected Arabs. Moreover, the appointment of Sir Herbert Samuel, a Jew, as Britain's first all-powerful High Commissioner for Palestine hardly displayed tactful even-handedness.

There were serious outbreaks of Arab–Zionist fighting immediately after the First World War. These reflected the uncertainty of the political situation, Arab disappointment at the rejection of their demand for independence, and their fear over what they saw as the potentially overwhelming tide of Jewish immigration. Conciliatory statements by the British and a fall in Jewish immigration (there was actually a net emigration in 1927) helped the situation remain calm until 1929.

As so often, the Arabs were not helped by divisions within their ranks. Their nominal leader was Amin al-Husseini, Grand Mufti (expert on Muslim religious law) of Jerusalem. His authority was weakened by traditional rivalry with the an-Nashasibi family and by the fact that his positions as mufti and president of the Supreme Muslim Council were both British appointments. Opposition to Zionism was divided between several organizations, such as the Husseini-led Arab Executive and the Nashasibi-led National Defence Party. When ancient town–country, tribal and religious divisions are added to the mix, the failure of the Palestinian Arabs to present a united front is understandable.

The Jews were less divided. During the 1920s they generally co-operated with the British, setting up the apparatus of a distinctively Jewish state: elected assembly, trade unions, schools, industrial enterprises and so forth. They even had their own defence organization, the Haganah. Nevertheless, rifts were starting to appear within the Zionist ranks. The majority followed the more moderate ('Labour') leaders of the World Zionist Organization, Chaim Weizmann in London and David Ben Gurion in Palestine. They sought a socialist Jewish state in Palestine separate from a Palestinian Arab one. The Haganah would be needed to defend this state, but force was not an integral part of it.

Opposition to this Labour view came from Ze'ev Jobotinsky and his World Union of Zionist Revisionists. These hardliners attracted considerable support during the late 1920s and set up a militant security force of their own, the Irgun. They followed what came to be termed the 'iron wall' policy, based on four principles. First, the Jews were the standard-bearers of a superior Western civilization into the Middle East. Second, Zion had to comprise all Palestine on both banks of the Jordan ('Greater Israel'). Third, the Arabs would never voluntarily accept this. Fourth, the only answer, therefore, was force: Zionists had to carve out their state and secure it behind an iron wall. Only then, when the Arabs knew they could never win, would they accept the presence of the Jewish state in the Middle East. When present-day observers wonder why peace between Arab and Israeli is so elusive, they have only to consider the iron wall views of the Revisionists to grasp at least part of the answer.

1930s

The uneasy post-war peace collapsed in 1929. The trouble was sparked off, oddly enough, by furniture. Jews believed that the 'Wailing Wall' in old Jerusalem represented the only tangible relic of the ancient kingdom of Israel. At this place of prayer and sometimes painful remembrance (hence 'wailing') Jews had met for centuries, bringing with them chairs and other items of furniture to make their observances more comfortable. Unfortunately, the same piece of architecture was also charged with deep significance for Muslims.

The wall and its environs, the third most sacred site in the Islamic world, were owned by Muslims. Broadly interpreting the words of the Koran, tradition held that the Prophet Mohammed had one night ascended to heaven from an outcrop near the wall now graced by the Dome of the Rock. It was also believed that Mohammed's holy horse had been tethered to the wall itself. Not only that, but immediately above the wall stood the al-Aqsa mosque. In short, in Muslim eyes it was not the sort of place where folding garden chairs were wholly appropriate.

Inter-community tension over co-usage of the sacred site was fired up by the taunting of extremists on either side. On 23 August, the Muslim community went on the rampage and indulged in a full-scale orgy of murder, rape and pillage in which 133 Jews and 116 Arabs were killed, the great majority of the latter by the British security forces as they struggled to restore order. Whatever slight hope there had been of Jew and Arab living together in a single harmonious Palestine was now gone.

During the rest of the 1930s, the situation deteriorated further as the British floundered from one expedient to the next. After the August Massacre, for example, they ordered a reduction in Jewish immigration only to reverse the decision under Zionist pressure. Similarly, when Jewish refugees from Nazi Germany began flooding into Palestine (30,000 in 1933 rising to 61,000 in 1935), the British again cut immigration before increasing it once more. The result was simply confusion and resentment. By the time of the Second World War there were some 300 Zionist colonies in Palestine. The 467,000 Jews, who owned about 15 per cent of the land, made up almost one-third of the population.

The Arab response was a national revolt. Husseini called a general strike, taxes were not paid, local government broke down, and violence in all its forms increased. This time it was directed at both Jews and the British. The former fought back with the services of the Haganah and the terrorist-like Irgun. The latter declared martial law and increased the Palestine garrison to over 20,000 troops.

One British officer went as far as to prepare Special Night Squads of Jews to attack Arab villages. Within four years perhaps 5,000 Arabs had been killed and 15,000 wounded.

The Arab revolt forced the British to accept the inevitable: they would not be able to prepare Palestine for independence as a single democratic state. The Peel Commission Report (1937) recommended that Palestine be partitioned into Jewish and Arab states, with Jerusalem and neighbouring Holy Places remaining under British control. Interestingly, a somewhat similar partition plan had been agreed by Chaim Weizmann and King Faisal 20 years earlier. It had been dropped after rejection by other Arab leaders; acceptance would have avoided an immense amount of blood and tears.

Although Labour Zionists cautiously welcomed the Peel proposal, Husseini and his advisors rejected it outright. Confused, the British government then put forward another idea: a Jewish homeland within an Arab state, and strict limits on Jewish immigration. This compromise was turned down by both sides. The Arabs were way beyond trusting the British, and it was now the turn of the Jews to feel betrayed.

By the outbreak of the Second World War, Palestine was in turmoil. Intolerance and incompetence had changed a complex two-sided struggle between Jews and Arabs into an impossible three-sided one in which Arabs, Jews and the British were all at loggerheads. If there was a way out of this slough, it was certainly not well signposted.

The State of Israel

PALESTINE IN WARTIME

The outbreak of war in 1939 had a considerable impact on the Palestinian situation. Moderate Arabs and Jews agreed to support Britain and its allies in their struggle against fascism, and inter-community conflict died down considerably. As many as 27,000

Jews and 25,000 Arabs (particularly the famous Arab Legion) fought with the British Army. With huge funds pouring into the mandate to support the 250,000 Allied troops based there, the economy flourished. The Jewish sector did particularly well, developing its industry to meet Allied war needs.

There were exceptions on both sides to this comparative harmony. The Grand Mufti drew down much disapprobation upon his head by making his way to Germany and entering into negotiations with the Nazis. His reputation tarnished, after the war he chose to settle in Egypt rather than Palestine. On the other side, Revisionist Zionists of the Irgun and the Stern Gang, a group of hard-line Zionist terrorists, carried out a series of attacks on British personnel and positions. Their most notorious achievement was the assassination of a British minister in Cairo.

Insight

Grand Mufti Husseini was among several prominent Arabs who sympathized with the Nazis. Others included leading Iraqis and Syrians who later formed the Baath Party, and Egypt's future president, Gamal Abdul Nasser.

Two things irked the more fervent Zionists. One was the proposed partition of their promised land; the other was Britain's attempt to curry favour with the Arabs by limiting further Jewish immigration. The British, as we have seen, had extensive interests around the Persian Gulf (see page 26). An uninterrupted oil supply from these protectorates and Saudi Arabia was essential for the war effort. Although large numbers of immigrants continued to arrive in Palestine (perhaps 40,000 in 1940), there were several high-profile tragedies involving boatloads of helpless refugees.

Another effect of the war was to draw the United States deeply into Middle Eastern politics for the first time. Like Britain, the US needed Arab oil and poured money into Saudi Arabia to keep it stable and on side. The pro-Arab stance of President F. D. Roosevelt ran contrary to the pro-Zionist feeling of the country at large. Following a visit of Ben Gurion to the US, the Biltmore

Programme of support for the Zionist project gained widespread backing, even from Congress and presidential election candidates.

By the end of the war, as the full extent of the horrifying Nazi slaughter of some 6 million European Jews became known, the tide of support for Zionism ran even stronger. Both President Truman and his Congress urged Britain to take a more relaxed line over Zionist immigration.

Meanwhile, the Palestine question was having positive effects within the Arab world. In 1945, Egypt organized an Arab League that comprised itself, Syria, Saudi Arabia, Transjordan, Iraq, Lebanon and Yemen. The League's primary purpose was to foster unity and co-operation among Arab peoples. To begin with its activities were largely cultural, social and economic. Political activity was limited by the fact that only Egypt and Yemen were truly independent. Saudi Arabia and Jordan were reliant upon Western funds, while Syria, Lebanon and Iraq were still under occupation. Nevertheless, the League established a Higher Committee to lobby against Zionism. Given the massive worldwide sympathy for the Jewish people after the Holocaust, the League had to measure its efforts with tact and care.

END OF THE MANDATE

Post-war Britain, exhausted, impoverished and much weakened, clung to its Palestinian mandate. Its personnel were still subject to terrorist attacks by Zionist extremists, most notably when the King David Hotel in Jerusalem was bombed, killing 91 people. Immigration, much of it technically illegal, continued to swell the Jewish population. The British Labour government wished to shed its burden of responsibility and get out of Palestine as swiftly as possible, while maintaining sufficient bases there to protect the Suez Canal. At the end of 1945, therefore, it invited the US to form a joint committee to look into the situation in Palestine.

The committee's proposals, emerging as the Morrison–Grady Plan, were rejected by both Zionists and Arabs. Further plans, proposals, schemes and so on were thrown up and then rejected until Britain surrendered and handed over the entire Palestinian business to the newly formed United Nations (UN). A UN Special Committee on Palestine (UNSCOP) came up with a suggestion not unlike that put forward by the Peel Commission: separate Jewish and Arab states, united in an economic union, with Jerusalem and its environs under international control. 'Israel' was accepted as the name of the Jewish state-to-be. The UNSCOP proposal was accepted by the UN General Assembly at the end of 1947, with Britain and all Muslim countries voting against. After some uncertainty, Britain declared that its Palestinian mandate would end on 14 May 1948.

The boundaries of the two UN-arranged states were contorted to incorporate the wishes of both Jews and Arabs. Such mathematical frontiers were hopelessly unrealistic and, as soon as they were known, fighting broke out as each side strove to alter and extend them. In other words, the UN's intervention had polarized the position in Palestine rather than placated it.

The Zionist campaign was predominantly masterminded by the Jewish Agency, headed by Ben Gurion, which controlled the disciplined and relatively experienced Haganah forces numbering at least 40,000. The Irgun and Stern Gang terrorist groups worked more or less together with the official forces. The Palestinians were less warlike and certainly less well organized. Their own force of about 3,000 men, led by a Husseini relative of the Mufti, was poorly equipped. Many of its guerrilla attacks were on fellow Palestinians who had sold land to Zionists. The Arab League's contribution, an 'Arab Liberation Army' of 3,000 disorganized volunteers, contributed little. At one stage it refused to help the hard-pressed Husseini and even co-operated with the Haganah. Better motivated were 2,000 Muslim Brotherhood volunteers from Egypt.

Unfortunately for the Palestinians, few, if any, Arab states were really interested in helping them. Certainly three neighbouring countries – Egypt, Transjordan and Syria – all saw the chaos on their borders as an opportunity for territorial expansion of their own. So behind the scenes, while the world was shocked by hot-blooded killings such as the massacre of 254 Arab villagers in

Deir Yassin by the Stern Gang and the brutal ambush of a medical convoy by Palestinians, politicians were making a more cold-blooded appraisal of the situation.

Most startling were secret meetings between Abdullah, now the self-styled King of Transjordan, and a Ukrainian-born, US-educated Zionist politician named Golda Meir. Abdullah, having picked up his own kingdom through a stroke of British hard-nosed political chicanery, was nothing if not a realist. He shared with the more fervent Zionists the view that territory was what you could get, not what you ought to have. Consequently, he had no problem reaching an agreement with the equally realistic Mrs Meir. In the event of full-scale war between Israel and the Palestinians, he should take over Palestinian territory on the West Bank of the Jordan and leave the Israelis to grab what they could of the rest.

As the date for the expiry of the British mandate drew closer, the fighting intensified. The all too familiar pattern of terrorist attack, reprisal, counter-reprisal, and so on was by now commonplace. While it is impossible to say precisely who was primarily responsible for the escalation, there are indications that Zionist extremists were more to blame than most. By May 1948, Zionist forces had fought their way into the ports of Haifa and Jaffa, broken the siege of Jerusalem and defeated the Arab Liberation Army.

The Arab League now warned that if the Zionists made a unilateral declaration of independence, regular Arab forces would immediately attack the newly formed Israel. In secret, however, most Arab leaders feared that war would simply be an excuse for Transjordan to expand to the west. To make this more difficult, King Abdullah was given nominal command of the Arab League forces. He produced no co-ordinated plan of attack.

Nevertheless, the Zionists were alarmed that Arab pressure might force King Abdullah to break his pact with them. Golda Meir put herself in considerable personal danger and, disguised as an Arab woman, sneaked across the Jordan for another secret meeting with Abdullah. Clearly troubled, the wily monarch explained that it might not be possible to honour his previous agreement. He could not afford to fall out with fellow Arabs. After all, they had chosen him as their commander-in-chief ...

Meir returned safely to Zionist territory where her news was received with no surprise. Two days before the end of the British overlordship, the Zionist Provisional State Council met to decide the future. The Americans were strongly urging caution. Ben Gurion successfully advised his colleagues to reject their advice. The time had come, he declared, for the Jews to form what they had long dreamed of – the State of Israel.

Insight

The country we know as simply 'Israel' is officially the 'State of Israel' (Hebrew: *Medinat Yisrael*). The word 'Israel' originally referred to the Old Testament figure Jacob and meant one who had striven with God or been saved by God.

Israeli independence was declared on 14 May 1948, the day the last British High Commissioner left Palestine. The boundaries of the new country were not defined. Both Israelis and Arabs knew that they would be decided by the rifle, not the pen. The following day troops from Egypt, Transjordan, Syria, Lebanon, and Iraq invaded Israel.

THINGS TO REMEMBER

1 *Theories as to when a true Palestinian nation first appeared range from the 1830s to the 1970s.*

2 *By the later nineteenth century, a number of influential Jews, whose ancestors had been driven from Palestine in Roman times (the Jewish Diaspora), were talking of refounding a Jewish state ('Zion' or 'Israel').*

3 *The 'Zionist' movement was boosted by the publication of Theodore Herzl's* The Jewish State *(1896). Perhaps 35,000 Jews had settled in Palestine by 1914.*

4 *Taking over the Palestine mandate in 1920, Britain faced simmering Arab–Jewish hostility. In 1929, this erupted into serious inter-community violence.*

5 *Jewish immigration and Arab–Jewish hostility increased throughout the 1930s. By 1939, perhaps 15 per cent of the land of Palestine was owned by Jews.*

6 *With the publication of the report of the Peel Commission (1937), Britain came round to the view that Palestine had to be partitioned between Jew and Arab.*

7 *During the Second World War, soldiers from both the Arab and Jewish communities fought for Britain.*

8 *The slaughter of around 6 million Jews in the Nazi Holocaust created a massive tide of pro-Jewish sympathy that manifested itself in support for the Zionist movement.*

9 *No longer able to control the Palestine mandate, after the Second World War Britain handed it over to the newly formed United Nations.*

10 *The United Nations having drawn up a plan to partition Palestine, on 14 May 1948 the State of Israel was declared to be in existence.*

4

....

Gamal Abdul Nasser

This chapter will cover:
* *the First Arab–Israeli War*
* *the effects of this war on Middle East stability*
* *the rise of President Nasser in Egypt*
* *the causes of the Second Arab–Israeli War (1956).*

The First Arab–Israeli War

THE BALANCE OF FORCES

The formal war began immediately after the state of Israel came into being. The fighting was really just a continuation of that in progress since the United Nations passed its resolution on the partition of Palestine the previous year.

Crude statistics, looking at overall wealth, size of population and so forth, might suggest that the forces of Egypt, Saudi Arabia, Syria, Transjordan, Yemen, Lebanon and Iraq ought to have overrun Israel in a matter of days. But wars are fought by troops on the ground, not numbers, and in reality this was anything but a David versus Goliath conflict.

It is estimated that the non-Palestinian Arabs managed to put about 23,000 troops into the field. The better trained Israel

Defence Force (IDF), created by forcing the experienced Haganah, Irgun and Stern Gang to amalgamate, eventually rose to over 96,000. Particularly after the re-armament of the summer of 1948 (when weapons and ammunition of all kinds came in from Soviet-backed Czechoslovakia, France and private US sponsors), the IDF was better armed than the Arabs. It even secretly acquired three US Flying Fortress bombers with which it was able to attack Cairo.

Insight

Originally anti-Zionist, in 1948 the USSR back-pedalled to support the State of Israel. It believed that, as a socialist state, Israel would oppose Western influence in the region. Later, during the Cold War, the Soviets reinstated their hostile stance.

Despite cultural differences between Jews originating from North-East Europe ('Ashkenazim') and those from elsewhere ('Mizrahim' from the Middle East or Asia, 'Sephardim' from Spain, Portugal and North Africa), all Israelis knew that they were fighting for their very existence. This gave them a ruthless determination, sometimes known as the 'Holocaust syndrome'. Israelis had seen what had happened to the meek and conforming Jews who had trusted others – they had been exterminated. The 'fighting Jew' would never let this happen. Their toughness might make them feared – hated even – but it would keep them safe.

To the first generation of Israelis, the end justified the means – even if it meant attacking their own unarmed trucks in order to provoke further fighting with Egypt; even if it meant Haganah troops of future prime minister Yitzhak Rabin killing Irgun fighters who had rejected a unified command (another future prime minister, Menachem Begin, survived the attack); even if it meant extremist assassins commanded by yet another future prime minister, Yitzhak Shamir, killing the UN mediator because he seemed too pro-Arab; even if it meant Moche Dayan's forces terrorizing Arab villages outside Israel so that their inhabitants would learn to live in fear of their neighbours. All of these acts of desperate cruelty actually happened. Understandable but nevertheless abhorrent, they laid the foundations of a wall of hatred and mistrust that stands to this day.

Faced with such steely unity, the motley Arab forces stood little chance. As we saw in Chapter 2, their states were largely new creations, politically unstable and not yet able to cope with the strains of full-scale, long-distance warfare. Moreover, although some troops might have been inspired by feelings of Arab or Muslim unity, their leaders were not. The Mufti, sheltering in Egypt, did not get on with the Arab League and refused to allow his Palestinian guerrilla band to co-operate with it. The Egyptians sought as much land as possible on the Sinai side of the Suez Canal. The Syrians wanted fertile land in the Golan Heights and around the Sea of Galilee. The Saudis sent one paltry battalion; the Lebanese and Iraqis were there largely because it was politically less trouble than not being there. Commander-in-chief Abdullah of Transjordan, dreaming of one day ruling a Greater Syria, made sure that no Arab forces got in the way of his seizure of the land the UN had assigned to the Palestinians on the West Bank of the River Jordan.

THE COURSE OF THE WAR

During the first phase of the war, ended by a UN ceasefire mediated by Count Folke Bernadotte, the Israelis secured their state. When the fighting broke out again a month later, they were able to go on the offensive and drive back their dispirited enemies on almost every front. Only in Jerusalem did the British-led Arab Legion hold its own, targeting Palestinians as much as Israelis.

It was a bitty war, punctuated by ceasefires that both sides broke if they felt they could gain an advantage by doing so. The British commander of King Abdullah's Arab Legion called it 'an imitation war'. Its most unsavoury aspect was Israel's Plan D, or Dalet. This strategy, which had been in place before the declaration of independence, was based on the principle of overcoming the enemy within – the Palestinians – before tackling invaders. To achieve this, Israeli forces 'pacified' Palestinian villages and towns.

This involved either getting the community to put itself under total Israeli control or driving the population out and destroying the buildings: 360 Arab villages and 14 Arab towns were razed as a consequence of the Dalet. The Israelis said this was the only feasible way of safeguarding their security; to others it looked suspiciously like the insidious form of racism now known as ethnic cleansing.

Despite the murder of Count Bernadotte, the UN continued with its efforts to broker peace. This resulted in a series of separate ceasefires agreed between February (Israel–Egypt) and July (Israel–Syria) 1949. These matured into more durable armistices with every state except Iraq. Totally in command of the military situation by the autumn of 1948, Israeli Prime Minister David Ben Gurion had considered pressing on with the campaign into the Sinai and West Bank. Only international pressure, particularly from the US, had held him back. In a very real sense, the next two Arab–Israeli wars (1956 and 1967) simply picked up the conflict where it had temporarily halted in 1949.

ISRAEL AND THE PALESTINIANS

The first and most obvious consequence of the conflict, known to the Israelis as the War of Independence and to the Arabs as the Palestine War, was the establishment of the State of Israel. Having absorbed 77 per cent of the UN's proposed Palestinian state, it was some 21 per cent larger than the state envisaged by the UN partition plan. Unlike the UN's Israel, the new one had defensible frontiers – though not as defensible as the military would have liked. The population comprised 717,700 Jews (the ratio of Ashkenazim to others being 6:1) and 165,000 Arabs (almost one-fifth of whom were Christian).

The remnants of the Palestinian state that had only ever existed on paper were divided between Egypt, which occupied the 6.5-km (4-mile) wide strip of Mediterranean coastline around the city of Gaza, and Transjordan, which had seized the West Bank. The international community, Israel excluded, eventually agreed to the West Bank

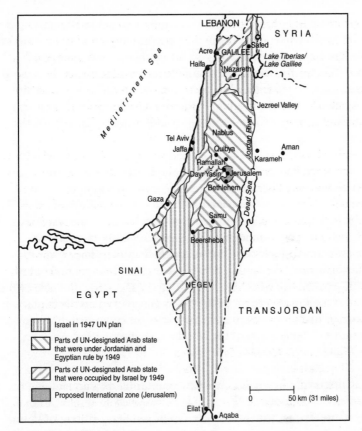

Figure 4.1 Palestine and Transjordan 1947–8.

being incorporated within Abdullah's original kingdom to form the Hashemite Kingdom of Jordan, or simply Jordan. Israel and Jordan divided the holy city of Jerusalem between them. Syria got nothing.

Insight

Middle Eastern politics are rarely translucent. Certain of defeat when it went to war in 1948, Syria probably called for an all-out Arab assault on Israel in order to divert King Abdullah from his plan forcibly to unite Syria with Jordan to form a Greater Syria.

Of all the Arab states, Syria was the most adamant about the need to go to war. In short, President Shukri al-Quwatli went to war not for pan-Arab notions of unity or brotherhood, but to prevent that very same spirit from undermining Syria's independence. He hoped to block King Abdullah from carrying out his Greater Syria unity scheme. During the first years of independence, Quwatli lived in constant fear that King Abdullah would invade Syria to unify the central Syrian lands.

What of the Palestinians? To them the events of 1948 were 'Al Naksa', the disaster. With terrible irony, the establishment of Israel, a country for refugees, had created a new nation of refugees. Precise figures are impossible to come by, but from the start of the fighting to the summer of 1949 perhaps close to 1 million Palestinians had left their homes and fled abroad. They went for many reasons. The Israelis drove out thousands; more fled out of fear, particularly when Arab politicians exaggerated the scale of the Deir Yassin massacre for propaganda purposes; some were pushed aside by invading Arab forces; the better off emigrated in relative comfort to other parts of the Middle East, Europe and America.

In all negotiations, the Israelis were adamant that no Palestinian might return. They had either left voluntarily, they argued somewhat obtusely, or they had been removed as a threat to the state. Sprawling, squalid refugee camps ran like a ribbon of shame around Israel's borders. Most were in the West Bank and Gaza, but they also appeared in Lebanon and Syria.

The Palestinians had never been an established nation, a people with a land, an anthem and a government of their own. They had never had the chance. But here, where half-naked children played between the cramped tents and insanitary washblocks of the refugee camps, a generation grew up inspired with a new and bitter Palestinian nationalism. As the Jewish founders of the state of Israel had done, so the Palestinians of the camps came to realize that only they could make their dream come true. Tragically, however, like the band of Zionists reporting long ago on the promised land, they too found that, 'the bride is beautiful but she is married to another man'. So began another set of bloody divorce proceedings.

A region of instability

The establishment of Israel, the war, and the flood of Palestinian refugees had a massively destabilizing effect on the Middle East. The humiliation of defeat helped undermine fragile regimes throughout the region. The situation was not helped by the fact that, despite secret talks and the efforts of third-party intermediaries, no peace treaties were signed. This meant that Arabs and Israelis remained technically at war. The Israelis rejected all offers of land for peace, declaring that having just fought for their country they had no intention of giving bits of it away. For their part, the Arab states refused to recognize Israel's existence. Impasse.

The region's problems were greatly exacerbated by the advent of the Cold War. This was the long period of superpower confrontation in which the Soviet Union, the champion of communism, stood toe-to-toe with the USA, the champion of democratic capitalism. It is generally said to have begun with Winston Churchill's famous statement, delivered at Fulton, Missouri, in March 1946, that an 'iron curtain' had fallen across Europe. The rivalry between the two sides of the curtain – communist East and capitalist West – fed wars, coups and terrorism all over the globe. As much by luck as judgement, it never quite escalated into the nuclear Third World War that everyone feared and many predicted.

Two matters tied the Middle East into the Cold War. One was the falling of a second iron curtain across the Palestine region, dividing Jew from Arab. It was inevitable that the superpowers would try to use the Arab–Israeli stand-off to increase their local influence. The reason why they sought this influence brings us to the second factor that made the Middle East such a vital battleground: oil.

The West was now running on oil, not coal, and the Middle East's share of world oil production was rising daily. To the US, which was rapidly taking over Britain's position as the major external influence in the Middle East, Arab oil was crucial. American policy, therefore, was to keep the Soviet Union out of the region, maintain trouble-free transport routes (both pipelines and seaways), and try to ensure that local governments remained on good terms with the US.

There was one major difference, however, between the way Britain and France had played their part in the Middle East and the way the US would do so. The former had usually dressed their power politics in the clothing of legality – treaties, mandates and so forth. The US was blessed with no such fig leaves. At that time the media back home did not want the US militarily embroiled in the Middle East, nor did the United Nations or the Soviet Union. Direct, overt interference risked a serious escalation of the Cold War. Therefore, competing with Soviet skulduggery, American administrations had to defend their interests in ways that were sometimes decidedly underhand. In short, that meant using the Central Intelligence Agency (CIA). As a result, the politics of the Middle East, always complex, became a game of bluff and counter-bluff, deceit and counter-deceit that not even the players themselves were able to control.

SYRIA

After the French withdrawal in 1946, the Syrians were eager to test their shiny new democratic constitution. They were soon disappointed. The country's complicated religious, social and economic diversity made stability unlikely. Defeat and outside intervention ensured its demise.

Shukri al Kuwatli's largely Sunni National Party, deeply corrupt but popular for leading the resistance to the French, clung on to power amid festering discontent. The disastrous defeat by Israel further undermined its already shaky credibility. The US State

Department was worried. Like Syria, Russia before the communist take-over in 1917 had been plagued by poor government, economic hardship and military defeat. Syria, a vital link in the pipeline route from the Gulf to the Mediterranean, might easily go the same way.

The precise role of the newly formed CIA in what happened next is understandably obscure. Nevertheless, there is plenty of evidence that they singled out a 'burly Kurd' named Colonel Husni al Zaim, a soldier of iron will and mind, as someone they could do business with. In March 1949, the tanks of the Syrian army rolled into Damascus, Kuwatli's elected government was removed and the iron Kurd installed in its place. Thus did the CIA oversee its first coup d'état, overthrow democracy, and help to power the Middle East's first modern military dictator.

Insight

The CIA-assisted change of government in Syria – 'If you cannot change the game, change the players!' – came as such a surprise to most Syrians that most of them did not even know the Arabic word for 'coup'.

Alas for American intentions! Zaim proved an unwise choice of ally. After strutting his stuff like a character out of *Bugsy Malone*, he was shortly removed by another coup. Syria now entered upon a prolonged period of instability marked by a succession of coups led by army officers. After changing hands five times in as many years, the baton of government finally ended up with Colonel Faisal al-Atasi, who restored the country's parliament.

Throughout this period, a new movement was gathering force in Syrian politics. This was the Arab Socialist Renaissance Party, better known as the Baath Party. It was fiercely anti-Western. Its Pan-Arabist manifesto claimed all boundaries between Arab peoples to be merely inconvenient Western devices. Not surprisingly for those who had once shown distinct Nazi sympathies, the Baathists were also intractably hostile to Israel.

LEBANON

Parliamentary democracy fared better in Lebanon, where the delicately balanced Muslim-Christian constitutional arrangement (see pages 34–5) survived the spat with Israel. The Christian leaders distanced themselves from the rest of Israel's enemies by declaring that Lebanon was not really an Arab country and had never wanted to go to war in the first place. A Syrian-backed coup attempt was foiled.

Thereafter, despite an assassinated prime minister and a president removed by a general strike, the system survived. Lebanon did not join the Second Arab–Israeli War and, to the intense annoyance of other Arab nations, refused to break off relations with Israel's allies, Britain and France.

IRAQ

Iraq fared better than Syria. Boosted by rising oil revenues, the country prospered. Its ragged form of democracy operated after a fashion, although it saw two prime ministers overthrown by popular uprisings and a period of martial law. Behind the scenes, regent Abdullah and the army continued to wield considerable power. Sadly, though, the stability and modernization anticipated when the British-educated King Faisal II came of age in 1953 failed to materialize. The young king lacked charisma and political instinct – a dangerous formula at any time, but potentially disastrous in post-war Iraq.

Diplomatically, Iraq's most significant move was entering into the Baghdad Pact just before the Second Arab–Israeli War (1956). The Pact started as an agreement with Turkey over the treatment of militant Kurds. It was then expanded to include Iran, Pakistan and Britain, and became known as the Middle East Treaty Organization (later changed to the Central Treaty Organization or CENTO). Its purpose was to act as a sort of North Atlantic Treaty Organization (NATO) of the Middle East, blocking any Soviet attempts at infiltration there. Pact members came and went, and it was never very effective. Most Arab countries mistrusted it because of British membership.

JORDAN

The end of King Abdullah of Jordan – 'the dog who sold Palestine to the Zionists' – might have been predicted. Indeed, the British representative in Aman had warned him that the al-Aqsa mosque in Jerusalem was a dangerous place to visit. But visit Abdullah did, for the site contained the grave of his father, Hussein, the sometime Sharif of Mecca.

The king was shot dead at point blank range on 20 July 1951. For a keen chess player, he had made the unusual mistake of not thinking far enough ahead. His killer was a fanatical Palestinian determined to slay the man whom he believed had betrayed not just the Palestinians but the entire Arab nation. There was some truth in this belief.

Two years later, Talal, Abdullah's schizophrenic son, was declared mentally unfit to rule. The crown passed to his son, another Hussein. The young man had been beside his grandfather at the time of his death and had narrowly escaped being killed himself in the wild hail of bullets that the royal bodyguard – too late – had sent in the general direction of the assassin.

The 18-year-old Hussein inherited all of his grandfather's political skills, and more. Educated at Harrow (Winston Churchill's school) and the Royal Military College, Sandhurst, England, he retained an affection for the country that had created his kingdom after the First World War. At the same time, he was too clever to let pro-British sentiment spoil his relations with his fellow Arabs. Though tempted, for instance, he refused to join the Baghdad Pact. After the Second Arab–Israeli War, he proved his Arab credentials by dismissing all British advisors and abrogating his grandfather's post-war Anglo-Jordanian treaty of friendship and co-operation.

Nasser

Defeat in the war with Israel left Egypt ripe for revolution. The
shaky constitutional monarchy handed down by Britain had
been seriously undermined by the extraordinary figure of King
Farouk. In his late teens he had been described by a British High
Commissioner as 'uneducated, lazy, untruthful, capricious,
irresponsible and vain, though with a quick superficial intelligence
and charm of manner' (*History Today*, Vol. 52, no. 7, 2002,
page 55). Time had not improved him. Now in his early thirties,
his girth and lust for ladies as pneumatic as himself shocked and
offended his subjects.

THE FREE OFFICERS' COUP

Worse still, Egypt's bloated playboy monarch dabbled in politics
with dangerous ineptitude. The country's corrupt and inefficient
government was allowed to run on unchallenged, making the rich
richer and the poor poorer. An attempt to suppress the increasingly
popular Muslim Brotherhood in the middle of the disastrous war
with Israel led to the assassination of the prime minister and the
subsequent killing of the Brotherhood's leader by government
agents.

For a while, many Egyptians focused their fury on the British.
In accordance with the pre-war treaty, Britain still maintained
a strong presence in Egypt and full control over Sudan. In the
Suez Canal Zone they had no fewer than ten airfields and two
naval dockyards, defended by a large military presence. By the

early 1950s, guerrilla attacks on British positions had become commonplace.

When negotiations failed to make any progress, the Egyptian government unilaterally ended its treaty with Britain. This only increased the tension and terrorism. The severity of one British retaliatory raid, which left some 30 Egyptians dead, led to widespread demonstrations in Cairo. Muslim Brothers, communists and frustrated ordinary citizens joined forces in an orgy of destruction. It began with an attack on Madame Badia's emporium for gambling and belly-dancing, and ended with assaults on banks, the British Council and other buildings, even cinemas, vaguely associated with the Western way of life. As Cairo burned, King Farouk enjoyed an extended luncheon for 600 guests. Only when it was over did he call out the army to suppress the riots in his capital. Over the next six months, he went through four prime ministers. Something had to give.

Enter a group of 89 well-meaning Egyptian army personnel by the name of the Free Officers. Their leader was a tall, handsome veteran of the Israeli war, one of the few men who had emerged from the conflict with his reputation enhanced. His name was Colonel Gamal Abdul Nasser. For the time being, though, the 32-year-old stayed in the background and allowed attention to be focused on the group's nominal head, the higher ranking General Mohammed Naguib.

Officially, the CIA had no links with the Free Officers and there are still Egyptians who refuse to believe that the United States had a hand in the rise to power of one of their national heroes. The evidence, however, suggests otherwise. The coup that drove out Farouk and saw General Naguib installed as both president and prime minister was almost a carbon copy of the Syrian affair of four years earlier. It was welcomed by the State Department, and the US entered into a period of good relations with the Officers' seemingly moderate, pro-Western regime. Considerable sums of American aid found their way into the Egyptian treasury.

The Free Officers had come to power with a six-point plan that included free education for all and an end to colonialism. Their international outlook was officially non-aligned and much of their rhetoric was about Arab nationalism spearheaded by Egypt's National Union for Arab Socialism. Other political associations were banned, as was the Muslim Brotherhood. The latter was outlawed after a failed attempt to assassinate Nasser. The driving force behind the Officers' coup had already replaced Naguib and now headed Egypt as chairman of the Revolutionary Command Council, prime minister and president.

So far Nasser had done well. He had abolished the monarchy, redistributed land and initiated a large number of much-needed schemes to regulate and reinvigorate the economy. Foremost among these was the construction of a high dam at Aswan to control the waters of the Nile. For this the Americans and British had promised a hefty $270 million. What had annoyed the Brotherhood was the president's agreement with Britain that allowed Sudan to become independent and the British to leave the Suez Canal zone gradually. Hard-line Islamists and nationalists had demanded union with Muslim Sudan and an immediate withdrawal of all foreign forces from Egyptian soil.

Nasser had never enjoyed good relations with the British, Egypt's former masters, who still clung to the fanciful notion that they were a major power. Any thawing produced by the Canal agreement was immediately re-frozen when Nasser heard of the Baghdad Pact (see page 66). He called it an insult to the Arab nation and a 'festering crime'. He would not join, nor would he countenance Jordan doing so. Britain, he believed, no longer had a role in the Middle East and should quit the region for good – as long as they left behind their contribution to the Aswan Dam.

Thus far the successful son of a postmaster from Alexandria had enjoyed something of a honeymoon with the US. Because of the Holocaust and the power of the Jewish vote in certain states,

American policy had always been pro-Israel. As President Truman had bluntly put it, 'I have no Arabs in my constituency'. That did not preclude friendship with Arab states, however, and Truman's successor, Eisenhower, tried to remain even-handed. As we have seen, the US had offered funds for the Aswan Dam project and after the Qibya Massacre (see page 73) Eisenhower withheld $75 million of US aid to Israel.

Eisenhower's cordial relations with Nasser ended suddenly when the Egyptian premier was tempted into infidelity. The bait was arms. Ever since the war with Israel, Egypt had wished to re-arm. The US and Britain, pledged to try to maintain a balance between Israel and her enemies, had provided some weapons but nowhere near as many as Nasser wanted. Early in 1955 he believed his point of view vindicated when, responding to the death of an Israeli cyclist in an Egyptian intelligence gathering mission, the IDF launched a massive raid on Gaza that left 38 Egyptian soldiers dead.

A chance conversation with the Chinese while on a visit to Indonesia appeared to solve Nasser's problem. Arms? The Chinese never had trouble obtaining arms. All he had to do was ask the Soviets, which Nasser promptly did. Within weeks, with Czechoslovakia acting as an intermediary, he was promised 100 self-propelled guns, 200 armoured personnel carriers, 300 tanks, 200 MIG 15 fighters, 50 bombers … and all $300 million's-worth in exchange for cotton rather than scarce hard cash. For the ambitious president, it was precisely what the doctor had ordered.

As far as the US was concerned, the move was an irritating betrayal that brought the Soviet Union into the heart of the Middle East. The following year, British and American funds for the Aswan Dam were frozen. Nasser responded with a move that sent shockwaves of disbelief humming around the world. Speaking to an enormous crowd in Alexandria, he announced that he was nationalizing the Suez Canal. The charges collected from the waterway's shipping, he explained, would be used to make up the shortfall on his dam project.

The move made Nasser the darling of the entire Arab world. He expected to be challenged, of course, but not quite as violently as he was.

The Suez crisis

ISRAEL AFTER THE FIRST ARAB–ISRAELI WAR

Life was hard in Israel after the war. Two years later 100,000 of its citizens were still living in tents, and immigration was continuing apace. By the fourth year of its existence, however, things had begun to improve with increased foreign aid, notably from private Jewish foundations, the US and (West) Germany.

Unlike most of its Arab neighbours, Israel enjoyed some political stability under Labour coalition governments headed by the old war-horse Ben Gurion and the more urbane Moshe Sharett. Tension continued between Labour and the hard-line Herut Party, successor to the Revisionists, although Ben Gurion's robust style of leadership attracted less criticism from the right than Sharett's more inclusive approach. Other sources of friction were uneasy relations between the Ashkenazi and other immigrant groups, and the degree to which the new state should embrace the Orthodox Jewish faith. The problem was partly side-stepped by not producing either a written constitution or a bill of rights.

Insight

Like Britain, whose influence on the thinking of Israel's founding fathers was considerable, Israel has a flexible parliamentary system evolved through legislation, practice and executive orders rather than a written constitution.

TENSION WITH ARAB NEIGHBOURS

The state's most serious danger was the continued threat from the surrounding Arab states. Arab governments did what they could to hurt the new state economically, boycotting its products and, where possible, impeding its commerce. Actual terrorist activity was limited. The bulk of the early Arab so-called 'infiltrations' into Israel were tragic cases of desperate Palestinians sneaking back to collect possessions, harvest crops or even just set eyes on the homesteads they had lost.

Aggressive infiltration began in 1950, when a dozen Israelis were killed. Thereafter, the number of victims was about 50 a year. Israel responded to all intrusion, pacific or not, with an iron fist. Unmarked borders were mined and suspects shot on sight. The bodies of those slain were booby trapped to kill relatives coming to collect them. Over six years, perhaps as many as 5,000 Palestinians, most innocent civilians, had been killed.

Disproportionate Israeli response also took the form of reprisal raids, mainly into Jordan and the Gaza Strip. The most vicious of these destroyed the Jordanian village of Qibya and killed 69 people, half of them women and children. Ben Gurion lied that the atrocity had been carried out by local Jewish settlers provoked by Arab attacks. The Qibya operation had been led by an ambitious young officer named Ariel Sharon. The following year the same man led two IDF commando squads that shot up a Gaza refugee camp, killing 20 civilians.

So the violence was cranked up yet again. By the time of Nasser's arms deal with the Soviets, his relations with Israel had reached a new low. An Israeli attempt to implicate Egypt in anti-Western terrorism – the Lavon affair – was badly bungled, leaving the Israelis exposed as an international menace. Later, in the year of the Gaza raid, Nasser also closed the Strait of Tiran. This prevented access to the Red Sea from Israel's southern port of Eilat. The Israelis regarded it as tantamount to a challenge to combat.

THE ALLIES' PLAN

By the autumn of 1956, it was not just Israel that was itching for a showdown with Nasser. The French were fed up with the assistance that Egypt was giving to independence fighters in the French colony of Algeria. (As we saw in Syria, the French rarely gave up a colony without a fight.) They wanted Nasser removed, at almost any price, and Israel was the ideal ally in such an enterprise. They had already supplied arms and were negotiating to build an Israeli nuclear reactor. The British, although less gung-ho, were also sick of the Egyptian premier. Prime Minister Anthony Eden dubbed him 'the Muslim Mussolini' and was furious with the way he had scorned the Baghdad Pact and pressured Jordan into not joining.

Two-thirds of Europe's oil and one-third of Britain's passed through the Suez Canal. As a commercial enterprise, it was also a source of revenue for the British and French governments. The sudden nationalization of this vital waterway had been totally unacceptable, despite Egypt's mutterings about compensation. The US put pressure on both sides to come to some sort of compromise but their desultory talks got nowhere. Equally ineffective were attempts by the French, British and Israeli secret services to eliminate Nasser by foul means.

The deadlock was broken by a cunning plan. It brought together France, Britain and Israel – the latter two becoming the most unlikely of allies – in a top-secret anti-Egyptian coalition. The preparations involved a build-up of British and French troops in the Mediterranean and a clandestine visit to France by British Foreign Secretary Selwyn Lloyd (sporting a false moustache) for a meeting with Ben Gurion and Israel's one-eyed Chief of Staff, Moshe Dayan.

Dayan and the IDF were in confident mood. The French had always kept them supplied with more weapons than was made public. As a counter-balance to Egypt's Soviet weapons, France had recently delivered a fresh consignment of tanks and aircraft. Dayan and his fellow hawks were eager to use them before Egypt's re-armament was complete. The prospect of doing so in alliance with Britain and France was even better. In fact, they couldn't wait.

THINGS TO REMEMBER

1 *The emergence of Israel turned the Jewish–Arab conflict into a full-scale Arab–Israeli War that lasted until July 1949.*

2 *The unco-ordinated Arab forces, nominally led by King Abdullah of Transjordan, were outnumbered and outgunned by the ruthless Israel Defence Force.*

3 *Israel's Plan D for the 'pacification' of Palestinian areas within Israel led to the destruction of hundreds of Palestinian villages and created around 1 million Palestinian refugees.*

4 *By July 1949, when the war was over, Israel had absorbed 77 per cent of the state that the UN had designated as Palestine.*

5 *The First Arab–Israeli War sparked widespread instability around the Middle East, beginning with the first of many military coups d'état in Syria.*

6 *Allying with the shaky monarchy it had established in Iraq, Britain organised an anti-communist Baghdad Pact.*

7 *Following the assassination of King Abdullah and the abdication of his immediate successor, in 1952 the throne of Jordan passed to the young King Hussein.*

8 *In 1952, Egypt's corrupt and incompetent monarchy was overthrown by a coup d'état of the 'Free Officers' movement.*

9 *When Anglo-American funding for the new Aswan Dam across the Nile was withdrawn, Egypt's President Nasser nationalized the Suez Canal.*

10 *Britain, France and Israel launched surprise attacks on Egypt in 1956, launching the Suez or Second Arab–Israeli War.*

5

War to war

This chapter will cover:
- *the Second Arab–Israeli War and its consequences*
- *the political instability of the Middle East, 1957–66*
- *the plight of the Palestinians*
- *the re-arming of the Middle East and preparations for another war.*

The Suez War

On 29 October 1956, taking up where they had left off eight years earlier, the Israelis attacked across Sinai towards the Suez Canal. Within a week they had captured Gaza and the entire Sinai peninsula. Meanwhile, Britain and France had expressed mock concern for the security of the canal. The Israelis and Egyptians must withdraw to within 16 km (10 miles) of the international waterway, they demanded. Their ally duly obliged. Nasser, on the other hand, would have none of it: just as the Anglo-French plan had predicted.

Upon Nasser's refusal, British and French fighter-bombers attacked Egyptian positions for almost a week, during which time 95 per cent of the country's new air force was destroyed. One bomb sank a ship in the canal, blocking it. The Egyptians completed the job by sinking concrete-filled hulks alongside it. From now on, whatever the outcome of the campaign, the canal would be useless for some time.

When the bombing stopped, British and French marine and airborne troops landed near the canal; 36 hours later a ceasefire had been negotiated. The assault force was home by Christmas and Nasser remained in possession of the canal. He had won.

The Anglo-French Suez plan had failed for four main reasons. First, the operation had been too slow. A sudden seizure of the canal within, say, three days would have given the attackers the upper hand in further negotiations. As it was, the prolonged bombardment allowed UN and domestic opinion to turn almost unanimously against the venture.

Insight

The author can remember the jingoistic chanting of 'Nasser is a twerp ... All his army have gone barmy!' in his primary school playground, while back home his parents bemoaned the reintroduction of petrol rationing.

Second, the invasion had taken place with no diplomatic or propaganda preparation. Britain and France's allies, the press, electorate and political supporters had not been consulted, and all felt understandably annoyed. Third, the operation brought an overstretched Britain perilously close to bankruptcy. A fuel crisis loomed, too. Not only was the canal blocked but Syria, in a gesture of Pan-Arabism, had also cut the oil pipeline that ran from Iraq to the Mediterranean.

Finally, the US was in the throes of a presidential election in which the incumbent, Dwight Eisenhower, was running on a peace ticket. He was furious that his NATO allies had launched a major campaign without even so much as informing him. The Soviet Union had responded to the aggression by threatening missile attacks on Britain, France and Israel unless the fighting stopped immediately. There was no way Eisenhower was going to risk a

Third World War in support of the crude neo-colonial thrashings of his European allies.

Such was the economic and political power of the US, that when it backed a UN ceasefire and demanded that Britain and France do the same, they had little option but to oblige. Rather, Britain obliged and thereby forced the reluctant French to do the same. How were the mighty fallen.

The consequences of Suez

ISRAEL

Before the start of the Suez campaign, Prime Minister Ben Gurion had dreamed of a new political order in the Middle East. Israel would conquer and assimilate all Sinai and the West Bank. Iraq would be allowed to swallow up Jordan on condition that it made peace with Israel. Egypt, crushed and humiliated, would ditch Nasser and accept Israel's peace terms. The Lebanese would follow suit. Finally, left out in the cold, Syria would be forced to do the same. Then Israel would be at peace with its neighbours behind secure and defensible frontiers.

In the face of Soviet hostility and US anxiety, the plan came to nothing. Israel was obliged to return all its conquests, although it did get a UN force (the United Nations Emergency Force – UNEF) to patrol the Israel–Egypt border and a US guarantee that the Strait of Tiran would be kept open. More importantly, the flow of US aid continued unimpeded.

Within Israel the campaign was seen as a triumph. In response to Arab terrorism, the Israelis had thumped their bullying neighbour and proved that they were the Middle East's superpower. Ben Gurion's philosophy of aggressive defence had triumphed over Moshe Sharett's diplomacy. The impact of this political victory would affect the politics of the Middle East for the rest of the century and beyond.

THE WEST

The Suez campaign was an almost farcical final fling of Anglo-French imperialism. Anthony Eden resigned within weeks and the humiliated French Fourth Republic collapsed the following year. The inhabitants of Britain and France's remaining overseas colonies, noting the weakness of their masters, pressed harder for independence.

The Cold War had long been extending its icy fingers across the Middle East. Oil had brought the US into the region during the Second World War. East and West clashed in Iran immediately thereafter. By the time of Suez, the Soviets had a considerable presence in Baathist Syria. In the meantime, accepting domestic sympathy for the Israeli cause, the US had developed close economic ties with Israel. The Soviet–Egyptian arms deal had then extended Soviet influence to Israel's southern flank. When Soviet Premier Nikolai Bulganin threatened attacks on Britain, France and Israel, and Eisenhower responded with the 'Eisenhower Doctrine' (see pages 87–8), the Middle East had become a major theatre of Cold War operations.

Insight

The US has provided economic aid to Israel in the form of grants and loans every year since 1949, but no military aid was forthcoming until 1962, during the presidency of John Kennedy.

Two reservations need to be made lest we get the over-simplified impression of a US-backed Israel battling against Soviet-backed Arabs. First, the Soviet Union was an atheistic state – an anathema to Muslim Arabs. Second, several conservative Arab regimes were strongly opposed to communist or even socialist thinking. In 1956 these included the monarchies of Saudi Arabia, Jordan and Iraq, as well as small sheikhdoms like Kuwait and Oman. One reason why the politics of the Middle East were so complicated is that the Arab–Israeli conflict frequently cut across political and religious boundaries.

EGYPT

The Suez War did wonders at home and abroad for President Nasser's reputation. He dismissed his military losses as insignificant. What were they compared with retention of a nationalized Suez Canal? Among Egyptians, fellow Arabs and anti-imperialists everywhere he was hailed as the underdog who had triumphed. Having successfully seen off the fading might of Britain and France, he was the undisputed leader of the Arab world.

Between the wars

Almost 11 years elapsed between the Suez War and the next major crisis in the Middle East, the Six Day War. Technically speaking, throughout this period the Arab nations were still at war with Israel, previous conflicts having been halted only by armistices. Moreover, all Israel's neighbours continued to deny its right to exist. The Saudi government was not alone in meticulously blacking out all references to the Jewish state in maps, books and articles.

In truth, however, most Arab states did not really want another large-scale armed confrontation with Israel. Politicians and generals talked about it, threatened it, even planned and postured for it – but they were unwilling to face the possibility of further defeat, loss and humiliation.

YEMEN AND SAUDI ARABIA

That a low-born army officer with links to the Soviet Union might claim leadership of the Arab world was abhorrent to the monarchies of Saudi Arabia and Jordan. The extent of this gulf was vividly illustrated when a civil war broke out in the tiny Yemen Arab Republic (North Yemen).

On one side was the country's conservative imam ruler; on the other were rebellious army officers. These forward-thinking young men had been trained in Egypt, where they had picked up republican and socialist ideas. King Abdulaziz having died, the Saudi government was headed by his conservative, palace-building, pleasure-seeking son Saud. Not wishing to entertain a revolutionary republic on his south-western border, he backed the imam.

Insight

The border between Saudi Arabia and Yemen, officially settled by the Taif Treaty of 1934, remains troubled. The exact position of the frontier is less significant than the presence of precious oil reserves nearby and the Shia persuasion of the Houthis of northern Yemen.

The issue divided the Saudi royal family. The king's brother, Faisal, who would eventually remove his elder sibling in a palace coup, was a modernizer. He opposed the policy of supporting religious traditionalists. Such men (and they always were men in a strict Muslim society) rigorously resisted the sort of modernization, like setting up television broadcasting, that Faisal sought for Saudi Arabia.

With the Saudis divided, Nasser responded to the Yemeni rebels' request for help with 70,000 troops and a great deal of equipment. This was sufficient for them eventually to win the five-year civil war. There is a further twist to the complex tale. While the Egyptians and Saudis were still fighting a proxy war in Yemen, they found themselves on the same side in the Six Day War with Israel.

EGYPT

Nasser's bid for Arab leadership received a major boost when he announced that Egypt and Syria had agreed to flout geography and history and become one country. The 1958 amalgamation was seen as the first step towards the formation of a single Arab nation. Egypt was designated the 'Southern Province' and Syria the 'Northern Province' of a United Arab Republic (UAR). Not surprisingly, after the wedding confetti had been swept away, the new partners took a long hard look at each other and realized that their marriage had been entirely about convenience and not affection, let alone love. Divorce came with yet another military coup in Syria three years later, although the Egyptians retained the grandiose UAR title for a further ten years.

Through all this, Nasser continued to make politically correct anti-Israeli noises – 'I announce from here, on behalf of the people of the United Arab Republic, that this time we will exterminate Israel' (1959) – but took no steps to turn rhetoric into reality. With the UNEF guarding his Sinai frontier and economic progress funded by substantial aid from both the Soviet Union and the US, the Egyptian president had no wish to do anything that might rock his even-keeled boat.

SYRIA

Compared with Egypt's plain sailing, the voyage of the 'Northern Province' – Syria – was tempestuous. Colonel Faisal al-Atasi's Baath Party espoused a curious cocktail of anti-imperialism, non-alignment in the Cold War, pick-and-mix features of Islam, and socialist egalitarianism. Above all, it was authoritarian and highly centralized.

The army cashed in on popular resentment at the state of Syria's economy and its subordinate status in the UAR, and in another coup re-established Syria as an independent country. The new, nominally civilian government soon fell foul of the army Baathists who engineered yet another coup in 1963. Under the strain of all this regime change, divisions were starting to open up within the Baath Party itself. Some members remained avidly pro-Nasser, others had close links with the Baathists in neighbouring Iraq.

A third group was keen to emphasize the party's specifically Syrian nature.

All factions claimed to have the cause of Arab unity closest to their hearts. In the end, the Syrian Baath Party came out on top, crushed all opposition, set up a police state, and diverted attention from domestic affairs by vigorously playing the anti-Israeli card.

IRAQ

Matters were just as chaotic in Iraq. Here, despite extensive public works provided by mounting oil revenues, the rule of King Faisal II failed to hold public support. In the eyes of the bulk of the population, joining a British-backed Baghdad Defence Pact and opposing the formation of the UAR were major political own goals. In 1958, a well-organized military coup removed the monarchy, slaughtering the king and leading members of the royal family. Power was placed in the hands of Brigadier Qasim. He survived for five years until ousted (and executed) by the Baath Party, whose influence had spread east from Syria.

Over the next few years the country was torn between ambitious army officers, passionate Pan-Arabists, socialists, and those seeking to establish stable civilian rule. The Soviet Union waded in and brought Iraq into its sphere of influence with grants of weapons and aid. Nevertheless, given its uncertain domestic situation, Iraq was in no position to do anything but shout from the sidelines during the Six Day War (see page 95).

JORDAN

Amid the surrounding mayhem, the young but politically astute King Hussein of Jordan managed to cling on to power. He walked a dangerous diplomatic tightrope. At one stage he was close to a Pan-Arab union with Faisal's Iraq, at another he was maintained in office with the help of US aid ($100 million p.a. by the early 1960s) and British paratroops.

Hussein's most intractable problem was the West Bank and East Jerusalem, the territories his grandfather Abdullah had seized in the First Arab–Israeli War. As well as 400,000 new subjects, they had brought him hundreds of thousands of Palestinian refugees, and a frontier with the sworn enemy of all Arabs. It was across that frontier, snaking along the yellow-brown hills above the River Jordan, that the iron of the Israelis met the flint of the Palestinians. To Hussein's dismay, the collision generated sparks that eventually flared into war.

The Palestinians

In all this sorry saga, the Palestinians remained the losers. They were still the forgotten people, pitied by all, wanted by no one. By the end of the Suez War, it was clear to some of them that they were unlikely to get anywhere if they left matters in other hands, specifically in those of their fellow Arabs. Despair bred resentment, and resentment bred violence.

As we have seen, guerrillas had been operating in and around Palestine for decades. The tradition continued during the early 1950s when the discredited Mufti of Jerusalem, then established in Gaza as leader of an 'All-Palestine Government', had openly urged young Palestinian Arabs to attack the Israeli usurpers of their land. The sporadic and fairly ineffective attacks of these *fedayeen* ('fanatics' or 'self-sacrificers') had been an excuse for Israel's Suez offensive.

After the 1956 war, as Nasser tightened his grip on Egypt, he clamped down on militant Palestinians as he had previously done on the Muslim Brotherhood. He did not want their enthusiasm threatening his policy of saying one thing while doing another. At the end of the 1950s – in events that are still, perhaps deliberately, shrouded in mystery – a group of young Palestinians gathered in British-run Kuwait (to this day no one is sure how they obtained visas) to form a new organization dedicated to the destruction of

Israel and the formation of a Palestinian state. Its name was Fatah ('Victory' or 'Conquest').

Among Fatah's leaders was a Palestinian engineer and political activist who would play a key role in Middle Eastern affairs for almost 40 years. His full name was Mohammed Abdel Rahman Abdel Raouf Arafat Al Qudua Al Husseini. To the world he announced himself simply as Yasser Arafat.

YASSER ARAFAT

At first glance, Arafat did not have a lot going for him as a potential leader of the Palestinian nation. Although from a Palestinian family, he had been born and educated in Cairo and spoke with an Egyptian accent. He was small (1.65 m/5 ft 4 in) and any pretension to good looks was marred by bulging eyes and a protruding lower lip (these were a considerable handicap in the burgeoning age of television). What's more, Arafat was not a distinguished public speaker, tending to rant and repeat a string of ill-assorted facts, observations and exhortations. This reflected his fractured academic training.

All these drawbacks Arafat overcame with an exceptional vitality that combined passion, determination, charm and bravery. There was no better salesman in the business. When meeting Saudi Arabia's King Faisal to request money for Fatah, for instance, he might reasonably have expected the Saudis to match Kuwait's few hundred thousand dollars. In fact, Arafat came away with millions. By the mid-1960s, Fatah was by far the best funded, if not the best organized, of all the Palestinian guerrilla groups.

About Arafat's physical bravery there could be no doubt. As a student he had volunteered to fight in 1948, and in the Suez War he had served in Gaza. Once Fatah was up and running, he personally participated in a number of raids. The adoption of the *kuffiya* head-dress (originally a white cloth, which later changed to a chequered one), worn by the Palestinians who fought the British in the 1930s, reinforced his warrior image. So too did the assumption of the name 'Yasser' – borrowed in customary Arab style from a doughty warrior friend of the Prophet Mohammed.

> **Insight**
>
> 'Arafat's personality was characterized by combined contradictions: peace and resistance, religion and secularism, relations with the West and East at the same time, and relations with the regimes and opposition movements.'
> www.islamonline.net, (Article dated 20 November 2007.)

To the Palestinians who eked out their existence in squalid refugee camps, Arafat came across as a fighter. He would rather die, he swore, than betray their cause. In return, they gave him their trust. Thousands of young Palestinians flocked to join Fatah. The movement armed them, trained them, filled their heads with anti-Israeli vitriol, and by the mid-1960s was using them on hundreds of pin-prick raids into Israel from bases in Jordan, Syria, Lebanon and Gaza.

Unlike the Mufti, Arafat would let himself become beholden to no Arab state or leader. He would use their territory as a base and take their money, but he would be no puppet in their political games. Shortly after receiving Saudi funds, in an extreme example of this reckless independence, he attempted to blow up the kingdom's oil pipeline to the Mediterranean. Similarly, when the first ever summit of Arab leaders, meeting in 1964, accepted Nasser's idea for an over-arching Palestine Liberation Organization (PLO) and Palestine Liberation Army (PLA), Arafat would have nothing to do with either.

Arafat saw quite clearly that Nasser needed the PLO in order to control the Palestinians and curb their guerrilla activity. Unlike the Egyptian president, Arafat eagerly sought another Arab–Israeli war. Earlier, matching the ruthlessness of his Israeli enemies, he had written, 'Violence is the only solution.' Nasser, more of a realist, accepted what Arafat would not: in open warfare the disunited Arab forces would stand little chance against the well-organized Israeli military machine. In the end, though, Arafat got his war.

Nasser was proved right and the Palestinians were left in an even worse plight than before.

ARMING THE MIDDLE EAST

There could have been no large-scale Middle East war in 1967 if the rest of the world, particularly the US and the USSR, had not armed Israel and its enemies to the teeth. Soviet arms, including sophisticated MIG fighter planes, had found their way into a number of Arab states. Egypt and Syria were the chief beneficiaries. Sometimes the weapons came direct from the USSR, and sometimes via Czechoslovakia or another state belonging to the Warsaw Pact, the Soviet Union's answer to NATO.

By 1967, the forces of the Arab nations facing Israel were 50 per cent larger in terms of manpower and boasted 100 per cent more tanks and aircraft. It was such comparisons, ignoring the forces' scattered disposition and unco-ordinated war plans, that persuaded Arafat and his ilk that the Arabs really could overwhelm the Israelis.

Since Israel's foundation, France and West Germany had been among its most reliable arms suppliers. France had taken on this role in order to maintain a presence in the Middle East. German assistance, which paid some 30 per cent of Israel's overseas trade deficit, came as reparation payments for the Holocaust. The hardware the West Germans provided was good, too. When US President Lyndon B. Johnson offered the Israelis American tanks in 1964, they politely replied that they would prefer German ones. The rebuff was ignored and 210 US tanks were delivered the following year, together with 48 Skyhawk bombers.

The US decision to arm Middle Eastern states came after Soviet intervention in the region at the time of Suez. Reflecting upon the crisis, President Eisenhower announced a change in US policy: henceforward his country would give economic and military aid to any Middle Eastern government that felt itself threatened by Communism. Some $200 million was allocated to this fund.

The 'Eisenhower Doctrine' led to US troops being sent to Lebanon in support of President Camille, and to an increase in US arms and funds for Israel. President Kennedy, helped to office by the Jews of Massachusetts, also felt obliged to assist Israel. Although the State Department remained wary of falling out with oil-producing Arab states, by the time of Kennedy's death a special relationship was developing between the US and Israel.

Insight

Although Jews comprise only three per cent of the American population, their concentration in key states such as Pennsylvania, California and Florida, their high voter turnout, and their tendency to vote en bloc, give them a heavily disproportionate influence in US elections.

US backing gave the Israelis a feeling of security. The US, they believed, would never allow the Arabs to overwhelm them. That, and President Johnson's remark that the Israelis would 'whip the hell' out of their enemies if war came, was in the minds of the Israeli government as it contemplated a massive pre-emptive strike.

The path to war

THE WATERS OF GALILEE

Israel had fought its neighbours over the waters of the Sea of Galilee and the River Jordan since Biblical times. The issue arose again the moment the new state was founded in 1948. The US tried to find a compromise solution in the early 1950s, but Ariel Sharon's attack on Qibya so poisoned Arab-Israeli relations that the plan failed (see page 73).

Not long afterwards, the Israelis devised a bold and technically challenging scheme to pump water from the Sea of Galilee and carry it in a vast conduit the entire length of the country.

After many years' work, the pumps were switched on in the summer of 1964.

Meanwhile, the Syrians had been working on counter measures. As the Israelis built their conduit, so Syria had constructed dams across two rivers feeding the Jordan's waters. These barriers, when their sluices were closed, would divert a considerable flow of water into Jordan's River Yarmouk, by-passing the Jordan and Sea of Galilee.

The Israelis were not amused when, as they began taking water from the Sea of Galilee, the Syrians severed the streams that fed it. For two years the new dams were regularly bombed and shelled by the Israelis, forcing the Arabs to abandon their irrigation project. When Israeli forces captured the Golan Heights in the Six Day War, the rest of the world mistakenly assumed they did so for their strategic importance. As Israeli commanders were to admit later, the true importance of the Heights was not military but economic – more specifically, aquatic.

MOUNTING TENSION

We are now in 1965. Israeli planes are attacking Syrian installations. The Golan Heights reverberate to repeated artillery exchanges. To the south and west, Arafat's Fatah are stepping up their raids into Israel, not doing great damage but increasing Israeli demands that the government of Prime Minister Levi Eshkol, Ben Gurion's successor, take firm action.

Matters are not improved when the Syrians find an Israeli spy – Eliahu Cohen – in the higher echelons of their government. He is hanged, but the fall-out of the scandal helps topple the Syrian government the following year. This brings into power a group of vigorously pro-Palestinian Baathists. Fatah, temporarily excluded by the previous regime, is welcomed back, re-occupies its bases and renews its attacks on Israel across the Syrian border.

Given the increasingly bellicose rhetoric against which this is happening, it is clear that all-out war is not far away. It will not come, however, without Egypt – and Nasser is not keen. There is little chance that Arafat and the Palestinians will be able to persuade him to change his mind.

IDF PROVOCATION

The first of two crucial Israeli actions took place towards the end of 1966. The previous months had witnessed a number of guerrilla attacks on Israel and some strong IDF reaction. Its retaliation of 13 November, however, was without precedent. In response to a terrorist bomb in Hebron that had destroyed an Israeli military vehicle, killing three soldiers and injuring a further four, a large Israeli force, including many tanks, descended on the West Bank village of Samu in broad daylight.

Reports of the massive destruction vary, but perhaps 5,000 villagers lost their homes, their clinic, school and mosque. Several were killed and injured. Jordanian forces rushing to investigate were ambushed and more than 50 of them were killed and wounded. A plane of the Royal Jordanian Air Force was shot down. Other villages in the area were badly damaged.

World opinion swung sharply against Israel. Its cruel bullying of defenceless civilians was roundly condemned by the UN Security Council. More significantly, Israel lost the confidence of King Hussein, who had come close to being overthrown in the furious rioting that followed the Samu debacle. The attack had taken place on his birthday, killing one of his friends. It was scant reward, he mused bitterly, for all his efforts to keep Fatah out of the West Bank. He wanted war with Israel no more than Nasser did, but the Israelis had to show him some respect.

With the US now wedded to Israel, it suited the Soviets to throw their weight unequivocally behind the anti-Israeli movement. While not getting anywhere with Saudi Arabia or Jordan, they had found Nasser's Egypt and Baathist Syria receptive enough to their blandishments and offers of aid. Against his better judgement, at the end of 1965 Nasser had allowed Soviet diplomats to steer him into a defensive alliance with the UAR's former 'Northern Province'.

The Egyptian premier probably believed this would enable him to dampen down Syrian war talk. In fact, the opposite occurred. Instead of pulling back his partner by the handcuffs that linked them, Nasser found himself dragged into positions he did not wish to adopt.

The second act of IDF tactless overkill – or deliberate provocation – took place the following spring. When an Israeli tractor ploughing land within the demilitarized zone between Israel and Syria was fired upon, the Israelis began an artillery duel. Shortly afterwards, Syrian Soviet-built MIGs and Israeli French-built Mirages appeared in the skies overhead. An unequal dogfight took place in which four MIGs were swiftly downed. When the rest fled inland, the Israelis followed and shot down two more within sight of the Syrian capital. The air battle of 7 April 1967 was a massive humiliation for which the Syrian government and its people demanded revenge.

SOVIET MISINFORMATION

At this point, the Soviets made an already dangerous situation worse by lobbing a diplomatic hand-grenade into the mêlée. Anwar Sadat, a senior Egyptian aide, was told on a visit to Moscow that Israeli forces were massing on the Syrian frontier in preparation for an invasion. The Soviets urged Nasser to take steps to assist his ally. The reason for issuing such a blatantly false report (the Egyptians saw through it straight away) remains a mystery. Explanations range from the influence of vodka to a wish to promote a Middle East war that might further embarrass the US as it was wading deeper into the Vietnam mire.

Whatever its intended purpose, the Soviet warning was Nasser's Catch 22: either act in support of his ally or massively lose face before the entire Arab world. For the self-appointed leader of the Arabs, the second option did not bear thinking about. With a heavy heart, therefore, he asked the UN to withdraw the protective UNEF from part of Egypt's Sinai border with Israel. The reason was clear: if Israel attacked Syria, he would be free to launch a counter-attack from the south.

CLOSING THE STRAIT

The UN, led by Secretary General U Thant, conducted a series of delicate negotiations with both Israel and Egypt. After various options had been rejected, U Thant tried calling Nasser's bluff. Instead of a partial withdrawal, the UNEF was pulled back from all its positions in Sinai, Gaza and Sharm al-Sheikh, the position that guarded the narrow Strait of Tiran. The ploy failed. With UN forces out of the way at his request, Nasser felt obliged to re-occupy Sharm al-Sheikh. In May 1967, he declared the Strait of Tiran closed to Israeli ships and those of other nations carrying military supplies to Eilat. It was the Suez Crisis all over again.

Nasser backed up his action with yet another salvo of verbal aggression: 'The Jews threaten war; we tell them: Welcome! We're ready for war.' It was not really what he meant at all. The high-blown phrases and flamboyant action were a calculated gamble intended to please his Arab audience without pushing Israel over the edge. Sadly, although he knew his own people, Nasser misjudged his enemy. In the eyes of the Israeli government the closing of the Strait was tantamount to a declaration of war.

It was a war that Israel's military establishment had sought, too. They wanted defensible frontiers; they wanted the land they had taken 11 years earlier but had been forced to abandon; they wanted to show their enemies once and for all that the humble, meek, subservient Jew was a creature of the past.

The Soviet Union threatened retaliation if Egypt were attacked. King Hussein of Jordan flew to Cairo and made a defensive pact with Nasser. Other Arab nations expressed solidarity. Nevertheless, US President Lyndon B. Johnson stood by Israel – he had little choice when American public opinion was united in hatred of the 'Hitler of the Nile'. Even so, Johnson continued negotiations, although with little hope of a successful outcome. 'They're going to go,' he said of the Israelis. 'Yes they're going to hit. There's nothing we can do about it.' He was particularly fearful of what the Soviets might do if their client states were hard pressed.

In Israel the mood was tense. 'Live or perish' was the watchword. Perhaps reluctantly, Prime Minister Eshkol was carried along with the nationalistic tide and handed the post of minister of defence to the piratical militarist Moshe Dayan. The cabinet knew that Nasser had no intention of starting the fighting. His hostile words, though, were enough to lead the outside world to believe that he might. What was needed, therefore, was an Israeli 'anticipatory counteroffensive' – doublespeak for an attack.

At 7.45 a.m. on Monday, 5 June 1967 the Israelis launched an offensive of Blitzkrieg dimensions. By lunchtime the war was as good as won.

THINGS TO REMEMBER

1 *Rapidly capturing Sinai and the zone around the Suez Canal, the Anglo-French-Israeli coalition was forced into humiliating withdrawal when its campaign failed to attract superpower backing (Oct–Nov 1956).*

2 *During the Cold War, the states of the Middle East were armed by both East and West.*

3 *In 1958, Egypt and Syria joined together in a short-lived United Arab Republic (UAR).*

4 *The 1950s saw the emergence in Syria and Iraq of the distinctive nationalist and socialist Baath Party.*

5 *By the 1960s, Palestinian militancy, headed by Yasser Arafat's Fatah, was on the rise.*

6 *Seeking to control the Palestinian movement, in 1964 Arab heads of state established the Palestine Liberation Organization (PLO).*

7 *Not until the presidency of John F. Kennedy (1961–3) did the US play a major role in the arming of Israel.*

8 *By the mid-1960s, there was serious tension in the Golan border region between Syria and Israel.*

9 *Israeli reprisals for Palestinian attacks reached a peak of harshness with the attack on the village of Samu in 1966.*

10 *When Egypt talked openly of war and closed the Strait of Tiran, Israel launched (on 5 June 1967) a massive pre-emptive attack on its Arab neighbours.*

6

....

Divisions and developments 1967–73

This chapter will cover:
- *the course and consequences of the Third Arab–Israeli War*
- *the Arab world, 1968–73*
- *the rise of Palestinian militancy*
- *the causes and course of the Fourth Arab–Israeli War.*

The Six Day War

Israel's victory in the Six Day War of June 1967 was one of the most startling in modern military history. As with the first two Arab–Israeli wars, however, it is important to separate the myth from the reality. The map (Figure 6.1, page 98) shows a tiny Israel surrounded by vast expanses of Arab-held territory: surely this time Goliath would crush the puny David?

But Israel was not a puny David. By 1967, it was more an outpost of the West. The governments and people of the US, France and West Germany sustained, armed and guarded it. Israel was a state created by war and preserved by war. It had been fighting in one form or another since its inception, often as the aggressor. Its commanders knew exactly what they were doing. If they called for war, as they did in 1967, it was because they knew they would win.

> **Insight**
> 'It was in our power to set high price for our blood, a price too high for the Arab community, the Arab army, or the Arab governments to think it worth paying.'
>
> Moshe Dayan, Israeli minister of defence at the time of the Six Day War.

THE AIR ASSAULT

The war began with a massive unannounced Israeli air strike against Egypt, Jordan and Syria. Its purpose was to gain immediate air superiority by destroying as many enemy planes as possible while they were still on the ground. The mission's success was almost total.

Taken utterly by surprise, the Arabs lost 189 planes in 80 minutes. In all, 393 of their 416 aircraft were destroyed and Israeli air space was never once penetrated. Virtually the entire Jordanian and Egyptian air forces were wiped out, and those of Iraq and Syria rendered ineffective.

The Israelis cynically insisted, falsely, that their strikes had been in retaliation for threatening Arab moves. The aggressors, intent on a massive land-grab, also kept the extent of their success secret. The last thing they wanted was for the watching world to pressure them into an early ceasefire. The general mood in the US, the most important spectator, was one of admiration for 'plucky little Israel'. Memories of Pearl Harbor had apparently long since faded.

THE SINAI CAMPAIGN

The rapid Israeli advance across the Sinai towards the Suez Canal and Sharm al-Sheikh was more target practice than war. Deprived of air cover, in the barren terrain Egyptian tanks, guns, vehicles and troops were sitting ducks for Israeli warplanes laden with cannon shell, high explosives and terrifying napalm bombs.

In little over three days Sinai was in Israeli hands. They had destroyed 80 per cent of the equipment of the Egyptian army, including about 700 tanks. Up to 11,500 Egyptian soldiers had been killed, many incinerated by napalm. The Israelis lost about 300 troops and 60 tanks. Nasser, his reputation in tatters, had little option but to accept a ceasefire on 8 June.

> **Insight**
>
> 'Napalm' is used loosely to describe the deadliest component of modern fire-bombs. Specifically, it is usually jellied gasoline mixed with **na**phthenic and **palm**itic acids, which act as thickening agents.

JORDAN

King Hussein of Jordan requested a ceasefire the moment he knew what had happened to his air force. Resistance, he knew, would mean mere slaughter. The Israelis rejected his plea and overcame the West Bank and East Jerusalem in three days.

The West Bank was put under military occupation while East Jerusalem was swiftly joined with its counterpart in the west and incorporated into the state of Israel. Palestinian homes were flattened and their occupants driven out to make way for Israeli settlers.

SYRIA

After destroying its capacity to fight in the air, Israel left Syria alone while it concentrated on its more southerly targets. For their part, the Syrians made no move. However, by the time the Israelis were ready to shift their campaign to the north and make an attempt on the Golan Heights, the UN was waking up to what was happening and demanded that hostilities stop immediately.

Soviet Prime Minister Alexei Kosygin made the new Kremlin–White House hot line glow red with his threats and denunciations. President Johnson, who had enough on his plate with the Vietnam debacle,

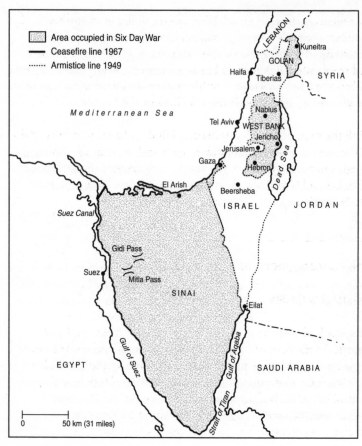

Figure 6.1 Israel's borders after the Six Day War.

urged the Israelis to comply with the wishes of the international community. Further conquest, he warned, might force the Soviets to intervene militarily.

But the Israelis had not quite finished. They wanted the Golan Heights with their precious water supply. Outrageously, to prevent the US learning that their attack on Syria would be unprovoked, they attacked and rendered inoperative the US intelligence-gathering vessel *USS Liberty* that was patrolling in the Mediterranean. It was all a 'sad accident' they explained to their unconvinced paymaster. Deeply embarrassed, President Johnson had the incident hushed up. His most important unofficial ally had all but sunk an American warship, killing and wounding 205 of its crew – and no one outside the US Navy or the Pentagon knew.

With the bulk of the US population blind and deaf to reality, the IDF made up an excuse to attack Syria and overran the Golan Heights in two days. As many as 115,000 refugees fled the region. With US and Soviet warships now on a collision course in the Mediterranean, a ceasefire came just in time.

The consequences of war

ISRAEL'S GAINS

The war had cost the lives of perhaps 20,000 Arabs and 766 Israelis. In six days of fighting the Israelis had captured the entire West Bank, Sinai (closing the Suez Canal again) and the Golan Heights. This more than doubled the amount of territory they controlled. It did not increase the size of Israel itself by much because, of the land it had captured, only East Jerusalem was officially assimilated. The rest was simply occupied.

The reason for this was straightforward. Although some 323,000 more Palestinians had become refugees, in the West Bank alone more than twice that number had neither fled nor been driven out, and so now came under Israeli governance. If their land were absorbed into Israel and they were given the vote, the Palestinian Arabs would gain sufficient political power to threaten the concept of the Zionist state. On the other hand, if the Israelis absorbed the conquered territories but denied the inhabitants political rights, they would be guilty of apartheid. Thus the West Bank and the Gaza Strip remained 'occupied territories'.

NO PROGRESS

The war had settled nothing apart from giving the Israelis what they believed were more defensible frontiers. This was a purely military matter because neither the 1948–9 frontiers nor the new 1967 ones had been enshrined in international treaty. They had been declared unilaterally and therefore were still theoretically open to negotiation. The Palestinians, inside Israel and without, remained an unwanted, stateless people.

As the Arabs were still technically at war with Israel, they continued to deny its existence. Armed with thick black pens, armies of clerks all over the Middle East went on scrubbing out the word 'Israel' from all imported books, maps, magazines and brochures. Their superiors refused to accept that resultant blotches only made the reader more aware of the censored enemy.

Total Israeli victory and total Arab humiliation was no recipe for negotiation. US President Richard Nixon's Secretary of State, William Rogers, hoped otherwise and tried unsuccessfully to persuade the Israelis to accept a land for peace deal as outlined in UN Resolution 242. In 1970, Nixon responded by handing the situation over to Henry Kissinger, his national security advisor.

Instead of trying to bring Arabs and Israelis together, Kissinger's prime concern was to keep Soviet influence in the Middle East to a minimum. To this end, he believed that the best Middle East policy for the US was preservation of the status quo. He hoped that this would show the Arabs that, as had happened to Egypt and Syria in 1967, friendship with the Soviet Union could offer no lasting benefit and might even bring disaster. All forms of US support for Israel grew appreciably.

As we will see, Kissinger's policy was only partly successful. By failing to support peace moves, particularly that of Anwar Sadat, he unwittingly promoted yet another war.

RESOLUTION 242

After months of discussion, in November 1967 the United Nations Security Council agreed Resolution 242 as a framework for solving the Arab–Israeli situation. At its heart was the concept of land for peace. It also said that it was illegal to obtain land by war, and that each nation in the region had the right to live at peace within secure boundaries. Finally, it called for a 'just settlement' of the problem of Palestinian refugees.

Land for peace would, years later, form the basis of Arab–Israeli agreements. For the time being, though, the balance of power between the two sides was too uneven for progress. Moreover, Resolution 242 did nothing for the Palestinians, who rejected it out of hand. This heralded one of the major changes in the Middle East situation over the next 15 years: the gradual collapse of Pan-Arabism and the increase of Palestinian nationalism as the main threat to Israel's security.

Insight

Resolution 242 has provided international lawyers with a field day regarding its precise interpretation. Note, for instance, the slightly more specific 'des' in the French translation of the first clause:

English: Withdrawal of Israeli armed forces from territories occupied in the recent conflict;

French: Retrait des forces armées israéliennes des territoires occupés lors du récent conflit.

Upon such apparent trivialities can history turn!

Enter Sadat and Assad

The Six Day War dampened down talk of 'liberating' the Palestinians. Humiliation in three wars had proved that the Arab states were simply not militarily strong enough to tackle Israel. Instead, the rhetoric of Arab governments tended to reflect what had always been the reality – that national self-interest came before all else.

EGYPT

Of all the Arab countries, Nasser's Egypt had suffered most. Its army and air force had been annihilated, it had lost vast swathes of territory, and the potentially remunerative Suez Canal remained closed. Most significant of all was the damage done to Nasser's personal credibility as leader of the Arab world. When great words are followed by feeble actions, the audience is not inclined to heed the speaker a second time.

Because the Israelis sought continually to remind the Egyptians of their inferiority, and because Nasser wished to show that he had lost a campaign but not the war, in 1968 a 'War of Attrition' began between the two countries. Fought in a spasmodic manner across the Suez Canal, it led to heavy casualties on both sides before being brought to a halt in 1970. While it was in progress the Soviets rebuilt Egypt's armed forces with modern technology, including powerful SAM 3 anti-aircraft missiles, and even permitted Soviet pilots to fly Egyptian jets against Israeli aircraft.

Nasser died of a heart attack in 1970. He was greatly mourned in the Arab world. Despite the disaster of 1967, he more than anyone had worked to ensure that the Arab peoples were respected beyond the Middle East. He was no dictator, and behind occasionally bombastic speech lay a heart that genuinely cared for the welfare of his people.

The same might be said of Nasser's successor, Anwar Sadat, although he did not go in for the same hyperbolic rhetoric. He was a thinker and a realist – during the Second World War he had even flirted with the Nazis in the hope that they would drive the British from Egypt. Shortly after coming to power, he offered Israel a peace treaty on the basis of Resolution 242. Prime Minister Golda

Meir and her cabinet thought about the suggestion then rejected it outright. So did the US.

When vice-president to Nasser, Sadat had not been taken seriously at home or abroad. He now set about raising and improving his profile. First he began undoing Nasser's cramping socialism. Then, as we have seen, he made overtures of peace towards Israel. When these were rejected, fed up with the level of support offered by the Soviets, he ended Egypt's partnership with them and ordered their advisors from the country.

Sadat made little headway in improving the unresponsive Egyptian economy. Discontent was widespread. Despite initial failures, the president was sure that the answer to all his country's problems was a permanent and lasting peace with Israel. This would enable him to divert millions of dollars from the military to schemes of more obvious benefit. But with Israel unwilling to talk and the US, thanks to Kissinger, happy to let things rest as they were, what was Sadat to do? With his patience running out, he came up with a desperate plan to prove that Israel was not the invincible military behemoth everyone believed it to be.

SYRIA

Not surprisingly, military defeat and loss of territory had undermined yet another Syrian government. The coup came in 1970 when the minister of defence, Hafiz Assad, quietly removed the government and inaugurated a series of measures that led to his election as president the following year.

Assad's early training as a night fighter pilot ideally suited his style of rule. A member of the Shia minority Alawite community, he remained largely in the dark, an unseen, low-profile figure who pulled the strings of power with total ruthlessness. In this he was not unlike his Israeli opponents, except that his aim was different. Above all, the unsmiling dictator sought to remain in power. After that came recovery of the Golan Heights, the expansion of Syrian power, and the crushing of Israel. When Sadat cut his links with the Soviet Union,

Assad was content to become the Soviet's primary client state in the region. It was not communism that appealed to him but arms.

> ## Insight
> While Alawis say their faith is a branch of Shia Islam, conservative Sunnis deny that they are Muslims at all. Certainly, a number of Syrians (the majority of whom are Sunnis) were horrified when they found themselves under an Alawite head of state, Hafiz Assad.

Palestine militant

The Six Day War and UN Resolution 242 marked a major turning point in the history of the Palestinian people. Divided between exile, crowded refugee camps and a stateless life in the occupied territories, they now knew for certain that there was little or no chance of fellow Arabs coming to their rescue. If anything was to be done, they had to do it themselves.

PALESTINIAN ORGANIZATIONS

It is estimated that in 1970 there were at least 30 Palestinian groups operating in Jordan alone. A few were independent; most were backed by one or more Arab states or by an outside power such as the Soviet Union or Communist China. Many were infiltrated by the Israelis, the CIA or both.

The leading Palestinian, Yasser Arafat, was unable (or, some say, unwilling) to provide a centralized leadership. He made matters still more complex by founding a Muslim splinter group of his own – Islamic Fatah. The confusing diversity and complexity go a long way to explaining why the Palestinians rarely spoke with one voice or followed a consistent strategy. For this particular failing Arafat must be held primarily responsible.

The Palestinian umbrella organization was the PLO, established in 1964 under Egyptian auspices to co-ordinate Palestinian activities.

It had a president, a legislature (the Palestine National Council), a charter and, in 1968, the Palestine Liberation Army. Before the 1967 war, it had been very much in the pocket of its Arab League paymasters. Thereafter it took a more distinctively Palestinian line. Yasser Arafat was elected PLO chairman in 1969.

Fatah was Yasser Arafat's guerrilla organization that had been in existence since the late 1950s. Based in Damascus, it operated mainly out of Syria, Jordan and Lebanon. Following Arab humiliation in the Six Day War, the next year it gained considerable prestige by the way it fought off an IDF attack on Karameh, Fatah's Jordanian headquarters. By 1970, Fatah was the largest and wealthiest of the Palestinian organizations, dominating the PLO.

Al Sa'iqah ('Thunderbolt') was a small Syrian socialist guerrilla group established in 1968. The Popular Front for the Liberation of Palestine (PFLP), led by the uncompromising Marxist George Habash, attacked Israel and Western interests in general from the late 1960s onwards. It specialized in aircraft hi-jacking and rejected all negotiation with Israel ('that lap dog of capitalist imperialists') or its supporters. The Democratic Front for the Liberation of Palestine (DFLP) was an extreme left-wing political movement established by the Jordanian Christian Marxist Naif Hawatmeh. It worked with the PLO and by the 1970s was engaging in particularly indiscriminate acts of terrorism.

BLACK SEPTEMBER

In the late 1960s, Arafat and other Palestinian leaders took a two-pronged approach. They continued the guerrilla attacks on Israel while at the same time building up a sense of Palestinian nationhood by providing schools, clinics, training centres and other practical assistance. The Israelis rejected out of hand Arafat's serious proposal that Israel and the occupied territories should become a single, secular, democratic state. In fact, Israel refused even to recognize the PLO, dubbing it an illegal terrorist organization.

Nor was King Hussein of Jordan enamoured of the PLO and its multifarious branches. He disapproved of their left-wing politics and their refusal to contemplate accord with Israel. Most of all, he objected to their lawless ways within Jordan. They have been described as a state within a state. More accurately, they resembled badly co-ordinated gangs of armed ruffians who terrorized, raped and pillaged the local population. Thousands were killed in regular clashes between Palestinian militants and the Jordanian army.

At one stage Hussein tried to bring the Palestinians on side by offering to make Arafat his prime minister. The PLO chairman was flabbergasted. Prime minister? Run a government? Non-plussed by the offer and alarmed by the thought of respectable and accountable responsibility, he turned it down. Compromise rejected, the king determined to bring the Palestinians to heel by less delicate means.

Arafat knew that Hussein despised him. Nevertheless, he felt that Assad's Syrian and Iraqi forces still based in Jordan would come to his aid if there was a showdown. The crisis came in September 1970.

The PFLP hi-jacked four Western airliners. One was blown up at Cairo; the other three were flown to Aman where they too were eventually destroyed. The passengers were subjected to a crash course of lectures in Palestinian politics, but were physically unharmed. The purpose of the hi-jackings was to free captive Palestinians in an exchange and draw the world's attention to the Palestinian cause.

For Hussein, this was the last straw. Using his capital's airport for anti-Western terrorist activities – and even renaming it in the process – was totally unacceptable. Either he or the whole rag-bag of Palestinian activists had to go. The king declared martial law, stopped all rights of political expression and sent in the army. Arafat called for Hussein to be deposed and the Palestinians to lead the revolution.

The fighting was tough. Reinforced with some deserters from the Jordanian army, at first the Palestinians were on top. The Iraqis did not get involved, however, and advancing Syrian armour was swiftly recalled when the US and Israel made it clear that it would not reach Aman intact.

By the end of the month ('Black September' in Palestinian parlance) the Palestinians had been defeated. Arafat and some 4,000 supporters eventually made their way to Lebanon, where they would cause even greater civil upheaval (see Chapter 7). The PLO leader himself claimed to have fled Jordan in disguise. The Jordanian authorities said they knew all along who he was and where he was headed. They were only too delighted to see the back of him. The whole unsavoury incident reflected badly on Arafat, the Palestinian militants and the Arab world as a whole.

Sadat's patience runs out

TERRORISM AND COUNTER-TERRORISM

As after previous wars, there were those in the Israeli establishment who believed that after the 1967 conflict the security of their land depended on constantly reminding the Arabs that Israel was all-powerful. Their political spokesperson was Menachem Begin, while in the military they were best represented by the ruthless Ariel Sharon. As far as this duo was concerned, Israel should never hand back any of the land it had taken in the Six Day War.

Prime Minister Golda Meir, who had replaced Eshkol in 1969, was more moderate. Heading a conservative Labour coalition (because of the country's proportional electoral system, all Israeli governments were coalitions), Meir felt that Israel should keep hold of Gaza and East Jerusalem, but that there might be room for negotiation over other occupied areas. This division in Israeli ranks was in part due to the pressures ordinary Israelis felt at living in a land constantly under siege.

The feeling of siege arose from continual terrorist attacks. These, as always, drew reprisals of disproportionate force. Sharon was the foremost exponent of these, 'thinning out' Palestinian refugee camps, clearing away Arabs to make way for Jewish settlements and, on occasion, destroying entire villages. The devastation of the Syrian village of Dail in January 1973, for instance, left an estimated 500 dead.

The previous September, Fatah had carried out its most daring mission. The motive was Arafat's desire to raise the profile of his group after recent headline-grabbing PFLP missions. His target was the Munich Olympic Games, about as high profile a target as one could get. Like many of Arafat's projects, the attempt to take Israeli athletes hostage was poorly planned and bungled in operation. Eleven Israelis and five Fatah terrorists were killed. In the predictably terrifying IDF reprisals perhaps 500 Palestinians, Syrians and Lebanese lost their lives. Neither side came out of the episode with its reputation enhanced.

THE ARAB PLAN

Without drawing attention to what was going on, Sadat had rebuilt Egypt's armed forces. In particular, his anti-aircraft defences could now cover an area extending 16 km (10 miles) beyond the Suez Canal. Simultaneously, the Soviets had been pouring arms into Syria, giving Assad's army a considerable but largely unnoticed tank advantage on the Golan Heights. Golda Meir's government, on the other hand, could not believe that the Arabs posed a real threat. Certainly Israeli intelligence, normally so efficient, had reported nothing alarming.

In the south, Israeli confidence was based on a gigantic wall of sand, steel and concrete topped with blockhouses. This supposedly insurmountable 'Bar Lev' ran for 160 km (100 miles) beside the Suez Canal. To make doubly sure, the Israelis were ready to pump oil into the canal and set light to it, producing an impassable barrier of fire. Egyptian engineers studied the problem carefully. Yes, they informed their president, they could almost certainly tackle both the firewall and the Bar.

Sadat was not looking to recapture Sinai, let alone march on Jerusalem. All he wanted was a symbolic victory to show the world that the Israelis were not invincible. Then, he believed, a realistic negotiated peace might be possible. Assad, with whom Sadat made a secret military pact, had much narrower aims. He wanted to retake the Golan Heights. He had been Syria's defence minister at the time of their capture, and was eager to expiate this slur on his competence.

The Fourth Arab–Israeli War

The synchronized Egyptian-Syrian attack began on 6 October 1973. This was the Jewish holiday of Yom Kippur. For once, surprise was with the Arabs. Egyptian frogmen blocked the pipes through which oil was to be pumped into the canal. High-pressure hoses blasted away sufficient sand from the Bar Lev for Egyptian tanks to storm through. Above, Soviet-made anti-aircraft missiles downed scores of Israeli aircraft attempting to halt the advance.

In just over two days the Israelis lost 500 tanks and 49 planes, and a despairing Dayan told his prime minister, 'We are heading for a catastrophe.' For the first time, Arab forces had inflicted a major defeat upon the Israelis. 'You have made us all proud,' King Faisal of Saudi Arabia told a smiling Egyptian premier.

Sadat, his point made, would have been happy to end the war there and then. Unfortunately for him, his ally Assad had fared less well. After significant initial advances, his forces were being driven back down the Damascus road. To help him, Sadat ordered an advance beyond the screen of the air defences. The result was a predictable slaughter as superior Israeli aircraft shot up unprotected men and armour.

When the fighting began, Iraq sent 20,000 men to Syria. Jordan, Kuwait, Morocco, Algeria and Saudi Arabia sent only token forces to the front. The PLA, though not under Arafat's command, had operated on both fronts. More significantly, the US and the USSR swiftly reinforced their respective sides.

US President Richard Nixon assisted Israel despite a warning from King Faisal that the Arab oil-producing states might be forced to

impose an oil embargo on states supporting Israel. This became
a reality when Nixon went further and gifted Israel a staggering
$2.2 billion. He wanted to ensure that Israel could defend itself
without having to resort to nuclear weapons. The Israeli nuclear
capability, though never used, always hung ominously over Middle
East crises.

Insight

With clandestine assistance from France, which allegedly
believed it 'owed' Israel a nuclear capability after letting it
down over Suez (1956), Israel developed nuclear weapons
that were, supposedly, being fitted to missiles as early
as 1966.

Sharon had now rallied the southern Israeli forces and was
planning to cross the canal into Africa. The manoeuvring of
a gigantic bridge into position was poorly handled and in the
end only a comparatively small number of Israeli tanks made it
to the other side. Here they met with stiff Egyptian resistance.
Meanwhile, Sadat had admitted that he could not fight the Israelis
and the United States together and accepted a ceasefire.

The Israelis broke the agreement, repeatedly. Soviet leader Leonid
Brezhnev called for a UN peacekeeping force, provided by himself,
to stand between the opposing armies. Nixon refused to accept
Soviet troops in the Middle East. The nuclear arsenals of the two
superpowers were put on alert. Fortunately, before anyone could
press the button, a compromise solution was agreed. Troops
were not needed as United Nations observers would monitor the
ceasefire outlined in Resolution 338.

Once again, a Middle East crisis had threatened to plunge the world
into nuclear catastrophe. This time all concerned – Americans,
Russians, Israelis and Arabs – were keen that it should not happen
again. The conditions for a settlement were much more favourable,
too. In defeating the Israelis on the battlefield, albeit temporarily,
and bringing the West to its knees with the oil embargo, the Arabs
had finally won the right to be taken seriously.

The oil weapon

On 17 October 1973, the Organization of Petroleum Exporting Countries (OPEC), a mostly Arab group, raised the price of crude oil by 70 per cent. At the same time it cut production by 25 per cent and banned all sale of its products to the US and the Netherlands (prominent supporters of Israel). Scarcity sent oil prices even higher. In 1972, a barrel of crude oil had cost $3.00. By the end of the following year, the price had risen to $18.00.

The effect was devastating, far greater than OPEC had anticipated. Most obviously, there was a worldwide oil shortage. British industry was put on a three-day week to save fuel. Many Western nations imposed speed limits on their roads to cut the consumption of petrol and diesel. Filling stations ran dry and long queues formed outside those still operating. There were reports from the US of angry motorists shooting each other as they fought for a place in the line.

The global economy stagnated. Unemployment soared as many countries went into recession. Inflation, caused by rapid price rises, hit at the same time. The resultant 'stagflation' caused widespread misery, hitting the poor hardest. It was a full ten years before the worldwide recession finally lifted. By then the West had made considerable efforts to diversify its sources of energy, developing nuclear power and exploiting oilfields of its own, such as those in Alaska and the North Sea.

POLITICAL REACTION

OPEC's use of the oil weapon presented the West, and the US in particular, with a tricky dilemma. For many years they had maintained close ties with Saudi Arabia because it controlled an estimated 30 per cent of the world's oil deposits. But there had always been those who had questioned this friendship because of the Saudis' domestic tyranny and support of Palestinian terrorism. This problem was now dragged into sharper focus.

By and large Western governments turned a blind eye to what was going on within oil-producing countries like Saudi Arabia, claiming that a state's domestic affairs were its own responsibility. At the same time, they were liberal in their criticism of what was going on inside communist states. One rule for the rich … That said, the oil crisis did make Kissinger's Middle Eastern policy of upholding the status quo no longer realistic. OPEC action might not have helped the Palestinians (it was hardly intended to help them, anyway), but it did initiate the process that eventually produced a lasting peace in some areas.

THE IMAGE OF THE ARAB

The world's image of the Arab had undergone a dramatic make-over. OPEC action made oil-producing states even more fabulously rich than they had been before. Millionaires, whose fathers had herded camels and whose mothers had been born in a tent, wore their robes with pride as they were driven around Western cities in vast limousines, buying up property and funding all kinds of commercial enterprise.

The Saudi oil minister, Sheikh Ahmed Yamani, was lampooned in some areas of the Western press as a highwayman who demanded 'Yamani [Your money] or your life.' The irony behind the jest was that it was true. Love them or hate them, the Arabs mattered.

One story illustrates well the power of the new image. A small, run-down seaside town in Britain wished to boost its economy by developing its port. Capital for the project was hard to find. The enterprise needed a sponsor, someone whose participation would assure others that the idea was sound. Enter an actor in a chauffeur-driven car, wearing Arab clothes. He emerged at the port, was shown around the site, chatted to officials, smiled, nodded, and was driven off again. Immediately the rumour mill started running: an Arab billionaire was backing the project. Before long, sufficient funds were found for work to begin.

On a more solemn note, back in the Middle East the oil crisis widened two significant rifts. One was between the oil-producing states and the rest; the other was between those who embraced the Western-style liberal secularism that came with prosperity and those who adhered to the more puritanical ways of Islamic fundamentalism. From these twin chasms dragons would soon emerge to plague the ravaged Middle East still further.

THINGS TO REMEMBER

1 *In the Six Day War (5–10 June 1967), Israel inflicted a crushing defeat on the forces of the Arab world, most notably those of its neighbours, Egypt, Jordan and Syria.*

2 *During the Six Day War, Israeli forces took the Gaza Strip from Egypt, the West Bank from Jordan and the Golan Heights from Syria. They also occupied the entire Sinai peninsula.*

3 *The events of the summer of 1967 sent a fresh wave of Palestinian refugees pouring over the borders into Lebanon, Syria and Jordan.*

4 *The United Nations Security Council Resolution 242 – known as the 'peace for land' option – has been the basis of nearly all subsequent attempts to solve the Israeli–Palestinian impasse.*

5 *1970 saw the Alawite General Hafiz Assad come to power in Syria and Anwar Sadat replace Nasser as president of Egypt.*

6 *Palestinian militancy, fed on despair, expanded considerably after the Six Day War. Its most notorious exploit was the attack on the 1972 Munich Olympic Games.*

7 *In an episode known as 'Black September', the PLO, now dominated by Fatah and headed by Yasser Arafat, were driven from Jordan.*

8 *By the early 1970s, Egypt's armed forces had been re-equipped with the latest Soviet-built hardware.*

9 *The Fourth Arab–Israeli War (October 1973: also known as the October War) began with a startling Egyptian advance*

across the Suez Canal. It ended a few weeks later with the Israelis advancing on all fronts.

10 *In 1973, the politics of the Middle East – and the world economy – changed for ever when Arab oil-producing states wielded the 'oil weapon' for the first time, dramatically cutting production and refusing to supply states that supported Israel.*

7

Lebanon bleeds

This chapter will cover:
- *the gradual erosion of Lebanese stability during the 1960s and early 1970s*
- *the Lebanese civil war*
- *Israel's invasion of Lebanon, the expulsion of the PLO and the refugee camp massacres*
- *Lebanon's slow recovery in recent years.*

Uneasy peace

We saw in earlier chapters how Lebanon was created when the French divided up the Ottoman province of Syria after the First World War. The ancient Syrian links are important for they have re-emerged to play a major part in Lebanese history since 1945. We also saw how the country's constitution, linked with an inter-community power-sharing agreement, enabled the diverse but comparatively prosperous little state to weather the storms that beset so much of the Middle East after the Second World War.

During the 1950s, President Camille Chamoun fell foul of his Arab neighbours for Lebanon's perceived pro-Western, pro-Israeli stance. The political acumen of General Chehab, commander of the Lebanese army and, perhaps, the short-lived appearance of US marines prevented serious unrest. Chehab then took over the premiership. Under his presidency and that of his successor the country's stability held, enabling it to prosper as a vigorous entrepôt and financial centre serving the entire region.

'Welcome to Beirut,' declared a young Lebanese greeting a Western visitor in 1973. 'Our city is the Paris of the Middle East. Everyone is happy here. We have open minds and tolerate everything.' A charming city Beirut might have been, but not everyone was happy and minds were closing fast. Barely two years later, the place had become hell on earth.

SOURCES OF INSTABILITY

The key to Lebanon's stability was harmonious relations between the Christian and Muslim communities. More specifically, it meant the country's four main socio-religious groups – Christians, Druze, Sunnis and Shia – sharing power. Tragically, the conditions allowing this to continue had been gradually breaking down.

Rapid urbanization had led to 40 per cent of the population living in the Beirut conurbation. This had widened the gap between the largely Muslim countryside and the urban Christians. In Beirut itself, the separate ethnic and religious communities lived in distinct quarters. When trouble did flare up, the security services were notoriously heavy-handed.

Insight
One of the great cities of the world, Beirut boasts a history stretching back at least to the time of the pharaohs. Its ancient Phoenician heritage explains why some elements of the Lebanese population deny that they are part of the Arab world (see main text).

Lebanon refused to join the Arab cause against Israel in the Six Day War of 1967 and the October War of 1973. The decision had led to hostility towards Lebanon in the Arab world, and within the country towards the Christian minority (now reduced to around 40 per cent of the population) that controlled the most influential positions.

Among the Christians, the Maronites (about 23 per cent of the total population) were particularly prominent. There was talk of secret agreements between the Christians and Israelis. Ironically, the opposite was true: unbeknown to the Lebanese, Ben Gurion and Dayan had actually talked of invading Lebanon and dismembering it.

The influx of around 270,000 Palestinian refugees, driven out by war and Israeli policy, had greatly added to Lebanon's difficulties. By 1973, ten per cent of those living in the country were Palestinian. Some had done well. For example, the country's largest construction company, CCC, was Palestinian owned. The majority, however, were poor and landless. They shared many of the same grievances as the impoverished rural Muslims.

Then came Black September, bringing the PLO leadership and their many followers from Jordan (see pages 105–7). They came with weapons, their own organization and, above all, an independent, aggressive attitude. To many Lebanese, especially the Christians, they were unwelcome swaggerers. Just as in Jordan, they were a law unto themselves, collecting taxes, setting up road blocks and generally behaving as if they owned the place. In Beirut it was made worse by plentiful money and the city's cosmopolitan, easy-going atmosphere. The PLO bureaucracy became huge and corrupt – some of its workers grew rich by selling arms to the Christians. Arafat kept PLO accounts in a small notebook in his jacket pocket. He even found time in his life for women. It was all a long way from the rugged simplicity of Fatah's early years.

The chaotic reality of Beirut did not match the outside world's image of the PLO. The international profile of Arafat and his organization was rising. For some years Arafat had been playing down his terrorist image and presenting himself as a peacemaker. Although the change cut little ice with the US administration, elsewhere it bore fruit. A PLO plan for solving the Palestine-Israel problem by the creation of two states was generally well received. In 1974, an Arab League summit at Rabat declared the PLO to be 'the sole legitimate representative of the Palestinian people'. Later that year Arafat addressed the United Nations and the following year the PLO was given UN Observer status (see Chapter 8).

By a previous agreement signed in Cairo, the Lebanese government had given the PLO virtually a free hand in organizing the Palestinians in southern Lebanon – as long as it did not interfere in national politics. However, Palestinian attacks across the border into Israel, drawing heavy Israeli reprisals, inevitably involved the Lebanese government. The PLO's help with local medical, educational and other facilities also gave it political status. Its natural ally was the Lebanese National Movement (LNM). Led by Kamal Jumblatt, a Druze, this was a left-wing, largely Shia coalition of groups dedicated to improving the lot of the impoverished Muslim majority.

The spring of 1975 found the confrontation between the country's militia groups growing rapidly. Apart from the non-sectarian Lebanese army and the PLO, the most prominent military-political organization was the Christian Phalange. The motto of these inflexible, European-orientated and right-wing paramilitaries was 'God, the Fatherland, and the Family'. Regarding themselves as descendants of the ancient Phoenicians, not Arabs, the Phalange strongly rejected Pan-Arabism and hated the PLO. Their 10,000-strong militia was well armed and ruthless.

The story of the many horrifying conflicts that tore Lebanon apart in the last quarter of the twentieth century is indescribably complex. Furthermore, the nation's deep wounds are still not fully healed, so history merges with politics. The narrative that follows, therefore, is by necessity much simplified. It is also based on current thinking and knowledge, factors that may well change with the perspective of time.

Civil war

THE HORROR OF WAR

Arguments about who was responsible for the outbreak of the civil war persist to this day. The conflict did not start suddenly.

Rather, Lebanon slid into war: the fishermen of Sidon went on strike; clashes with the authorities turned violent; Maronites fired on Palestinians, Palestinians fired on Maronites; the PLO joined with the LNM after a Maronite attack on refugees; the Phalange of Bashir Gemayel clashed with the Phalange of his brother Amir; Sunni fought Shia who fought Druze. By May 1975, Lebanon was in total, bloody chaos.

One story among many illustrates the random, senseless nature of the killing. Christian militiamen were in the habit of stopping cars to check whether they were carrying Palestinians. As forged papers were easy to acquire, they set the occupants the language test. 'What is red and juicy and eaten with salad?' The terrified interogatee replied 'tomato'. If they did so using the Lebanese word, 'banadoura', they were allowed to go free. If they said 'bandoura', the Palestinian version of the word, they were instantly killed, or worse.

Central government collapsed and local warbands imposed what order they could. Arms poured into the country from around the world, particularly from Syria and Israel. The factions stockpiled sophisticated weaponry like rocket launchers and artillery as well as rifles and grenades by the container load. There had never been a civil war like it. The firepower in daily use was awesome, terrifying. Thousands of Lebanese fled abroad. Dwellings were shattered, businesses wrecked, communications cut. Around 70,000 people lost their lives, most of them innocent civilians.

FOREIGN PLAYERS

Many governments kept a close eye on the Lebanese situation. A significant number intervened with arms and money, some in a most unexpected way. The majority of the Arab oil producers, for instance, aided the Christians because they feared the communist leanings of some Palestinians. Israel and the CIA also helped the Christians. Iraq supported the PLO.

Today's readers, used to interpreting events in the Middle East largely in religious terms, may recall that, before Iran's Islamic Revolution (1979) and the collapse of the USSR (1990), the secular left–right (communist–capitalist) divide was as significant – perhaps even more so – than any Shia–Sunni–Alawite–Christian distinction.

No one watched what was going on more closely than Syria's President Assad. Until the end of 1975 he gave support to Muslim groups, mainly the LNM-PLO. By early the next year he was having doubts: if the Muslims won, as now seemed likely, Lebanon would either be divided or become a left-leaning state dominated by the PLO. Neither situation would be acceptable to Israel, which would certainly intervene.

To prevent this happening, Assad switched support to the Christians. This produced the extraordinary situation of Israel and Syria – sworn enemies and still technically at war – both backing the same side in a civil war on their borders. Assad received US assurance that the Israelis would not object, and sent 20,000 Syrian troops into Lebanon from the east. To the west, Israeli warships blockaded the coast and reinforced their strong links with Bashir Gemayel.

The Lebanese civil war sounded the death knoll of Pan-Arabism. It presented a most distressing image of Arabs to the outside world. Moreover, it played into the hands of Israel, giving it ample excuse to expand its northern frontier if considered expedient. Finally, the civil war was being exploited by Assad. At a time when he was vying with Egypt for leadership of the Arab world, it enabled him to pose as a defender of Muslims and a peacemaker.

Eventually, acting on a Saudi-Kuwaiti-Egyptian initiative, a ceasefire was agreed. Very roughly, the Muslims (LNM-PLO) and Druze were left controlling the south. Until his assassination the following year, Jumblatt was their overall political leader. The north was in

Christian hands. A 'Green Line' ran through the centre of Beirut dividing the Christian east from the Muslim west, and 30,000 Arab League troops, mostly Syrian, patrolled as peacekeepers.

Israeli intervention

INCOMPLETE CEASEFIRE

The ceasefire agreed in October 1976 brought a reduction in the violence but not its complete cessation. The Phalange were still under arms, as was the LNM, and clashes between them and smaller groups persisted. Syrian forces remained in the country, too. In the north and in East Beirut, Bashir Gemayel had combined most Maronite groups to form a fiefdom of his own. He was happy to receive Israeli support.

Insight

The Maronites, whose heritage dates back to the fifth-century St Maron, are a branch of eastern Catholicism that recognizes the authority of the Pope. They claim, if the Lebanese diaspora is included, to be Lebanon's largest single religious group.

OPERATION LITANI

The PLO's strength was predominantly in the south of the country. After the Lebanese civil war it had increased its governmental role, using some of the funds provided by supportive states and organizations to help restore electricity, water and communications in areas shattered by the conflict. The less corrupt PLO operatives also sought to build for a better future by expanding the network of schools and medical clinics in Palestinian areas. Furthermore, Arafat had agreed with the Lebanese and Syrian governments to cut back on Palestinian attacks on Israel (the Shtaura Accord). Despite his poor organizational ability, Arafat was trying to put forward the PLO as a viable government for a separate Palestine.

This tied in with three developments beyond Arafat's control, two alarming, one potentially favourable. The former were the growing accord between Egypt and Israel (see Chapter 8), and the election of Menachem Begin as Israel's prime minister (1977). This ex-Irgun commander now headed the Likud Front, a right-wing, nationalist coalition. These two setbacks were to some extent balanced by the election of Democrat Jimmy Carter to the US presidency in 1976. One of his first actions was to declare himself in favour of a 'Palestinian homeland'.

Arafat's state-building efforts with the PLO were a total anathema to Begin. Like its Labour predecessor, the Likud government maintained pressure on the PLO by constant and fairly indiscriminate cross-border attacks. These were not just retaliatory. Rather, in the light of the PLO's restraint, they were intended to provoke. (The Israelis themselves called them 'preventative' – similar to the protagonists' language at the time of Anglo-American invasion of Iraq in 2003. See Chapter 14.) The Israeli government did not want the PLO quiescent – it wanted it removed, disbanded, liquidated. It therefore sought to stir up PLO attacks on Israel as an excuse for further missions of its own.

Arafat was never consistent, nor did he have control over all Palestinian terrorist activity. In March 1978, an 11-man Fatah hit squad made their way down the coast and landed near Haifa. They had intended to reach Tel Aviv and were confused by their surroundings. In due course, finding the main road between Haifa and the capital, they decided to make the most of their opportunity. Their attack on a bus left 37 dead and a further 78 injured.

This was just the excuse Begin needed. He ordered the IDF to advance into southern Lebanon and destroy the PLO bases there. Arafat led the resistance in person, fighting, as he always did, with immense bravery. It was to no avail. Two thousand people were killed, almost all of them Palestinians and Lebanese. Around one quarter of a million people were rendered homeless. Operation Litani, as it was called, established a security zone south of the

River Litani patrolled by an Israeli-backed South Lebanese Army. This accomplished, the IDF withdrew. Henceforward the PLO had to tread more warily in the south, although its bases further north were unharmed.

Israeli invasion

THE ADVANCE OF THE RIGHT

The positions of extreme Israelis and Palestinians had much in common. Each rejected compromise and denied the right of the other to exist. Both saw the conflict between them as a fight to the death. By 1980, however, the bulk of Palestinians, including Arafat, realized that they would never be able to wipe Israel from the map. Hence Arafat's 'two state' solution – Israel and Palestine as separate, independent countries. In the circumstances, it was the best he could hope for.

It was not the best the Israelis could hope for. Their deal with Egypt (see Chapter 8), exchanging land for peace, was still the desired template of most mainstream politicians. It involved handing back some land to those from whom it had been taken – Jordanians and Syrians – but not to the Palestinians. To this end, hard-line Israelis were prepared to go to almost any lengths to reduce the power and influence of the PLO.

In the early 1980s, the Israeli right was riding high. First, Begin was re-elected as prime minister. Second, two hardliners, Yitzhak Shamir and Ariel Sharon, entered the government as foreign and defence ministers respectively. Third, Jimmy Carter had fallen foul of the media and the new militant Iranian regime of Ayatollah Khomeini (see page 156), and failed to get re-elected. His place had been taken by Ronald Reagan. The Republican president and his measured (some said slow-witted) Secretary of State Alexander Haig regarded Israel as a 'strategic asset' in their battle against communism. This meant publicly supporting the Likud administration in almost all it did, even though it might disagree in private.

ISRAELI PROVOCATION

In 1981, Begin's government officially annexed the Golan Heights. Next, showing how ruthless it was prepared to be in defence of its country's interests, it ordered the destruction of an Iraqi nuclear plant that was under construction at Osirak. In Operation Babylon, Israeli F-16 fighter-bombers, with F-15 fighter protection, completely destroyed the site with 900-kg (2,000-lb) bombs. Israeli planes then tackled the PLO headquarters in Beirut, leaving 300 civilians dead. A US-promoted ceasefire was declared, broken, and agreed again.

Insight

Israel's Golan Heights Law of 1981 extended Israeli law and administration to the region but stopped short of integrating it fully within the State of Israel. The law was condemned by the UN Security Council (Resolution 497).

Shamir and Sharon were determined on an all-out invasion of Lebanon. Its purpose would be three-fold: final destruction of the PLO, the establishment of a pro-Israeli government in Lebanon (headed by Bashir Gemayel), and a war with Syria that would force it to accept peace on terms similar to Egypt's. Jordan would have no choice but to follow suit, they reasoned, leaving Israel secure, the PLO feeble and homeless, and non-Israeli Palestinians obliged to become citizens of the states in which they lived.

Arafat refused to play ball. Despite repeated Israeli incursions into Lebanon, the PLO did not retaliate. The Israeli command was finally relieved by events in London, England.

On 3 June 1982, the Israeli ambassador to Great Britain was shot and wounded outside the five-star Dorchester Hotel. The gunman belonged to Abu Nidal, a terrorist gang whose leader had been expelled from the PLO for attempting to assassinate Yasser Arafat.

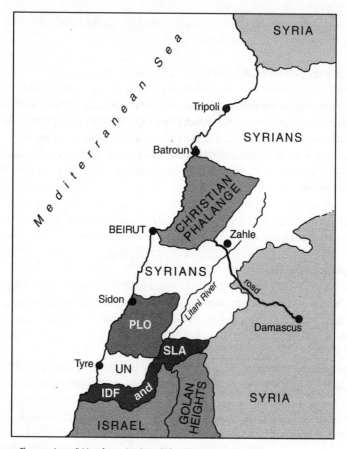

Figure 7.1 The approximate division of power in Lebanon before the 1982 Israeli invasion.

Begin had no time for such details: to him all Arab terrorists were the same. Three days after the London shooting, 1,240 Israeli tanks roared over Israel's northern border into Lebanon.

PEACE FOR GALILEE

The Israeli invasion was named Operation Peace for Galilee, although there had been little or no fighting in Galilee for years. It was just another example of skilful Israeli propaganda: however unjustified the assault, the combination of 'peace' and 'Galilee' instinctively warmed the hearts of Christians the world over, not least those of the mainstream United States.

In military terms the advance was a blistering success. The invaders did not stop in the south, as they had said they would, but powered on to Beirut to link up with the Maronite forces of Bashir Gemayel. Resistance from the PLO, Muslim groups and the Syrians was crushed, the Syrian air force losing dozens of planes. Thousands were killed, mostly Arabs and many of them civilians. Assad accepted a ceasefire almost immediately and the Lebanese government soon followed suit.

The international outcry against the invasion was loud and virtually unanimous. Words, however, were not enough. The only country with the power and influence to limit Israeli policy, the US, was reluctant to ditch an ally pursuing a policy to which it had given tacit approval. US funds that permitted Begin to pay for his $1 million-a-day venture remained largely intact. As a gesture, though, supplies of some US-made weapons, such as deadly cluster bombs, were cut.

Short of military intervention, there was little anyone else could do. Certainly the Arab states were not prepared to get involved. We have seen before how they had little love for the Palestinians, nor were they willing to risk much for a country that had stood on the sidelines in 1967 and 1973. Egypt, at peace with Israel (see Chapter 8) and expelled from the Arab League, did nothing. Jordan saw no point in intervening. Saddam Hussein's Iraq, already at war with Iran, had neither the desire nor the means to get involved (see page 164).

BEIRUT UNDER SIEGE

By 1 July, the PLO fighters were holed up in West Beirut, surrounded by Israeli-Maronite forces. The Israelis did not want to get involved in deadly street-to-street fighting. Instead, as previously agreed, they asked their ally Gemayel to go in and root the enemy out. Gemayel refused. The Israelis began to realize that they had underestimated the man: he wanted to govern a fully independent Lebanon, not a puppet state. He no more wanted his country dominated by Israel than by the PLO.

The siege of West Beirut intensified with regular bombing, artillery and rocket attacks. Supplies of water and electricity were cut. Prime Minister Begin, it seems, was under some sort of illusion that the heart of Beirut was akin to Hitler's bunker in Berlin during the Second World War. 'I feel as a Prime Minister,' he telegraphed President Reagan, 'empowered to instruct a valiant army facing "Berlin" where amongst innocent civilians, Hitler and his henchmen hide in a bunker deep beneath the surface' (Avi Shlaim, *The Iron Wall: Israel and the Arab World*, 2001). By equating Arafat with Hitler, this remark demonstrates just how rigidly men of Begin's generation were tied to their hideous past. They were unable to see the present for what it was, regarding it instead as a form of nightmare, endlessly repeating what had been.

In this most desperate of situations, once again Arafat showed extraordinary bravery and a remarkable instinct for survival. The Israelis wanted him dead. Time and again their spies marked the building where he was supposed to be – in came the warplanes – the building was destroyed – he emerged somewhere else, smiling, his shoes defiantly polished, his distinctive head-dress intact. Journalists and soldiers alike testified to his unique ability to rouse the shattered Palestinian forces, taking men by the arm, encouraging them, assuring them that in the end victory would be theirs. 'Beirut will be the Hanoi and Stalingrad of the Israeli army' he quipped with irrepressible optimism.

Once, when it was certain the PLO was on the verge of surrender, a group of high-ranking Lebanese officials came to wish Arafat bon voyage. Introducing them, a Palestinian official told his leader that the delegation had come to say goodbye. 'Ah!' Arafat replied, 'Where are they going?' The whole room burst out laughing. The remark itself was not particularly amusing. What so attracted those present was the sheer joyful indestructibility of a man whose immediate prospects were just about nil.

Eventually, on 12 August, President Reagan called Prime Minister Begin in person. The fighting in Beirut had to stop at once, he warned. Did the victims of the Holocaust really wish to be the perpetrators of another such horror? The guns fell silent almost immediately. An international peacekeeping force of mainly American, French and Italian troops was called in to supervise a ceasefire. The PLO and its supporters were escorted from West Beirut and into exile in any country that would take them. Arafat, a sad and lonely figure, sailed away to Tunisia where he re-established his PLO headquarters.

MASSACRE

In order to get elected as president of Lebanon, Bashir Gemayel had denounced the Israeli presence in his country. Begin's policy was clearly beginning to unravel. True, the PLO had been driven from Lebanon, but there was nothing to stop them or similar groups returning, and the economic and political cost had been enormous.

The vast reservoir of international sympathy for the Jews, present since the Holocaust, had all but run dry. US friendship had been sorely tested. Syrian forces remained in eastern Lebanon, supporting PLO remnants in the Biqa Valley. Unnecessary Israeli aggression had made enemies of the Druze and the Lebanese Shia. The creation of Hezbollah ('Party of God'), an Iranian-backed terrorist organization that would prove even more intractable than the PLO, can be traced directly to Israeli attacks on previously neutral Shia villages. Worse was to come.

The removal of the PLO had left the Palestinians alarmingly vulnerable to attacks from their Maronite enemies. One spark would be enough to re-ignite the fire and inspire the Christian militia to another orgy of slaughter. What came, in fact, was not a spark but a bonfire: president-elect Bashir Gemayel was blown to tiny pieces by a bomb that destroyed the Phalange headquarters. His body was so mutilated that his wife had to identify him by a wedding ring on a severed hand.

The Phalange were rocked to their very core. Many of them refused to believe that their leader, the man who symbolized all they stood for, was dead. Rumours soon circulated that he had been seen walking uninjured from the ruins of the building where the bomb had gone off, making his way to a mysterious ambulance. One day, when his people were in great danger, he would return like King Arthur to save them.

For the time being, the Phalange sought revenge. Everyone in Lebanon knew this. The Israeli forces knew it, too, as did their political masters back home.

What happened next is still disputed. Nevertheless, it seems clear that Sharon and Israeli military leaders on the spot approved the entry of armed Phalange bands into the Palestinian camps of Sabra and Shatila. As their escorts were well aware, it was not a social call. They remained there for three days, engaging in a ghastly orgy of slaughter, torture, mutilation and rape. The IDF, knowing full well that something terrible was happening, did not intervene until they tired of the screams. The death toll will probably never be known, but it is thought to amount to around 2,000 men, women and children.

Insight

Elie Hobeika, the Phalange leader at the time of the Sabra and Shatila massacres, was assassinated in 2002. Arab commentators alleged Israeli involvement because Hobeika had been due to give evidence in a Belgian court of Sharon's involvement in the killings. In 2002 Sharon was prime minister of Israel.

Israel's Lebanese policy was in tatters. An estimated 400,000 Israelis filled the streets of Tel Aviv to protest at the IDF's role in the killing, passive or otherwise. Their government condemned the massacre, too, but denied all responsibility. Public pressure eventually forced Sharon to leave his post in the defence ministry, although he remained in the cabinet. A government inquiry exonerated the IDF from blame. The Sabra and Shatila massacres were investigated by many others, including international bodies and Israeli journalists. None of their reports supported the view that Sharon and his forces were entirely innocent.

Towards settlement

CHAOS RETURNS

In the May following the Sabra and Shatila massacres, Israel negotiated an armistice with President Amin Gemayel, brother of the assassinated Bashir. It lasted only a year until abrogated under Muslim and Syrian pressure. In that time the increasingly unpopular IDF, subject to violent and persistent attacks from all sides, had begun its painful withdrawal to the southern security zone which it had established during its previous invasion.

Meanwhile, the international peacekeeping force was also coming under attack. In the spring of 1983 a number of Americans, Italians and French were killed by a group whose name meant nothing at the time: Islamic Jihad. Within weeks it would be on everybody's lips. In April an Islamic Jihad suicide bomber drove a truck laden with explosives into the American embassy in Beirut and blew away the central section of the building. Human remains were found floating in the Mediterranean. In total 63 people died, including all the leading CIA agents in the region. A telephone message to a press agency announced with great clarity: 'The operation is part of the Iranian revolution's campaign against the imperialist presence throughout the world.'

President Reagan, would-be gunslinger that he was, immediately went on the offensive. His men were no longer in Lebanon as part of a peace mission. They were there to defend President Gemayel and crush his enemies, the Druze, Syrians and Shia. All of them used Soviet-made weapons, Reagan argued, so they must be communist sympathizers. This was not just a civil war in Lebanon, it was part of the US's worldwide crusade against the Evil Empire of the red flag.

The crusade failed, despite the best efforts of the American forces in the area. Nothing symbolized American impotence more than the massive 40-cm (16-inch) guns of the battleship *USS New Jersey* pounding Druze positions from a safe distance offshore: a great deal of sound and fury only served to make the enemy more determined. Shia suicide bombings increased, killing over 300 American and French peacekeeping soldiers in their bases. Bewildered, hurt and humiliated, the international forces left the country in 1984.

The withdrawal of external forces led to five more years of turmoil. The remnants of the PLO fell out with the Shia, the Syrians gradually increased their hold on the country while the Maronites, when not squabbling among themselves, did their best to resist them. The economy went from bad to worse.

When Amin Gemayel's term of office ended and it proved impossible to choose a new president, the country found itself with two prime ministers. The more forceful of them, General Aoun, announced a War of Liberation against the Syrians in an attempt to bind all Lebanese together.

THE TAIF ACCORD

Following a ceasefire, in 1989 the Saudi government invited the Lebanese parliament to meet in the hill town of Taif to work out a new power-sharing agreement. The multi-billionaire Lebanese businessman Rafiq al-Hariri, a prominent member of the Shia community, funded the visit. It eventually produced a fresh compromise – but no immediate end to the instability or the fighting. A new president was elected and promptly assassinated. General Aoun rejected the Taif Accord, giving Syrian forces a reason to re-enter the country. This time they were regarded by most parties as a necessary inconvenience.

The country was exhausted. Over 25 per cent of its population had fled abroad. About 150,000 had been killed. Hundreds of thousands had been made homeless. Not a family in the land had escaped suffering and loss. Hariri, now prime minister, set about getting Lebanon back on its feet again. His wealth, business acumen and worldwide contacts made him in many ways the ideal man for the task. Nevertheless, the probity of all the deals made by 'Mr Miracle', as Hariri was known, did not always bear scrutiny.

Although there was a definite decline in violence and a marked economic recovery in northern Lebanon, less progress was made in the south where the borders of Lebanon, Israel and Syria met. Eventually, though, the IDF left the region in May 2000. The withdrawal left some issues unresolved. Among these were ownership of an enclave on the Golan Heights known as the Sheba Farms, the continued presence of Syrian forces in Lebanon, and the ongoing anti-Israeli activities of Hezbollah and Islamic Jihad (see page 242). At the dawn of the twenty-first century, real and lasting peace was still a long way off.

THINGS TO REMEMBER

1 *By the 1970s, demographic changes were undermining the delicate political balance between Lebanon's religious communities.*

2 *Lebanon's instability increased when the PLO moved its headquarters there in 1970.*

3 *In 1975, Lebanon disintegrated into a long, bitter and extremely complex civil war in which foreign powers, notably Syria and Israel, played a major role.*

4 *With Syrian peacekeeping troops already operating there, in 1978 Israeli forces also entered Lebanon to tackle the threat posed by the PLO.*

5 *By the 1980s, Israeli society was becoming more polarized between left and right.*

6 *Launching Operation Peace for Galilee, Israel invaded Lebanon a second time in 1982 and advanced to besiege the PLO in Beirut.*

7 *Surrounded and facing annihilation, Yasser Arafat and the remnants of the PLO were allowed to leave Lebanon for Tunis.*

8 *Following the assassination of President-elect Bashir Gemayel, Phalange (Christian extremist) fighters perpetrated dreadful massacres in the Sabra and Shatila Palestinian refugee camps near Beirut. Israeli forces failed to intervene to stop the killing.*

9 *During the 1980s, Hezbollah, the Iranian-backed Shia Islamist party, emerged as a major force in Lebanon.*

10 *The Lebanese civil war finally drew to a close with the Taif Accord of 1989, mediated by Syria and Saudi Arabia.*

8

Camp David

This chapter will cover:
- *how the conditions at the end of the 1973 war made Arab–Israeli peace talks possible*
- *US Secretary of State Henry Kissinger's shuttle diplomacy*
- *President Sadat's historic visit to Israel*
- *the Camp David agreement and its repercussions.*

'We can negotiate'

At the end of the Fourth Arab–Israeli War (known in Israel as the Yom Kippur War), the Egyptian chief of staff addressed the Israeli deputy chief of staff with the remark, 'Look, this is the first time a war between us has ended in equality ... From here we can negotiate.' The comment was as prophetic as it was perceptive. Five years later, Israel and Egypt reached an historic agreement that marked the beginning of what has been called the Middle East peace process.

POST-WAR ISRAEL

Both Egypt and Israel claimed to have won the war. Technically speaking, because it was advancing into Egypt and Syria when President Nixon and Secretary of State Kissinger ordered a halt to the fighting, Israel was the victor. Politically, though, the victory was Egypt's.

The IDF had lost 3,000 men and women. Some had been captured, others were missing in action. The mightiest power in the Middle East, the state built by war and for war, had been caught napping and was driven back. Although an inquiry into what went wrong did not finger out the political leadership, Prime Minister Golda Meir's tarnished Labour government resigned the following year.

The new Labour administration was led by Yitzhak Rabin, the first Israeli-born politician to head the country's government. A native of Jerusalem, he had fought with the Haganah against the Palestinians and, briefly, against the dissident Irgun of Menachem Begin (see page 58). After independence he had attended staff college in Great Britain and made a name for himself as chief of staff in the 1967 war. On retiring from the army, he had served as ambassador to the United States. Having been elected to the Knesset (the Israeli parliament) only in 1973, he lacked political experience. An awkward manner made his job even more difficult. Henry Kissinger remarked in *Years of Upheaval* (Little Brown & Co, Boston, 1982), that Rabin 'had many extraordinary qualities, but the gift of human relations was not one of them'.

Because of the oil crisis and the world economic recession (see page 111), Rabin predicted seven lean years for Israel. He was correct. Inflation and unemployment rose. Overseas friends, notably the apartheid regime in South Africa, fell away under threat of an Arab oil embargo. Internal divisions widened, not just between Ashkenazim and other immigrants (see page 58), but between an emerging peace movement and extreme nationalists who sought a 'Greater Israel'. Among the latter was the Gush Emunim movement, which encouraged the building of Jewish settlements on occupied territory close to areas populated by Palestinians.

Insight

Gush Emunim is an extreme Jewish religious movement whose followers believe that the imminent arrival of the Messiah will be hastened if settlements are made on land given to the Jewish people by God – that is, on the West Bank.

Rabin's government was supported by a small majority in the Knesset and frequently divided over policy issues. Its slogan 'continuity and change' was an attempt to appeal to as many Israelis as possible. Sometimes Rabin was hawkish, as when he approved the successful 'Raid on Entebbe' (a daring mission by Israeli commandos to rescue the passengers of a hi-jacked Air France plane). At other times, as in his relations with Egypt, he was more accommodating.

EGYPT, SYRIA AND THE PLO

Life was no easier on the other side of the Suez Canal. Sadat's personal status rose dramatically as a result of his country's efforts in the Yom Kippur War, but this did not help him with Egypt's immediate economic difficulties. These were deeper rooted than those of Israel. Within a few years, the popularity of the 'Hero of the Crossing', as Sadat was known, had given way to violent anti-government demonstrations and unrest. Further dismantling of the repressive Nasser regime and an attempt to introduce limited democracy had little immediate impact. As far as Sadat was concerned, much depended on the anticipated 'peace dividend' of his foreign policy.

Syria's President Assad had lost further territory in the Golan Heights area as a result of the 1973 war, although this was never admitted to his people. In the words of his propaganda, 'He led the Liberation War of October 1973 in which our Armed Forces and people achieved great victories and emancipated the will of the Arabs and destroyed the enemy's arrogance' (found on several sites, such as the semi-official www.cafe-syria.com). Unlike Sadat and Arafat, Assad was not prepared to woo the Americans. Instead, he preferred to remain in the Soviet camp, giving moderate support to the Palestinians and pressing his case to be seen as leader of the Arab world.

Assad's erstwhile client, Yasser Arafat, was trying to move in a different direction. In keeping with his new, non-aggressive stance, the PLO had kept a relatively low profile during the Yom Kippur War.

As it continued to embed itself into Lebanese political and economic life, its international standing rose with official recognition by the Arab League and the UN. The international recognition that Arafat really wanted was that of the US State Department. Here he met with no success at all. Three times before the war and even in the middle of it, Arafat tried to contact Secretary of State Kissinger. The best he got was a warning not to employ his terrorist activities against US interests. He – and with him the Palestinian people – were being frozen out.

Shuttle diplomacy

Paradoxically, Sadat had gone to war in 1973 because he wanted peace. He wanted to open the Suez Canal, he wanted to cut back on military expenditure, he wanted himself and his people to be able to concentrate on making their country stable and prosperous, not always looking over their shoulders in the direction of Sinai. The first step towards achieving all these things was to settle Egypt's differences with Israel.

The first attempt to find a peaceful post-war settlement was a grand conference in Geneva, Switzerland, co-hosted by the UN, the USSR and the US. Neither Syria (self-excluded) nor the Palestinians (not invited) were present. After a few days of grandiose-sounding statements from all sides, the conference fizzled out. A comprehensive peace for the Middle East was beyond anyone's capacity to organize. Enter Henry Kissinger.

President Nixon's indefatigable and infinitely patient Secretary of State, Henry Kissinger, was keen to defuse the situation in the Middle East as swiftly as possible. The region's tensions were expensive and dangerous. Besides, a US-brokered settlement would enhance his country's position in the world and leave the Soviets looking like warmongers.

Having witnessed the Geneva fiasco, Kissinger abandoned the 'big plan' idea in favour of a step-by-step approach towards implementation of UN Resolution 242. To this end he spent many months flying backwards and forwards between the capitals of the Middle East, relaying offers and counter-offers, making suggestions of his own, and, when he felt it appropriate, using the big stick of US economic power to bring the parties round to his way of thinking.

Insight

Henry Kissinger, a US citizen of German-Jewish stock, entered political service after a first career as a Harvard professor. He is credited with being the first diplomat to use 'shuttle diplomacy'.

SINAI I AND II

Assad, as might be expected, proved the most intractable. It took almost a year to work out terms of disengagement on the Golan Heights. After that, negotiations ground to a halt. Neither Israel nor Syria would contemplate the sort of concessions necessary for a fully fledged peace treaty. The question at the back of both sides' minds was water – as we have seen (page 89), whoever controlled Golan had their hands on a vital water supply.

Negotiations between Israel and Egypt went better. Rabin went along with Kissinger's suggestions as long as it did not look to his electorate as if he was bowing under pressure. In private the Israeli prime minister was also prepared to admit that in the end his country would have to release not just land taken from Egypt but also that taken from the Palestinians. For his part, Sadat played the 'crossing' card with skill: Egypt's initial breakthrough on the Suez Canal had seriously undermined Israeli self-confidence, making them more amenable to compromise. Rabin was also softened by Kissinger's pledge that he would never include the PLO in negotiations until it renounced all violence and recognized Israel.

Under Kissinger's auspices two far-reaching disengagement agreements were reached, Sinai I and Sinai II (1974 and 1975). The armies pulled back, peacekeepers went in, and the Suez Canal was opened for the first time since 1967. After this the talks lost momentum.

According to Kissinger and President Gerald Ford, who had replaced the disgraced Nixon following the Watergate scandal, it was Rabin's tactlessness and inflexibility that blocked progress. This is not strictly true. The astute, French-educated King Hassan II of Morocco agreed to act as a secret go-between in Rabin–Sadat approaches that by-passed the Americans. Rabin took up his offer. Heavily disguised, he sneaked into Morocco with a message for the Egyptian president. It was taken on by Hassan's trusted commander of the royal guard, but evoked no response. Sadat would do nothing without US backing.

Early the next year it was Egypt's turn. Hoping to break the diplomatic deadlock, Sadat's vice-president approached Rabin's deputy, Shimon Peres. This time it was Austria's Jewish chancellor, Bruno Kreisky, who acted as an intermediary. Again, nothing came of the initiative. The peace process was stalled.

Elections in the US (1976) and Israel (1977) brought Act I of the peace drama to its anti-climactic close. At the time no one was even sure that there would be an Act II. Nevertheless, the curtain did rise again, and with different actors in key roles the second act was even more momentous than the first.

A moment in history

JIMMY CARTER

In the autumn of 1976, Republican President Ford was defeated in the polls by Democrat Jimmy Carter. Carter was an idealist, a 'big picture' man. Not for him the cautious shuttle diplomacy of Kissinger with its piecemeal results that left the major questions unanswered. To Carter's way of thinking, the longer the Arab–Israeli problem remained unsolved, the more intractable it would become.

Not only that, but Carter was a reader. Before taking office in January 1977, he did his homework, brushing up on the relative merits of each side. In the course of this swotting, he decided that the Palestinians had a case.

Early in his presidency Carter met with Yitzhak Rabin and said that he believed the Palestinians would be better off with a homeland of their own. The word 'homeland' set alarm bells ringing in Rabin's mind. Like all Israelis, he remembered every detail of his people's struggle towards statehood. He knew full well the British Foreign Secretary's famous Balfour Declaration of 1917, in which he had supported the idea of a 'homeland' for the Jews in Palestine. Just as the Jews had interpreted Balfour's use of 'homeland' as a codeword for 'state', so Rabin interpreted Carter's remark as backing for a Palestinian state. The shutters came down.

MENACHEM BEGIN AND LIKUD

The situation was saved in a most unexpected way. Rabin's wife had illegally kept open a US bank account she had opened when her husband was ambassador in Washington. The scandal came on top of others and Rabin resigned in the midst of the 1977 Knesset elections, handing over leadership of the Labour coalition to Shimon Peres. Rabin's resignation was not enough to save Labour. After the elections, for the first time in Israel's history, Labour was unable to form a government. Its place was taken by a right-wing coalition known as Likud.

Likud had been formed four years earlier in an effort to break the Labour monopoly of power. At its heart were the old Liberal and Herat ('Freedom') Parties. Likud's intellectual position was inherited from Russian Jewry, notably Jabotinsky's revisionist and Greater Israel philosophy (see page 48). In practical terms, its foreign policy might take the same course as that of Labour. The difference between them was intellectual. Both made national security their number one priority. For Labour, though, it was essentially a pragmatic issue, while to Likud it was ideological. As we have already noted, Rabin understood that one day Israel's security would be best served by handing back some of the West Bank and Gaza. To Likud this was impossible – a hideous betrayal of the solemn trust imposed upon them by the 6 million victims of the Holocaust.

Leadership of the Likud fell upon Menachem Wolfvitch Begin, sometime leader of the Irgun terrorists who had once exchanged fire with Rabin. Begin had been born in Poland in 1913. He had trained as a lawyer and had been an active Zionist before fleeing to Soviet territory to escape the Nazis at the start of the Second World War. One of his brothers and both his parents failed to get away and died in concentration camps. After being held in Siberia by the Russians, in 1941 he joined the Free Polish Army and was taken with them to Israel. Here he became the first head of Herut, the party he helped found.

The experiences of the first 40 years of his life had left a deep imprint on Begin's thinking. As we saw in the last chapter, his mind automatically linked opposition to Israel with anti-Semitism on the Nazi scale. His was a siege mentality. Embattled Israel, surrounded by enemies, had to defend itself within an iron wall.

The metaphorical wall encompassed both the West Bank and Gaza. Over those two pieces of land there could be no discussion. This was a point of view Begin shared with Ariel Sharon, his minister of agriculture. In many administrations the agriculture portfolio might not be a position of great importance. Not so in Begin's. Agriculture meant water and that meant retention of the Golan Heights, the West Bank and Gaza. Beneath the latter two lay about one-half of the area's underground water.

Likud retained power with the support of ultraconservative religious and nationalist groups. They supported the government's refusal to negotiate over Gaza and the West Bank for different reasons. These lands, together with much of Jordan, had been part of the ancient realm of King David which they, the Jews of the twentieth century, were gloriously recreating. God's chosen people were coming into their own once more. To hand away what God had given would be sacrilege. With Sharon's blessing, the number and scale of Jewish settlements in the occupied West Bank grew markedly.

SADAT'S FINEST HOUR

It was widely believed that Begin's election marked the end of the Middle East peace process for the duration. To the surprise of many, however, he declared himself willing to talk. At this point, President Carter, intellectually sound but still diplomatically naïve, set the process back by suggesting the Soviets be involved. The idea was not well received in the US, Israel or Egypt.

Sadat and Begin took up the running on their own. Once again Hassan II acted as clandestine facilitator. Begin found that he and the king, a prominent figure in the Arab world, shared certain key opinions. When the subject of Yasser Arafat and his organization was raised, the king declared bluntly, 'The PLO is a cancer in our midst. Their fate does not concern me at all.' Begin could only nod in total agreement.

After some initial exchanges, it was clear to Anwar Sadat that his Israeli counterpart was dragging his feet. What was needed was some dramatic, very public act that would force Begin into moving the process forward. Just as he had gambled by ordering an attack across the Suez Canal four years earlier, Sadat gambled again by laying his cards squarely on the table in full view of the whole world.

Speaking before the Egyptian National Assembly on 9 November 1977, Sadat pronounced these historic words:

> *You heard me saying that I am prepared to go to the ends of the earth if my doing so will prevent any of my officers or men being killed or wounded. I really am ready to go to the ends of the earth and Israel will be amazed to hear me say that we do not refuse – I am prepared to go to their very home, to the Knesset itself and discuss things with them ...*

Kirsten E. Schulze, *The Arab–Israeli Conflict*, 2008 page 110

It was a brilliant move. The world applauded and awaited Begin's
response. He had to accept. Sadat was invited to Israel and asked
to address the Knesset, just as he had said he would. His speech
called for an 'overall peace', not just one between Egypt and Israel.
This 'durable peace based on justice' would involve Israel handing
back the conquests of 1967 in return for full recognition by the
Arab world and binding peace treaties with its neighbours. The
Palestinians should be granted self-determination, establishing a
state of their own if that was what they wished.

Begin refused to be carried away by the emotion of the moment.
The tone of his speech in reply was a stark contrast to that of the
Egyptian president. His tone was tight and mean. He talked of the
past, of injustices done to the Jewish people. There could be talks,
he agreed, but with no pre-conditions. He gave away nothing and
did not once mention the Palestinians. Clearly, there was still a
very long way to go.

Just how far apart the Arabs and Israelis were became apparent over
the next few months. Begin suggested a partial Israeli withdrawal
from Sinai, then promptly allowed further Jewish settlements to be
built on occupied territory there. At the same time, more settlements
were appearing in the West Bank and Gaza. Sadat was at his wits'
end. To make matters worse, hostility against him was rising in
the Arab world. It was feared that he was prepared to go it alone,
abandoning the united Arab front that had more or less held firm
since 1948.

The deadlock was broken by Jimmy Carter. In a move that was
almost as dramatic as Sadat's speech to his parliament, he sent
personal invitations to the president of Egypt and the prime minister

of Israel. Would they please visit him at the presidential country retreat of Camp David, Maryland, to discuss their differences? It was an invitation neither man dared refuse.

Camp David

The Camp David talks marked a fundamental milestone in the recent history of the Middle East. Before the agreement, the Arab–Israeli story had been one of hatred and wars; afterwards, solid and enduring peace was at least a possibility. Camp David showed the way by cutting two knots. One had bound Arab to Arab in a solid front against Israel, the second had tied Israeli to its conquests. On their severance, much of the rest of the bitter tangle could begin to unravel.

The exception, as so often, was the Palestinian problem. This difficulty was glossed over at Camp David because Sadat knew that he could not have peace with Israel if he tried to fight the Palestinians' cause as well as the Egyptians'. Later, other Arab states were to follow his pragmatic example. One by one the Palestinians' Arab allies fell away, until they were faced with a reality that many of them had known in their hearts all along: whatever they wanted they had to get for themselves. Precisely the same realization had motivated the founders of Israel in the middle of the century.

SHANGRI-LA

Camp David is situated within the elevated and densely wooded reaches of the Catoctin Mountain Park in Maryland. Established by F. D. Roosevelt as a summer refuge from the heat and humidity of Washington DC, its original name of Shangri-La had been changed by President Dwight Eisenhower to the more prosaic one it bears today.

Three features of the camp were important for the talks' success. The first was its air of informality. This meant the negotiators could behave as if on holiday, dressing casually and wandering or cycling around the extensive grounds as they wished. There was not a reporter or a press camera for miles. Aliza Begin and Kihan Sadat were invited to attend with their husbands, although Mrs Sadat was unable to accept. The wife of the US president, Rosalynn Carter, accompanied her husband and played a key role in maintaining a cordial, relaxed atmosphere.

Camp David is just what it says it is – a complex of many buildings spread out over several acres. This gave each party separate and discrete accommodation where they could retire to put their feet up or hold private discussions. Finally, Camp David is remote. Except in thick fog, access is by helicopter. The site is surrounded by a high and heavily guarded protective fence to keep out intruders. This isolation and security also make the camp a difficult place to leave. Begin described it as an 'elegant jail'. Had it been possible simply to walk out, it is quite likely that the talks would have failed as at one time or another both parties felt that a resolution was unobtainable.

All this made President Carter's choice of venue for the talks a masterstroke. Once he had got the two parties to his dacha, isolated from outside pressures and influences, he was determined not to let them go until agreement had been reached. His role was more than just that of a facilitator – at times he was almost an enforcer.

CHEMISTRY AND QUOTATION

Carter's unusually united team was headed by himself, his Secretary of State Cyrus Vance, and his National Security advisor Zbigniew Brzezinski. Vice-President Walter Mondale was brought in at the end because of his perceived friendship with Israel. As well as Begin, the Israeli delegation also contained Foreign Minister Moshe Dayan, Defence Minister Ezer Weizman, and Attorney General Aharon Barak. Prominent among Sadat's delegation were Foreign Minister Muhammad Ibrahim Kamil and Osama El-Baz.

The chemistry of the assembled parties was complex and at times explosive. There was no love lost between Sadat and Begin. Their initial discussions ended up as shouting matches. Fortunately, Sadat liked and trusted Carter. His favourite member of the Israeli party was the ex-RAF fighter pilot Weizman.

Perhaps because they were both of Polish origin, Begin and Brzezinski seemed to get on well. On the evening of the fifth day of the talks, the two sat down to a game of chess. Begin sighed and confessed that the game brought back vivid memories: the last time he had played was just before his arrest and deportation to Siberia by the Soviet secret police. His beloved Aliza let him down. Entering the room some time later and seeing the game still in progress, she announced with delight that Menachem loved to play chess. He had obviously been playing all his life and the story about the game at the time of his arrest was just a ploy to gain sympathy.

Chess was not the only diversion. To lower the temperature, on day six Carter took his guests to visit the Gettysburg battlefield. Sadat, who as a cadet had studied the battle in great detail, was delighted. To Begin it meant nothing until they came to a memorial of President Lincoln's Gettysburg Address. 'Fourscore and seven years ago our fathers brought forth on this continent a new nation ...' began the Israeli prime minister. He knew the speech by heart and continued right through to its famous ending: '... that this nation under God shall have a new birth of freedom, and that government of the people, by the people, for the people shall not perish from the earth.' It looked as if Lincoln and Begin shared the same dream.

TO THE BRINK AND BACK

The talks lasted 14 days. Two basic issues were at stake: one, the return of Sinai and the normalization of Israeli–Egyptian relations; two, the return of other occupied territories, specifically the West Bank and Gaza, and the right of self-determination for the Palestinians living there. From the outset, Begin's position was the strongest. He had something to give (Sinai) and would not lose too much face back home if he returned without agreement. Carter was eager for a foreign policy triumph to bolster his flagging presidency. Sadat, having been the prime mover in the peace process, had the most to lose.

During days one and two, each side set out its positions. Sadat showed his lack of experience as a negotiator by revealing to Carter the concessions he was willing to make. The face-to-face meetings of Carter, Sadat and Begin on days three and four produced little but hostility. Thereafter the Americans acted as shuttle diplomats, ferrying messages and suggestions between the sides. By now it was clear there could be no firm agreement over the Palestinian question, so it was set aside for the time being. On strictly Israeli–Egyptian business, Begin's unwillingness to hand over settlements and airfields in Sinai was proving a major obstacle to progress.

By day ten, the two sides were still unable to agree and Carter feared the talks would fail. Begin, at his most adamant, had declared, 'My right eye will fall out, my right hand will fall off before I ever agree to the dismantling of a single Jewish settlement.' Later, Carter retorted that the Israel prime minister was throwing away peace for 'a few illegal settlers on Egyptian land'.

On day 11, Sadat and his entourage packed their bags and announced that they were leaving. Carter put on a jacket and tie and went to confront the Egyptian delegation in their lodge. If the talks collapsed, he warned, he could not guarantee that US aid to Egypt would be maintained. Moreover, Sadat would have made a fool of himself before the Arab world. Was he sure he wouldn't stay, just for a few days?

From then on the end was in sight. The US agreed to build new airfields for the Israelis and to guarantee their access to Sinai oil – but the settlements there had to go. US aid to Egypt amounted to about $1 billion a year during the 1980s.

The fate of the Palestinians was left in the air. The final text of the Camp David Accords spoke of what should happen to give the Palestinians their rights as outlined by Resolution 242, but there was nothing about what would happen. Although the Accords said that the 'peaceful and orderly transfer of authority' should begin when a 'self-governing authority … in the West Bank and Gaza [was] established', they contained no timetable for this to happen. Negotiations on the Palestinian issue dragged on long after all parties had left Camp David, but little substantive progress was made.

THE AFTERMATH

Back at the White House, all parties signed the Camp David Accords on 17 September 1978. Sadat and Begin shared the Nobel Peace Prize for their ground-breaking agreement, a reward perhaps more deserved by Jimmy Carter. After a further seven months of detailed negotiation, Israel and Egypt signed a formal treaty. By its terms Israel agreed to withdraw from 80 per cent of Sinai over three years, retaining rights to the area's oil. A UN observer force would patrol the new border. Most significant of all, Israel and Egypt established full diplomatic relations.

Although the abandonment of the Sinai settlements drew down the wrath of conservatives on Begin's head, many Israelis welcomed the treaty as the first step towards full international recognition and an eventual all-embracing peace. The more cynical saw it simply as a ploy to secure Israel's southern frontier, leaving the IDF free for a full invasion of Lebanon in 1982 (see Chapter 7).

Israeli strikes against the PLO continued, notably the assassination by a hit squad of Arafat's most trusted subordinate and adopted son, Ali Hassan Salameh. Jewish settlements went on being built on the West Bank, where local Palestinian leaders had met roundly to denounce the treaty. Likud and Begin were re-elected in 1981. The year before, disappointed that the Camp David process had not been taken further, Ezer Weizman had resigned. Leaving Begin's office for the last time, he had noticed a peace poster on the wall. Ripping it down, he shouted, 'No one here wants peace!'

Sadat had a rougher ride. His fellow Arabs accused him of abandoning the Palestinians for the sake of Sinai. Egypt was expelled from the Arab League, which moved its headquarters from Cairo to Tunis, and was subjected to an Arab boycott. Interestingly, of all the Arab nations only the PLO maintained diplomatic relations with Egypt, albeit in secret. Arafat was still eager to cosy up to the US.

In Egypt itself, the reception of the peace treaty was mixed. Much would depend on the 'peace dividend' that Sadat had set so much store by. To his intense frustration and disappointment, despite all the US aid and cuts in military expenditure, the Egyptian economy showed few signs of a significant recovery. As the class gap widened still further, popular unrest grew. In an attempt to mollify his people, the president introduced an element of popular participation in the political system and announced that henceforward Egyptian law would be based on the Islamic Sharia Law. It was too little, too late.

Still the discontent rumbled on. In September 1981, Sadat took action to forestall a possible coup, arresting over a thousand of the country's political élite. The next month a massive military parade was organized to celebrate the anniversary of the crossing of the Suez Canal during the October War. Here, on 6 October, before thousands of his people, Anwar Sadat was killed by Muslim extremists.

Insight

The assassination of Sadat was an extremely bloody affair involving a truckload of assassins, grenades and rifle fire. A total of 12 people died, including foreign dignitaries. A follow-up popular rebellion in the south of the country was swiftly crushed.

Among his own people, Sadat was not liked. He had promised much but delivered little, and his regime was intolerably harsh. The West, however, saw a different Sadat. The title 'hero of the crossing' had taken on a double meaning. He had not just crossed the canal. With a great leap of faith he had crossed cultures, striding over a gulf of misunderstanding and mistrust to shake hands with the enemy. It was as brave an act as any on the battlefield.

THINGS TO REMEMBER

1 *Egyptian success at the start of the 1973 October War destroyed the myth of Israeli invincibility and paved the way for Israel and Egypt to talk as equals.*

2 *'Shuttle diplomacy' by the US Secretary of State Henry Kissinger produced the Israeli–Egyptian Sinai I and Sinai II disengagement agreements.*

3 *The possibility of an Israeli–Syrian accord foundered on the question of control of the Golan Heights.*

4 *In 1976, the Democrat Jimmy Carter was elected to the White House with a mission to seek peace in the Middle East.*

5 *Labour's hold on power in Israel was broken when Menachem Begin formed a right-wing Likud coalition administration in 1977.*

6 *When peace talks appeared to be stalling, in November 1977 Egypt's President Sadat shocked the world by saying he was prepared to go to the Knesset (the Israeli parliament) to talk peace.*

7 *Sadat duly visited Israel and set in train events that led to the first formal peace treaty between Israel and an Arab state.*

8 *When public negotiation seemed to be failing, President Carter invited Prime Minister Begin and President Sadat to his presidential summer retreat of Camp David, and there bullied and cajoled them into reaching an agreement.*

9 *In September 1978, the groundbreaking Camp David Accords, in which Israel and Egypt established diplomatic relations but which sidestepped the Palestinian issue, were signed in Washington DC.*

10 *The Camp David agreement aroused fury throughout the Arab world and led to President Sadat's assassination in 1981.*

9

....

Revolution and war

This chapter will cover:
- *Iran's White Revolution*
- *the overthrow of the Shah of Iran in the revolution of 1979*
- *the rise of Saddam Hussein in Iraq*
- *the Iran–Iraq War.*

Our attention now moves east, to the Persian Gulf. Iran and Iraq had as much impact on the late twentieth-century world as Israel-Palestine, but for very different reasons. Iran underwent a unique political, social and religious revolution, the impact of which was felt right across the Middle East and beyond. Iraq came under the rule of a dictator as ruthless as any we will meet. These two states, each representing a distinct form of tyranny, then clashed in one of the most senseless and costly wars of recent times.

_____

King of Kings

In Chapter 2 we saw how the absolute but well-intentioned young ruler of Iran, Mohammed Reza Shah Pahlavi, was trying to modernize his oil-rich state along Western lines. Opposition came principally from a traditional landed élite, often called the notables, and the Shia Muslim hierarchy. Domestic support, at first, came from a tiny group of Western-educated intellectuals and business people, and the landless rural majority.

Backing was always available from the West, eager for Iranian oil and keen to support a friendly bulwark against possible Soviet expansion. In 1953, for example, US support enabled the shah to recover his authority after it had been briefly undermined by Prime Minister Muhammed Mosaddeq. Thereafter the shah was very much the US's man.

THE WHITE REVOLUTION

Shah Pahlavi carried out what was termed a 'White Revolution' from above. The key was land reform: obliging wealthy landowners to hand over their land to impoverished tenants. One estimate suggests that some 12 million Iranians benefited from this move, increasing the proportion of owner-occupied land from 26 per cent to 78 per cent over a 12-year period. Those who lost land were compensated, sometimes in shares.

The profit-sharing principle was introduced into industry, and co-operative ventures were encouraged. Government grants and direct injections of capital came largely from the profits of the National Iranian Oil Company, a Western consortium led by BP. Mosaddeq had briefly nationalized the oil industry but the restored shah reversed the decision.

In an effort to diversify the economy, government help was given to vehicle and steel manufacture, mining, and construction. Dams were built and irrigation projects completed in double-quick time. Gross national product was rising at almost eight per cent a year by the mid-1970s. It has been estimated that the average per capita income rose from $170 to $2,500 in just 18 years.

The White Revolution was about more than economics. All sectors of education were expanded and university-level students encouraged to study abroad. Malaria was eliminated and the benefits of modern medicine extended. Literacy and health corps were established to benefit the many remote villages and smaller towns. A range of Western experts, from language teachers to civil engineers, flooded into Iran at the shah's behest. Iranian women were urged to set aside their traditional subservient roles and play prominent parts in all aspects of life. Pictures of the shah with his third wife, Farah Diba, adorned every loyal enterprise, from bazaar stall to ministry. This was not just royalist propaganda, but an effort to portray a woman as a working partner. The conscious effort to make Iran a Westward-looking country also brought all the peripheral glitz of Euro-American life: the flashy cars, the night clubs, the movies, rebellious teenagers, and so forth.

WHITE TYRANNY

A list of the achievements of the White Revolution looks impressive. Its cost, however, was unpleasantly high. First, there was the toll it took on the shah himself. He became a living example of the corrupting effect of power. In 1967, in a ceremony of vast expense and magnificence, he had himself crowned Emperor of all Iran and King of Kings. At the same time, Farah was created 'Shahbanoo' or Empress. The move was justified as necessary to promote the royal family as a unifying force. Within Iran and abroad, it was mocked as pompous tomfoolery.

The 1971 celebration of 2,500 years of Persian monarchy drew equally sceptical responses. The elaborate and costly show was staged amid the spectacular ruins of Persepolis, once the capital of the ancient Persian Empire. The site was chosen to link the Pahlavi dynasty with the country's glorious past. In the light of what was to happen to him, the shah might have been better advised while at Persepolis to reflect upon the transitory nature of earthly power.

Insight

The Shah's isolation from ordinary Iranians began early. He started his education in a private school established especially for him in the grounds of the royal palace, then moved to Switzerland for his secondary education.

Associating the ruling dynasty with a pre-Islamic past did not do much for Shah Pahlavi's already acrimonious relationship with his country's Shia hierarchy. Nor did another of his attempts at self-glorification: replacing the Islamic calendar with an 'Imperial' one that began with the foundation of the Persian Empire some two-and-a-half millennia before.

In carrying out his policies, the increasingly autocratic shah rode roughshod over the country's constitution. Ministers, in theory representative of the people, were merely his appointees. He talked of introducing democratic reforms but took no practical steps to do so. Savak, the state intelligence and security organization, rooted out opposition and dealt with its perpetrators with summary ruthlessness. Distorted by the power he wielded, the once-handsome shah came to look cold and cadaverous. It was as if the lymphatic cancer that eventually killed him had begun by attacking his soul.

The Iranian Revolution

MOUNTING OPPOSITION

There were two strands of opposition to the shah. One comprised those who supported his Westernization policy but believed it did not go far or fast enough. They sought more participation in the political process, for instance, and less state interference in business and industry. The second group was the Islamists, opposed to Westernization and calling for a return to Sharia. It is a measure of the shah's political ineptitude that he managed to unite these seemingly irreconcilable parties.

By the mid-1970s, the fairly apolitical bulk of the population, although they had benefited from the shah's rule in many ways, found their confidence in him melting away. As elsewhere in the world, rising oil prices fuelled inflation. This cut the value of wages and savings. Against this background the shah's massive military spending programme was criticized as tactlessly inappropriate. Most Iranians felt that too much oil wealth flowed into the pockets of the few rather than the many. No one outside the royal inner circle had a good word for Savak.

Informed of his people's unease, in 1977 the shah made the mistake of slightly relaxing his political control. One measure in particular – reducing the powers of the censor – served only to fuel demands for more reform. Public protests at the end of the year resulted in several deaths at the hands of the security forces.

The following January popular unrest surged again. Students in Qumm protesting against a visit by US President Jimmy Carter were fired on by the police; 70 were killed. The Shia branch of Islam has a particular respect for martyrdom. One of its traditions is that martyrs are commemorated 40 days after their death. So, 40 days after the Qumm slaughter, fresh protests broke out. This time the city of Tabriz saw more than 100 protestors slain. After another 40 days a similar number was shot at Yazd. By midsummer almost the entire country was consumed by protest.

The shah vacillated. After trying conciliatory tactics, in early autumn he ordered a crackdown. In Tehran hundreds were shot dead on what was immediately dubbed 'Black Friday' (8 September 1978). Martial law was introduced and thousands of arrests were made. Public protest gave way to strikes and within a short space of time the country's key industries ground to a halt.

AYATOLLAH KHOMEINI

By this time the protest movement had coalesced around the austere figure of Ruhallah Khomeini. Few late twentieth-century figures were more controversial than this scholar-dictator. Born around the turn of the century in the town of Khomeyn, from whence he took his name, he came from a long line of mullahs (Shia religious leaders). A learned but humourless student of Islam, in his fifties he was proclaimed an ayatollah – important religious leader – and ten years later a grand ayatollah.

Insight

Punctilious to the point of obsession, Ayatollah Khomeini's day was precisely regulated to the nearest minute: he is said even to have awoken at the same moment each morning.

Khomeini used his position as one of the country's leading Shia clerics to speak out against the shah's rule. For his opposition to the forced reduction of religious estates, he was imprisoned and then sent into exile. As the unsmiling firebrand was now in his mid-sixties, the shah must have thought he had seen the last of him. Not so – the older Khomeini grew, the more active he became. Moving from Turkey to Iraq and eventually Paris, France, the ayatollah kept up a constant barrage of criticism of the shah and his regime. By the late 1970s, illegally copied recordings of his unrelenting, earnest speeches were in popular demand throughout Iran.

Reason alone cannot explain Khomeini's popularity. Many of the things he advocated – women re-veiling, bans on alcohol and Western music, for example – had little obvious appeal to the students of both sexes who so adored him. He was certainly helped by his absence from Iran. Without the intrusion of awkward reality, his image became fantastically embellished in the popular imagination: Ayatollah Ruhallah Khomeini developed into the long-lost saviour who would one day return to rescue his people. The exile's nationalistic Shia roots contrasted favourably with the shah's pro-Western secularism, too. In short, Khomeini was everything the shah was not. The obverse of popular hatred for the shah was hysterical love of Khomeini. The two were part of the same tidal wave of emotion that swept across the nation. What elevating the revered mullah meant in practical terms, people only discovered when it was too late to do anything about it. By then they had given the unyielding puritan supreme authority for the rest of his life.

THE FLIGHT OF THE SHAH

Stirred up by Khomeini's vision of an Islamic republic, Shia fundamentalists became the most prominent and outspoken of the shah's opponents. At their head were the Mujahedin, 'Dedicated Fighters'. As 1978 came to an end, appeals to Khomeini to return to his native land multiplied. Waiting until such a move would be unopposed as well as universally welcomed, he refused to come home as long as the shah remained in the country.

During the especially holy month of Muhurram, beginning on 2 December, anti-shah protests reached a crescendo. The strikes escalated and literally millions took to the streets. Government buildings were occupied and ransacked, and officials assassinated. To the Mujahedin no task was too dangerous – if it led to death, so be it: there was no greater honour than martyrdom. In such conditions, the government could not operate.

Accepting the inevitable, on 16 January 1979 the shah left the country. At the time, officials announced that he was going on holiday. This was later changed. The new version said he had left Iran to prevent further bloodshed. Neither explanation was particularly convincing. The regency government that the shah left behind was unable to cope. By now the loyalty of the armed forces and police was shifting from the shah to Khomeini.

The saviour finally arrived on 1 February. Amid scenes of extraordinary mass hysteria, he made his way from the airport to Tehran through a crowd of several million. There seemed nothing he could not do. When the official government fled, he appointed a new one in its place. By the end of the year, Iranians had voted in a referendum to make their country an Islamic republic on a new model devised by their religious and political leader.

Insight

Iran's constitution is based on belief in:

'(1) The One God (as stated in the phrase "There is no god except Allah"), His exclusive sovereignty and right to legislate, and the necessity of submission to His commands; (2) Divine revelation and its fundamental role in setting forth the laws.' (Various sources)

Under the Khomeini constitution, the secular and the religious were merged. All government actions, from the passing of laws to making treaties with foreign powers, were subject to the scrutiny of a Guardian Council comprising the country's most learned Shia clerics. This reverend body was charged with ensuring that the government acted in accordance with the Koran. At the head of the Council, on the very pinnacle of the theocratic power pyramid, sat Ayatollah Khomeini. Against his judgements there was no appeal. In practice, therefore, Iran had come close to swapping one dictator for another.

THE NEW IRAN

Mercy was not Khomeini's favourite attribute of the Almighty. He gave his blessing to bands of young enthusiasts who patrolled the streets looking for backsliders, possible royalist sympathizers, or anyone just showing an interest in Western culture. Thousands of ex-royalists were reportedly executed. Women were beaten for not covering their faces, shopkeepers for being found in possession of Elvis Presley tapes. Thousands of better-off Iranians fled abroad. Human rights were no more respected than they had been under the previous regime.

One of the most destabilizing effects of the Iranian Revolution stemmed from Khomeini's determination to export it. Central to this process was an often declared fight with the 'corrupt' West and its 'evil' sympathizers. As straightforward battle was not an option, Iran became a training ground for Muslim terrorists prepared to embrace martyrdom. Thus international terrorism entered a new and more violent phase that would bear its most vicious fruit in the next century.

Meanwhile, an incident had occurred that turned nearly all democratic states against Iran's new government. When the shah visited the US seeking treatment for his cancer, Khomeini demanded his extradition. This was refused – the US had no extradition treaty with the new regime in Iran. In response, a gang of student extremists seized the US embassy in Tehran and took captive the 66 US citizens working there. President Carter demanded their immediate release. Backed by the frenzied anti-Americanism of the streets, Khomeini refused.

Carter applied economic pressure, freezing Iranian assets in the US and placing an embargo on the country's oil. Still the hostages were not released. Growing desperate, the president authorized a clandestine rescue attempt by helicopter. Incompetence and a sandstorm caused the mission to be aborted before it reached

Tehran – by which time eight Americans had been killed in the chaos of collision and fire. The world watched in disbelieving disgust as elderly ayatollahs gloated gleefully over the charred bodies. Following the death of the shah, Carter's defeat by Ronald Reagan, and the outbreak of the Iran–Iraq War, the hostages eventually came home in January 1981.

> ## Insight
>
> The hostage rescue attempt failed when a ground marshal directing a US helicopter moved back to avoid the sand blast churned up by the machine's rotor. The pilot believed he, and not the marshal, was in reverse, and so moved his helicopter forward – into collision with a laden Hercules refuelling aircraft. End of mission.

The rise of Saddam Hussein

The monarchy of the British-created state of Iraq was overthrown in 1958. The consequent five-year rule of Brigadier Qasim was bloody and troubled. After only a year in power, for example, he narrowly escaped assassination at the hands of Baath Party machine gunners. The wielder of one of these weapons was hit in the leg by a bullet but managed to make a daring escape on horseback and by swimming fully clothed across the Tigris. The hero of this adventure, which would one day be recounted ad nauseam in prose, verse, song and film, was a 22-year-old Sunni Muslim from the Tikrit district named Saddam Hussein.

THE ADVANCE OF THE BAATHISTS

Saddam Hussein, son of a peasant farmer who died around the time of his birth, was brought up in a tribal society which espoused loyalty and cruelty in almost equal measure. Single-mindedly ambitious, he joined the Baath Party while a student. He was not particularly attracted to the organization's socialist or nationalist principles, but saw it as a means to power.

After the failure of the 1959 coup attempt, Hussein fled abroad to Damascus then Cairo. His part in Iraq's next coup – if indeed he did have a hand in it – is obscure. Qasim had incurred the disfavour of the West by nationalizing part of Iraq's oil industry, threatening to invade Kuwait and leaving the Baghdad Pact. It is not surprising to learn, therefore, that the CIA played a significant role in his fall from power in 1963. The coup was carried out in the name of the Baath Party, with army assistance. Many of the conspirators were from the Tikrit region.

Shortly after pictures of Qasim's bullet-riddled body appeared on television, General Arif expelled the Baathists and took the reins of government into his own hands.

Hussein learned several lessons from each of the coups he witnessed. Two were particularly important: one, total control was possible only with the support of the army, security services, party and a strong local (tribal) power base; two, the first priority of anyone taking power was to eliminate all possible rivals as quickly as possible.

General Arif's failure to apply this last lesson cost him his position. In 1968 he was overthrown in yet another coup, organized by the Baath Party with the backing of Colonel al-Nayif, head of military intelligence. Had Arif been more ruthless and eliminated the Baath Party leader and deputy leader (the cousins Ahmed al-Bakr and Saddam Hussein) after he had arrested them in 1966, his period of power might have been longer. As it was, Hussein persuaded the guard ferrying him from the court house to prison to stop by a local restaurant. Here, with extraordinary good fortune, he escaped by simply walking out of the back door of the building.

PRESIDENT SADDAM HUSSEIN

The fall of Arif left al-Bakr as head of state and Hussein as his lieutenant, the strong man behind the scenes. Over the next ten years, Hussein eliminated possible opponents. Nayif, for example, who had helped the Baath come to power, was personally

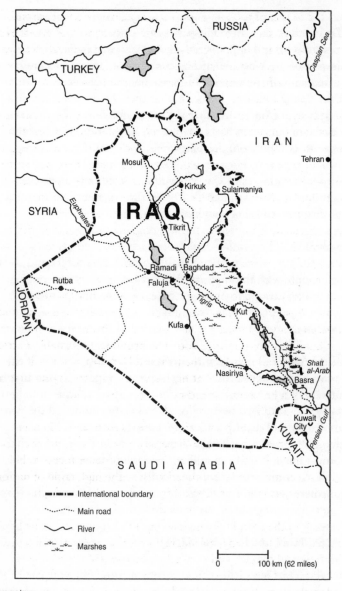

Figure 9.1 Iraq.

escorted to the airport by Hussein and told never to return to Iraq. Later, unsure that exile was sufficiently secure, Hussein had him shot dead in London. Ex-Defence Minister General al-Tikriti was assassinated in Kuwait. Many others simply disappeared. Membership of any opposition party was punishable by death.

Hussein struck on 10 July 1979. Prompted by his eager successor, al-Bakr announced to a meeting of the Revolutionary Command Council (RCC) that on account of his poor health he was stepping down as president. Hussein would succeed him. There was some opposition within the Baath Party and talk of a Syrian-backed coup. Barzan, Saddam's half-brother, investigated the rumours with torture-assisted thoroughness. One-quarter of the RCC were executed, along with 16 other possible opponents of the new regime.

The new president did not stop there. He wanted the purge to be a public warning to anyone who even thought of standing in his way. Suspects from all over the country were rounded up and killed. In many instances – a new departure this in Iraqi thuggery – their families were punished too. The prominent journalist Patrick Cockburn (2002) tells how the tortured body of one prominent Baathist was dumped back at his house with a note saying that he had died of a heart attack and mourning was forbidden.

Hussein did not want power simply for its own sake. He was determined that Iraq, hitherto little more than a somewhat chaotic second-rate Gulf state, should become the premier force in the region – a country to be reckoned with at the high table of nations. Immediate events in Iran seemed to play straight into his hands.

Glancing to the east, Hussein saw that the Khomeini regime had plunged Iran into chaos, considerably weakened its armed forces with fanatical purges, and severed all links with its previous backers in the West. Moreover, there was no chance of Shia fundamentalists doing a deal with the atheistic Soviet Union. Since both the West and the Soviets viewed with horror what was going on in Iran, Hussein reasoned, they might well support an attempt to unseat the ageing ayatollah. Besides, an attack would be the best way of preventing Iran's religious plague from infecting the Iraqi Shia, who comprised about 60 per cent of the population.

Confident of success but with no formal military knowledge or experience whatsoever, Hussein ordered a full-scale invasion of Iran in September 1980.

THE IRAN–IRAQ WAR (1980–8)

Animosity between Iran and Iraq went back a long way. The Bakr-Hussein regime's Friendship and Cooperation Treaty with the Soviet Union in 1972, for instance, placed Iraq on the opposite side in the Cold War to the US-backed regime of Shah Pahlavi. In 1973–4, the shah, with tacit US support, backed separatist Kurdish rebels in northern Iraq. Equally serious was the conflict over the Shatt al-Arab waterway, the broad estuary formed by the confluence of the Tigris and Euphrates Rivers.

Iraq's coastline is only 40 km (25 miles) long. The Shatt al-Arab, at its eastern end, is the country's vital link with the Gulf. A treaty made before the Second World War gave control to Iraq. After this had been abrogated by Iran, the Algiers Agreement (1975) between Hussein, then vice-chairman of the RCC, and the shah gave their two countries joint control over the waterway. Following these Iraqi concessions, Iran stopped supporting the Kurds in their struggle for independence. As a consequence, the Kurdish war soon ended.

This was the situation when Khomeini and Hussein came to power in their respective countries. A more contrasting pair of dictators it would be hard to imagine, so it comes as little surprise to learn that they were soon at war. Nevertheless, for a few months Hussein had gone out of his way not to react to his new neighbour's fiery taunts.

The Khomeini regime refused to recognize Saddam Hussein's secular and therefore unholy government. The ayatollah himself called on Iraq's Shia majority to rise up against a president whom he dubbed 'the main obstacle to the advance of Islam in the region'. Hussein, with rare humour, mocked the dusty old mullah as 'that mummy'. Shia assassins, recruited by Iran, slew numerous Baath Party officials, and Iranian support for Kurdish rebels began to flow once more.

We cannot be completely sure why Hussein did not react more swiftly to such blatant provocation. The most likely answer is that he wished to secure his rule before engaging in any dramatic foreign adventure. He had plans to spend some of Iraq's fast-growing wealth on large-scale projects that would boost his popularity, such as irrigation and health care. War would divert these funds into unproductive arms purchases.

Towards the end of 1979, Hussein's mind began to change. He expelled 100,000 Iraqis of Iranian stock and began supporting Iranian Sunni opposition to Khomeini. With fine irony, while battling against the Kurds at home, he backed the Kurdish independence movement within Iran. When these signals drew forth no response, military clashes along the Iran–Iraq border escalated. After Iraq had unilaterally abrogated the Algiers Agreement in September, all-out war was virtually inevitable.

THE COURSE OF THE WAR

The story of one of the most costly, cruel and protracted of modern wars is simply told. It began with an Iraqi operation intended to deliver a knockout blow, rather like that launched by Israel at the start of the Six Day War. Iraqi planning and execution fell far short of the Israelis', however. Although initial gains were made, Iran's armed forces remained very much operational. In fact, far more damage had already been done by Khomeini, whose purges had deprived the Iranian army of 12,000 officers and the air force of one half of its pilots.

After the first clashes, during which the Iraqi army had advanced a relatively short distance into Iran, a period of stalemate ensued.

This came to a close in the autumn of 1981. The Iranians launched an offensive that eventually retook much of the land they had lost and threatened Kirkuk in northern Iraq and Basra in the south.

In a significant development, the Iraqis first used poison gas in the defence of Basra. Delighted at the weapon's efficacy, they thereafter employed it on all fronts, especially against the Iraqi Kurds. In an attempt to hit the Iranian economy, Hussein stepped up the so-called 'Tanker War', striking at Iranian oil tankers and their port facilities.

By the time the war dragged into its sixth year, the situation for Hussein was looking extremely gloomy. Khomeini even issued a fatwa – religious command – demanding that his people win the war within the next 12 months. Iraq was saved by several factors, including massive foreign arms shipments and, paradoxically, a near-mutiny in its own army. The latter occurred when General al-Rashid was summoned to the presidential palace to explain why he had failed to make headway against the Iranians in the south. Normally, such a summons meant only one thing: removal and probable execution.

Rashid's officers were aware of this. They also knew that their commander had been unable to conduct the war as he would have wished because of continual amateur meddling from Baghdad. Before Rashid arrived at the palace, the officers sent a message to Hussein saying that if anything happened to him they would not be able to continue the war. When Rashid arrived at the palace, he found a smiling Hussein waiting to decorate him. Thereafter the president left the conduct of the war largely in the hands of the professionals.

The seventh year of the conflict saw Iraq on the offensive again and the UN Security Council voting unanimously for a ceasefire. Iraq accepted it but Iran wavered. Directed by US intelligence, which identified the weakest points in the Iranian line, the Iraqi army made notable gains. For the first time for years they found themselves on Iranian soil. The Iranian president, Ali Akbar Hashemi-Rafsanjani, implored the ailing Ayatollah Khomeini to call a halt to the slaughter. The old man was not yet ready.

Khomeini's mind was changed by a terrible accident. On 3 July 1988 the *USS Vincennes*, on duty in the Gulf, accidentally shot down an Iranian passenger jet with 290 people on board. The US offered compensation but would not apologize. Rafsanjani persuaded Khomeini that the incident demonstrated Iraq's alliance with the US, which was about to attack Iran. Saying it was like taking poison, Khomeini agreed to call a halt to the slaughter. His decision was also influenced by near-rebellion at home and Iraq's development of missiles that could rain chemical and biological warheads on Tehran and other major Iranian cities. Not even Khomeini was sure he wanted martyrdom on that scale.

THE TERRIBLE PRICE

The Iran–Iraq War was remarkable for a variety of unpleasant reasons. One was the extent of the slaughter. Around half a million people were killed, well over 50 per cent of them Iranians and their Kurdish allies. The number of wounded was at least twice as many. The war had cost an estimated $800 billion, leaving both countries heavily indebted. Iraq, for example, owed Saudi Arabia $25.1 billion, Kuwait $10 billion and other states another $40 billion. Hussein seems genuinely to have believed that as he had been defending the Arab world against Iranian fanatics, his fellow Arabs would forgive his debts. They did not.

In the thick of the slaughter were Iran's Revolutionary Guards, the Pasdaran, and its youth movement counterpart, the Basji. Both were imbued with their leader's extraordinary passion for the cause, even to the point of death. Believing that victory could be won only by 'blood ... and strength of faith', Khomeini advocated the murderous 'human wave' tactic – thousands upon thousands of foot soldiers pouring towards the enemy lines and eventually overcoming them by sheer weight of numbers.

The antics of the Basji particularly horrified those who encountered them. Drawn mainly from deeply religious, rural families, these young boys (some only 12 years old) carried on their person tokens of their coveted martyrdom: a piece of white cloth symbolizing their shroud and a plastic key (a gift from the ayatollah) to remind them that their entry into paradise was guaranteed. Lightly armed, if at all, they were used as human minesweepers or as decoys to draw enemy fire. They were shot down in their thousands.

THE INTERNATIONAL DIMENSION

The international repercussions of the war were extremely complex. On the surface, the West, headed by the US and France, joined with the Soviets in support of Saddam Hussein. The French built up especially strong commercial links with Iraq. The US, estranged during Bakr's premiership, re-established diplomatic relations with Baghdad during the war. The CIA regularly supplied Iraqi generals with invaluable reconnaissance material.

Of the handful of states siding with Iran by far the most surprising was Israel. The reason was simply that they did not want Hussein, with his capacity to reach Tel Aviv as well as Tehran with his lethal warheads, emerging as a major power in the Middle East. We have already seen how the Israeli air force got in a pre-emptive strike against Iraq's nuclear plant in 1981 (see page 125).

As so often the case in the murky world of diplomacy, the picture was less straightforward than it at first seemed. Britain, for instance, sold Iran spare parts for its tanks. In what is known as the Iran-Contra Affair, the chicanery of the US administration was even more cynical. During 1985–7 it emerged that senior US officials, possibly with the knowledge of President Reagan and Vice-President George Bush Sr, were selling arms to Iran via Israel. These weapons then found their way to Islamic terrorists operating in Lebanon, who in return freed Western hostages held there. The profits from the arms sales were used to fund the Contras – anti-communist guerrillas fighting in Nicaragua.

The Tanker War also brought the international community into the conflict. By the end of the war more than 50 warships were patrolling the Gulf to defend Iraqi, Kuwaiti and other tankers from Iranian air strikes. Meanwhile, Iraqi planes were free to attack Iranian shipping at will.

POST-WAR IRAQ

From almost every viewpoint, the Iran–Iraq War was a costly, tragic exercise in futility. By the time the two sides had finally finished haggling in 1990, the terms of their settlement were virtually the same as those of the previous Algiers Agreement. Strategically, therefore, all that bloodshed, all that misery, all that expenditure had achieved precisely nothing.

Billions of dollars of oil revenue that might have been spent on education, health or transport had been wasted on armaments. As far as Hussein's personal ambitions were concerned, however, the war had not been entirely a waste. It had allowed him to tighten his stranglehold on Iraq, eliminating thousands of Shia dissidents and innocent Kurds. His Kurdish policy came wickedly close to genocide. The chemical attack on the city of Halabja, for instance, left 5,000 men, women and children dead within 30 minutes.

Insight

Halabja fallout: The attack on Halabja helped fuel Western fears that Saddam Hussein had stockpiles of WMDs – weapons of mass destruction. The elimination of such weapons was given as a major reason for the US-led invasion of Iraq in 2003.

By the close of the war, the Iraqi army boasted 55 divisions and 4,000 tanks. This fulfilled another of Saddam Hussein's ambitions: he now ruled perhaps the most powerful state in the Gulf. His neighbours watched anxiously to see how he would exercise that newly acquired power.

THINGS TO REMEMBER

1 *Mohammed Reza Pahlavi, Shah (Emperor) of Iran since 1941, was seen by the West as a key bastion against the communist influence of the USSR.*

2 *In an attempt to modernize Iran's economy and society, Shah Pahlavi conducted a 'White Revolution' that alienated most influential groups in Iranian society.*

3 *Opposition to the shah coalesced around the austere figure of Ayatollah Khomeini, who in 1979 returned from exile in Paris and led a revolution that replaced the shah with an Islamic republic.*

4 *The Iranian Revolution impacted worldwide, marking the rise of anti-Western, militant Islam as a major force in global politics.*

5 *After the collapse of Iraq's shaky monarchy in 1958, the country was ruled by a series of military dictators.*

6 *In 1963, General Qasim was overthrown in a Western-supported coup led by General Arif, who in turn was overthrown by a Baathist coup led by al-Bakr.*

7 *Coming to power in Iraq on the retirement of President al-Bakr in 1979, Saddam Hussein established a ruthless police state and removed anyone who might threaten his position.*

8 *Border disputes led to the Sunni-secular regime of Saddam Hussein going to war with the neighbouring Shia-Islamist government of Iran in 1980.*

9 *Saddam Hussein survived the long and bloody Iran–Iraq War (1980–8) only with the tacit support of the West.*

10 *The Iran–Iraq War, which cost some 500,000 lives, left Saddam Hussein's oil-rich Iraq virtually bankrupt and needing to find employment for its huge military establishment.*

10

Intifada

This chapter will cover:
* *unsuccessful attempts to solve the Israel-Palestine problem in the 1980s*
* *the emergence of Palestinian nationalism*
* *the First Intifada*
* *the election of Yasser Arafat as president of the state of Palestine*
* *the Madrid Conferences and renewed hopes of a settlement.*

Fruitless negotiation

TIME OF STRIFE

During the early 1980s, the Middle East was as strife-torn as it had ever been. In the east, to satisfy the ambitions of their dictator-rulers, the people of Iran and Iraq were dying in their tens of thousands. Iranian fundamentalist fervour was beginning to seep west across the region, bringing with it a new wave of unstoppable terrorism in the form of the suicide bomber. Egypt's discontent had manifested itself in the assassination of its well-intentioned president.

The Israeli invasion of Lebanon had gone horribly wrong. It brought none of the political or strategic gains intended, and ended in a shameful withdrawal. The massacres at Sabra and Shatila left the Israeli government in deep disgrace and the nation bitterly divided. The PLO had been defeated and its leadership now languished in distant Tunisia. The people it purported to help remained stateless, impoverished and largely hopeless. The only beam of light, appearing in the middle of the decade, was the emergence of Mikhail Gorbachev as leader of the Soviet Union. His leadership would end the Cold War that had so often fuelled the Middle East's bitter quarrels.

LEBANESE ENDGAME

At about the time that Saddam Hussein was wondering whether war with Iran was such a good idea after all, several thousand miles away Yasser Arafat was also contemplating the future with some alarm. Now based in Tunis, for the first time in its existence the PLO had no common frontier with Israel. The armed struggle to replace Israel with a single democratic Palestinian-Jewish secular state had clearly failed.

Arafat, as PLO chairman and instigator of its policies, was inevitably blamed. Senior figures within the Palestinian National Council were tired of his inefficiency, favouritism and corruption. They wanted him removed. Back in Lebanon, open fighting broke out in the Biqa between remnants of Fatah loyal to Arafat and Syrian-backed PLO dissidents. Keen to be at the front, Arafat shaved off his beard, donned a smart suit and dark glasses and sneaked into the battle zone via Cyprus.

After Shia bombs killed 241 US marines and 59 French paratroopers, mediators were eager to restore some semblance of order to the battered country. Syrian forces eventually managed to separate the warring Palestinians and once again Arafat was packed off to Tunis, this time of a Syrian plane.

Insight

Arafat's second expulsion followed his arrest by the Syrians in Tripoli, and what President Assad described as 'slanderous' remarks directed towards him. At the time, many believed this signalled the end of Arafat's leadership of the PLO.

TALKS ABOUT TALKS

The bewildering details of the criss-cross network of proposals and talks going on at this time, some secret, some open, are too obscure to be relevant here. Many were simply talks about talks – efforts to decide an agenda and who would be allowed to participate before the negotiations proper began. The Israelis and the USA, for example, would not talk with the PLO because they regarded it as a terrorist organization. For this, Arafat had only himself to blame. Because he claimed, arrogantly and inaccurately, to speak for all Palestinians and control their paramilitary activities, he was also held responsible for their actions. This sometimes rebounded unpleasantly on him.

In 1985, for instance, a PLO hit squad – acting with or without Arafat's knowledge – killed three Israelis on a yacht in Cyprus. The Israeli government reacted by bombing the PLO HQ in Tunis, killing 56 Palestinians and 15 Tunisians. Small wonder several Arab states had said they were unwilling to harbour the PLO when it was expelled from Beirut. Arafat miraculously survived the raid on his Tunis compound. He was, he said, out 'jogging' at the time. Those who knew him smiled. Arafat was never a jogger – he had been simply taking a walk.

A few weeks later, Arafat was again put in a difficult position. This time it was by his friend Abu Abbas, the pro-Iraqi bandit and leader of the Popular Front for the Liberation of Palestine. Abbas arranged for four young, frightened and poorly trained would-be freedom fighters to hi-jack the cruise liner *Achille Lauro* as it sailed from Alexandria. On board were 556 passengers and crew, including some Americans. Arafat immediately took responsibility. He would, he told the world, sort the matter out peacefully and discipline the hi-jackers. In fact, he did neither.

The hi-jackers shot dead a disabled American passenger and dumped his body overboard. When the ship returned to Egypt, an Egyptian aircraft was ready to fly the hi-jackers and Abu Abbas to Tunis. US fighter aircraft intercepted it en route and forced it to land in Italy. The Italian authorities, not wishing to get involved, eventually released all the hi-jackers.

Not only were the Israelis and the Americans unwilling to talk to the PLO, but the PLO itself refused to accept the crucial UN Resolution 242 (backed by the 1973 ceasefire Resolution 338) which the US made a central pre-condition for negotiation. Arafat's understandable objection was that 242 talked of peace between the 'states' of the Middle East and not of self-determination for the Palestinians. Even when Arafat said he would accept Resolutions 242 and 338 in return for Palestinian self-determination, US President Ronald Reagan rejected the offer out of hand.

When Israel went into Lebanon in 1982, three peace suggestions were in the air. The Reagan Plan wanted to take matters on from where they had been left at Camp David. Another plan, drawn up at an Arab summit at Fez, suggested a return to the two-state solution envisaged by the UN in 1947. The third idea was that somehow Jordan should merge with Palestinian-inhabited territory to form a state or confederation. Something on these lines was agreed between Arafat and King Hussein in 1985. Two years later Hussein made another agreement, this time with Israeli Prime Minister Shimon Peres. Along with all the other proposals, neither produced any lasting or tangible result.

ISRAEL'S NATIONAL UNITY

Depressed by the death of his wife and haunted by what was happening in Lebanon, Prime Minister Begin resigned in 1983. He was briefly replaced by Yitzhak Shamir, the one-time Stern Gang member. After the following year's elections neither the Labour nor the Likud coalitions were able to form a stable government. With the country under pressure from its friends over Lebanon and inflation running at 400 per cent a year, a political crisis was the last thing Israel needed. A way out of the difficulty was found by establishing a Labour-Likud Government of National Unity. Labour leader Shimon Peres became prime minister, while Likud leader Shamir acted as his deputy and foreign minister. Then, 25 months later, their roles were reversed.

Peres initiated the phased withdrawal from Lebanon (see page 132), leaving a security zone in the south of the country under the nominal control of the South Lebanese Army. Both Peres and Shamir allowed the policy of planting Israeli settlements in the occupied territories, especially the West Bank, to continue apace. Indeed, Shamir refused even to talk of the 'West Bank' – to him it was 'Judea and Samaria', two provinces of the Old Testament Kingdom of David. The Jewish population in the area tripled between 1982 and 1986, bringing perhaps half of the land there and over 80 per cent of the water into Israeli hands.

Insight
The largest aquifer in Israel-Palestine, the Yarkon-Tanninim Aquifer, lies beneath the West Bank. Israel takes 340 million cubic metres of water annually from it, the Palestinians some 20 million cubic metres a year.

The motives for this were two-fold. First, settlements appealed to the ultraconservatives to whom the Likud was increasingly beholden for political support. Second, with each settlement built it became more difficult for Israel to abandon its conquests of 1967. By the end of the 1980s, the government could claim with some justification that things had changed so much since the Six Day War that proposals made immediately after it were no longer relevant. The answer, they suggested somewhat cynically, was not for the Israelis to leave the territories, but for the Palestinians to do so.

At this point, for the first time in the long and unhappy saga, the ordinary Palestinians took matters into their own hands. They had had enough of being a political football kicked about by Israelis, the PLO, the Americans, the Soviets, the Egyptians, the Syrians, the Jordanians, the Iraqis, and just about everyone else who took a passing interest in the Middle East. Despairing of ever being listened to amid the hullabaloo of international politics, they let out a long, instinctive, heart-rending scream of pain.

The Palestinians

THE WEST BANK AND GAZA STRIP

The Palestinians of the West Bank and Gaza Strip called their uprising the Intifada, meaning 'trembling' or 'shaking off'. With the benefit of hindsight, it is perhaps surprising that they endured so much for so long before losing patience. It may help, therefore, if at this stage we remind ourselves just who these people were.

When the State of Israel had been created out of the mandated territory of Palestine, the area contained some 1.3 million Arabs. Few of these people regarded themselves primarily as Palestinians. Rather, their first loyalties were to clan, tribe, faith, and the wider Arabic-speaking community. The enormous upheaval caused by the First Arab–Israeli War left around 150,000 Arabs within the new State of Israel. Although technically Israelis, they were very much second-class citizens. For almost 20 years, they lived under military controls. To discourage the development of a distinct Arab identity, the administration referred to them not as Arabs but as 'Druze', 'Bedouin' and so forth.

Insight

By 2008, those Israeli citizens identifying themselves as Arab had risen to about 20 per cent. The figure is rising fast, leading to predictions that Israel will have an Arab majority by the middle of the 21st century.

The remaining 1.15 million Arabs from the Palestinian mandate were scattered three ways. Over 20 per cent went to live in neighbouring Arab lands, settling either in refugee camps just over the border or in the towns. The largest group, around 100,000, went to Lebanon.

A second group fled to the West Bank, joining the Arabs already living there to swell its population to about 700,000. In this rugged region, with the city of Jerusalem on its south-western edge, they lived as shepherds, farmers, craftspeople, labourers and managers of small businesses. The hills of the north-west received sufficient annual rainfall for grazing and the harvesting of cereal crops. Elsewhere, water from the River Jordan or pumped from beneath the ground irrigated fields of fruits and vegetables.

The third group of Palestinian Arabs pressed into the Gaza Strip. With meagre boundaries determined by a 1949 ceasefire line, this was an area of 363 sq km (140 sq miles) that had surrounded Egypt's 1948 military headquarters. Only 8 km (5 miles) wide at its broadest, it was an arid band of poor and desperately overcrowded territory with little to recommend it. The bulk of the refugees lived in camps managed by the United Nations. Here, as on the West Bank, it was more than ten years before all the tents had been replaced by concrete huts. Water and sewage provision were poor. Education and medical facilities were generally rudimentary, and employment opportunities extremely limited.

For most of the time until the Six Day War, the West Bank was administered, though not formally annexed, by Jordan. Egypt ruled the Gaza Strip with considerable harshness. Its inhabitants, for example, were not given Egyptian citizenship. Jordanian rule in the West Bank was reasonably sympathetic.

THE EMERGENCE OF A NATION

Both the Gaza Strip and the West Bank were overrun by the Israeli army in 1967 and thereafter administered by Israel. Some Arabs fled the Israeli advance; others were forced to leave. Those who remained behind rapidly developed a national consciousness, becoming the first generation of true Palestinians.

Two factors helped the emergence of Palestinian nationalism. One was the PLO, with its network of semi-independent affiliates. The organization gradually became more than just a resistance movement.

Recognized as the voice of the Palestinian Arabs of the West Bank and Gaza Strip, it came to regard itself as a government in waiting. Its pronouncements and propaganda filtered through to the crowded dispossessed, instilling in them a sense of what they believed ought to be and hoped one day would be.

The second influence on the growth of Palestinian nationalism was the behaviour of the Israeli conquerors. For ten years, guided by Moshe Dayan, the occupied territories were governed with a comparatively light hand. Those dwelling in the West Bank benefited from new roads (built for military purposes but useful for getting goods to market), better housing, and improved medical services. This changed dramatically with the formation of Begin's Likud government in 1977.

ISRAELI OPPRESSION

The most obvious sign of the Israeli government's new approach was its settlement policy. In ten years the number of Jewish settlements rose from 36 to over 100. Most were small and the soil they farmed was generally poor, but to their Arab neighbours they were an obvious affront. The Israelis said the land they built on was either barren or not owned by anyone. The Arabs complained that, barren or not, the land was not just there for the taking. Furthermore, much of the land for which no owner could be found had belonged to Arabs who had fled during the various wars. New settlers dug bore holes that drew upon the West Bank's precious underground reserves of water. Some sources say the average Israeli was allocated 12 times as much water as the average Palestinian.

Israeli settlers were given grants and tax advantages, and provided with good roads, schools and medical services. Their Arab neighbours looked on with increasing resentment. The settlements attracted some of the most intolerant and racist elements of Israeli society, too. Vigilante groups, like Gush Emunim, attacked Arab shops and houses. When apprehended, the perpetrators of this anti-Arab terrorism were generally let off lightly. Arab resentment grew still more bitter.

Life was made difficult for the Arabs in all kinds of little ways, too. They were subjected to road blocks and strict searches of their vehicles and property. Large-scale meetings were prohibited and taxes were increased. Failure to pay led to imprisonment. If Palestinians tried to get redress, the legal system was weighted against them. Verbal and minor physical abuse were commonplace, adding to the general feeling among the Palestinian Arabs that they were an unwanted and despised people.

In 1985, the Israeli cabinet voted to tighten the screw still further. Its 'Iron Fist' policy, devised by Foreign Minister Rabin, had a double aim: to destroy all opposition to Israeli rule, and persuade Palestinians that life would be better for them outside Israeli-governed territory. This tied in with the 'Greater Israel' policy of gradually absorbing the occupied territories into the state created in 1948.

Iron Fist led to an increase in so-called 'administrative punishments', which included deportation and preventative detention. The latter meant holding people without trial or appeal on suspicion that they might commit a crime. The use of physical intimidation increased, too. Palestinian youths were regularly rounded up, beaten, tortured and made to confess to crimes they had never committed. The courts frequently turned a deaf ear to accusations of malpractice.

One comparatively mild example is illustrative of thousands of similar cases. The Palestinian lawyer Raja Shehadeh recalls the case of a 14-year-old shepherd boy who lived near Ramallah. One day, as he was grazing his sheep on the hills near Jenin, an anti-Israeli demonstration took place which involved throwing stones at Israeli soldiers. When he returned to Jenin, the young shepherd was arrested and taken to a special prison for youths that occupied a former British army barracks in the Faraa Valley.

He had done nothing, the boy told his interrogators. He had been out on the hills with his sheep all day. 'Confess!' screamed his persecutors. The lad did not even know to what he was supposed to confess. He was beaten until one of his arms fractured, then released. The Israelis believed such behaviour would break the back of Palestinian resistance. Not surprisingly, it had the opposite effect.

All this took place against a background of high unemployment (as much as 50 per cent in the Gaza Strip), poverty and lack of hope. The way the world's rich and powerful glibly discussed the fate of the Palestinians at high tables only served to unite the 'people nobody wanted' in their fury. They were not numbers or tokens, they insisted – they were people with as much right to a decent life as anyone else.

There were, needless to say, acts of cruelty on both sides. With the PLO advocating talks for a peaceful settlement, more militant Palestinian groups continued along the path of violence. These included the Syrian based PFLP, which organized the hang-glider attack on northern Israel in 1987 that led to the death of six Israelis. A new organization, Islamic Jihad, brought Iranian-style Shia fundamentalism into the equation.

The spark that ignited the bonfire flashed on 6 December 1987. On that day, Shlomo Sakal, an Israeli trader, was stabbed to death in a Gaza market. The next day an Israeli military truck ran into Palestinian workers at the Erez checkpoint between Gaza and Israel, killing four and injuring seven. The Israelis said it was an accident. The Palestinians did not believe them, claiming that it was deliberate revenge for the stabbing.

Rioting broke out on the Gaza Strip. The Israeli security forces reacted harshly. On 9 December, Hatem Sissi, a resident of the Jabaliya refugee camp in Gaza, was shot dead by Israeli soldiers chasing stone-throwing youths. More Palestinians took to the streets; more police and soldiers confronted them. The conflagration spread to the West Bank and before long the whole of the occupied territories were caught up in the protest. The Intifada had begun.

Intifada

VIOLENCE

The Intifada was a spontaneous, violent, revolutionary movement not dissimilar to that which had overthrown the French establishment in 1789. A major difference was that the Palestinian movement involved a high proportion of children. Wearing the distinctive kuffiya headdress that Arafat had made the symbol of the Palestinian cause, they came out in their thousands to taunt the occupying forces with words and stones. The stone-throwing was also symbolic, being a traditional Islamic way of warding off evil spirits.

The children of the Intifada were a new and desperate generation. Raised amid violence and cruelty, they too were violent. Without a sense of a better future – at least on earth – they were also relatively fearless. Mobile, organized, knowing the terrain infinitely better than their enemy, they were an impossible target. If the Israelis used force, the world condemned them as child murderers; if they hung back, the protests escalated as the attackers believed they were winning. It was one war in which the Israelis, for all their military might, could not triumph.

Backed by $40 million from Iran and Iraq, at the local level the Intifada was organized by the Palestinian United National Leadership (or Unified National Command – translations vary). This organization had come into being a few weeks after the start of the uprising. At the heart of its 14-point plan of action was self-determination for the Palestinians. Islamic Jihad also emerged into the open, organizing relief as well as anti-Israeli activities.

Another child of the Intifada was the Islamic Resistance Movement, commonly known as Hamas. Led by Sheikh Ahmed Yassin and Dr Abdulaziz al-Rantisi, Hamas had its roots in the Muslim Brotherhood (see page 30). It was organized into military and relief sections, responsible, respectively, for attacks on Israelis and assistance for the Palestinians. Like Islamic Jihad, it rejected all possibility of compromise with a state that it regarded as both illegal and an infidel virus within the body of a holy Muslim society. Ironically, the Israeli government had for a while been encouraging the growth of such Islamic groups as a counter-balance to the PLO. The policy's shortcomings were now apparent.

At first the PLO leadership in Tunis and Baghdad, where Arafat moved some offices in the late 1980s, was unsure what to make of the Intifada. When it became clear it was not just a flash in the pan, Arafat gave it his wholehearted support. He handed over daily responsibility for the PLO-Intifada operations to his lieutenant Abu Jihad. This competent and tireless administrator co-ordinated and assisted the uprising as best he could from remote Tunis. Elsewhere, the reaction of most Arab leaders, apart from President Assad, was the opposite to Arafat's. At first welcoming the Intifada, they were soon playing it down. Such an inspiring example of people power was not quite what the unelected heads of largely corrupt Middle Eastern regimes wanted plastered all over their national TV screens.

On the ground, the stone-throwing of the children was accompanied by demonstrations by women, illegal flying of the Palestinian flag, a tax strike, boycotts of Israeli goods and a host of other activities that rendered the occupied territories ungovernable. The movement was widely covered by the world's media which was almost universally shocked by Israeli tactics and sympathetic towards the Palestinians. The anger of ordinary people had drawn the world's attention to their plight far more effectively than their leaders had ever done.

COUNTER-VIOLENCE

To begin with the Israeli cabinet saw the Intifada as just another Arab disturbance that they would soon quell with the usual tactics. Curfews were imposed, arrests and detentions increased, and the security forces urged to use appropriate tactics to cow the rioters. Within a few weeks, it was clear that what was happening was more than just another round of troubles.

Seeking to break the resistance with what Rabin called 'might, power, and beatings', the government declared a state of emergency and called up reservists. Mass arrests were made, tear gas used to disperse crowds, universities and schools closed. Houses used by suspected leaders were blown up. Arabic newspapers were heavily censored. It is said that a deliberate attempt was made to break the fingers and legs of the stone-throwers.

Within two years, 626 Palestinians died, 37,500 were wounded, and around 40,000 were arrested – yet the fires of the Intifada blazed as fiercely as ever. A considerable number of Israelis began to view the occupied territories in a new light. Instead of being essential to the security of Israel, they were actually weakening the country. Three-and-a-half million Israelis were just not physically capable of holding down one-and-a-half million Palestinians. The cost to the Israeli economy was enormous. It was not simply a matter of expenditure, either. The call-up took people from productive work, and when the crossing points into Palestinian lands were closed, as often happened, Israeli businesses were deprived of labour.

Abroad, the reputation of Israel sank to an all-time low. At home, national morale collapsed. Comparisons were made between the racist behaviour of the IDF and other security forces, and the Nazis. A Peace Now movement gathered strength, calling for an immediate settlement with the Palestinians. The ultraconservatives reacted with renewed defiance and determination never to surrender to those perceived simply as terrorists.

In April 1988, the Israeli cabinet agreed a dramatic attempt to destroy the Intifada by eliminating its leadership. A submarine landed an Israeli hit squad in Tunisia. Aided by spies and aircraft, it sought out the organizing mind behind the Palestinian uprising. Before the horrified gaze of his wife and young child, Abu Jihad's body was shot through with 150 bullets. The action was condemned by governments around the world, while a funeral attended by thousands in the streets of Damascus announced the creation of yet another Palestinian martyr.

The state of Palestine

DIPLOMATIC ADVANCES

Diplomatically, the Intifada had dramatic consequences. When it had been active for about seven months, King Hussein of Jordan announced what had been a practical reality for years: he had no claim either to the West Bank or to represent the Palestinians. This significantly enhanced the authority of the PLO and Chairman Arafat.

> **Insight**
> While few took much notice when Egypt renounced its claims to the Gaza Strip, Jordan's abandonment of the West Bank was seen by some as a serious setback. Ever since 1967, an Israeli-Palestinian-Jordanian compromise deal over the region had been posited as a viable arrangement.

Armed with his new prestige, Arafat determined to use the Intifada as a springboard for a diplomatic triumph. In June 1988, one of his officials announced at an Arab summit that the PLO would accept UN Resolutions 242 and 338 in return for a Palestinian state. The offer evoked no dramatic response.

In November, Arafat went even further. Appearing as the Intifada's triumphant commander, he told a meeting of the Palestine National Council that the state of Palestine now existed. Jerusalem was its capital and he was its president. (His position would be confirmed by election the following year.) He went on to accept a two-state solution to the Palestine-Israel problem. Although the US and Israel remained sceptical, the UN invited Arafat to address its General Assembly. As US Secretary of State Schultz would not grant Arafat a visa to speak at the UN in New York, the General Assembly adjourned to Geneva. Here Arafat spoke on 13 December, making sweeping concessions.

A comprehensive Middle East peace settlement was needed, Arafat declared. He talked of the 'State of Israel', recognizing its existence.

He accepted Resolutions 242 and 338. He renounced terrorism. At a news conference the next day he went even further. Israel, he admitted, should be permitted to live in peace and security. When questioned further, he underlined the extent of his concessions with the famous words, 'Enough! Do you want me to do a striptease?'

At last, in renouncing violence and accepting Israel's right to exist, Arafat had uttered the words the US wanted to hear. Its response was immediate: American negotiators would begin talks with the PLO at once. Israeli premier Yitzhak Shamir, however, insisted that his country would not negotiate with terrorists. Coming from someone who had himself fought as a terrorist against the British, it was hardly a convincing argument. His real reason for stalling was an unwillingness to hand back 'Judea' and 'Samaria'.

THE FIRST GULF WAR

Under American pressure, cracks began to appear in Israel's National Unity government. Defence Minister Rabin (Labour) came out in favour of talks with the Palestinians. Prime Minister Shamir (Likud) then put forward a plan of his own that offered the Palestinians almost nothing. Despite the efforts of Secretary of State Schultz and his successor James Baker, no progress was made. The Israelis would not negotiate with Arafat, nor would they stop their programme of settlement building. The latter entered a new and more vigorous phase with the appointment of Sharon as minister of construction and housing.

Two acts of violence only made matters worse. The first was the shooting dead of seven Palestinians in the occupied territories by a young Israeli. The second was when the *Achille Lauro* hi-jackers, now with Iraqi backing, landed on a beach near Tel Aviv and were shot dead by Israeli security forces. On 13 June 1990, James Baker stormed out of talks with the Israelis shouting, 'Our telephone number is 202–456–1414. When you're serious about peace, call us.' A week later, he announced that he was breaking off talks with the PLO as well.

Surprisingly, the deadlock was broken by Saddam Hussein. Over the past few years, Arafat had become increasingly dependent upon the Iraqi dictator. This led him to make one of the biggest mistakes of his career. In the summer of 1990, Saddam Hussein's forces invaded and occupied Kuwait (see Chapter 11). The action was condemned by just about every country in the world, including the wealthy oil-producing Arab states. Arafat, however, went the other way and sided with Iraq. In doing so, he tied himself to an international leper. Worse still, the next year an American-led coalition drove the Iraqi forces from Kuwait and destroyed much of Hussein's military capacity. This left Arafat and his PLO isolated, impecunious and impotent. The only option left to them was to return to the negotiating table.

Hopes of settlement

As soon as the First Gulf War ended, US President George Bush Sr announced a new initiative to settle the Israeli-Palestinian question once and for all. Secretary of State Baker put forward a nine-point plan as the basis for an international conference. Arafat rejected it.

Arafat's move was little more than a gesture of independence. His position was considerably weaker than it had been before the war. His oil-rich backers had cut his funding, leaving the PLO close to bankruptcy. The image of Palestinians dancing at the sight of Israeli civilians killed by Saddam Hussein's Scud missiles had not gone down well internationally, either. Moreover, the Israelis had improved their tarnished reputation by not reacting to Iraq's unprovoked attacks.

Therefore, when peace talks co-hosted by George Bush and Soviet premier Mikhail Gorbachev were announced, Arafat had little choice: he could either attend or be cast into outer diplomatic and political darkness. To meet Israeli sensibilities, the Palestinians were represented by delegates from the occupied territories.

The PLO went as part of the Jordanian delegation, though without Arafat himself.

A series of conferences was held in Madrid, Spain. Not surprisingly, they soon ran into difficulties. The usual sticking points arose: Israeli settlements in the occupied territories, and the Palestinian desire for full statehood rather than just a vague autonomy. The Israeli hand was strengthened by the arrival in Israel of thousands of Jews from the collapsing Soviet Union. Where could they be housed, pleaded Shamir's government, if settlement was not permitted on the West Bank? Shamir was in no hurry to reach agreement, and the Soviet development made a useful bargaining point.

After a few months, as the talks were bogging down, elections were held in Israel. The Labour leader, Yitzhak Rabin, campaigned on the manifesto of bringing peace with the Palestinians within a year. From the man who had been an unflinching hard-line defence minister, this was difficult to believe. Nevertheless, the electorate placed the Labour coalition in charge of the Knesset. It was now up to Rabin, prime minister of Israel for a second time, to deliver on his pledge.

THINGS TO REMEMBER

1 *The 1980s were marked by violence throughout the Middle East, notably in Lebanon, Iran-Iraq and Israel-Palestine.*

2 *Beset with economic difficulties, in 1984 Israeli politicians established a Government of National Unity.*

3 *As no progress was made towards a settlement of the Israel-Palestine problem, the Palestinians of the occupied territories (Gaza and the West Bank) felt increasingly isolated, harassed, helpless and hopeless.*

4 *Despite the exile in Tunis of Yasser Arafat and the PLO leadership, Palestinian groups continued to attack Israeli targets, drawing Israeli reprisals of disproportionate force.*

5 *In 1987, the Palestinians of the occupied territories rose up in a spontaneous Intifada ('Shaking Off'). Stone-throwing children played a significant part in the anti-Israeli uprising, which also saw the emergence of the Islamist group Hamas.*

6 *Israel responded to the Intifada, which caused serious damage to its economy, with shootings, arrests and the destruction of Palestinian property.*

7 *Riding the worldwide wave of pro-Palestinian sympathy, in 1988 Arafat recognized Israel's existence, accepted Resolution 242, renounced violence and demanded a two-state solution to the Israel-Palestine problem.*

8 *Now that the PLO had renounced violence, the US worked to bring about an Israeli-Palestinian settlement. Neither side was willing to compromise, however.*

9 *In 1991, Arafat seriously weakened the international standing of the PLO when he supported Saddam Hussein against the UN-backed international coalition liberating Kuwait.*

10 *Seeking to take advantage of the 'peace dividend' that followed the collapse of the Soviet Union, in 1991 a large-scale Middle East peace conference opened in Madrid. It made little headway.*

11

....

Desert Storm

This chapter will cover:
- *the state of Iraq after the Iran–Iraq War*
- *Saddam Hussein's invasion of Kuwait and the international reaction to it*
- *the First Gulf War, 1991*
- *the repercussions of the war.*

Saddam bankrupt

By the end of the Iran–Iraq War in 1988, it is estimated that Iraq owed almost $100 billion to overseas agencies and governments, and that it would take a further $180 billion to repair the damage done to the country's infrastructure. With an annual income from oil revenues then running at around $10 billion, it would be almost a quarter of a century before the country was back on its financial feet again. In other words, Saddam Hussein's regime was to all intents and purposes bankrupt.

Financial difficulties were only one of the dictator's worries. There were grumblings from the Shia majority in the south, which had suffered decades of Sunni domination and persecution by Hussein's secular government. At the other end of the country, the Kurds – the largest national group in the world not to have their own state – remained as dissatisfied as ever with their lack of autonomy.

In the country at large the deprivations brought on by the recent war fuelled discontent within a regime that totally disregarded the rule of law and human rights, and maintained itself by fear and torture. Some sources say there were no fewer than four attempts to assassinate Hussein in the two years following the ending of the war with Iran – one from within his army's élite Republican Guard.

Sensing the weakness of his position, Hussein made grand announcements about liberalizing his government. He established a committee to prepare a new constitution that guaranteed multi-party government and freedom of the press. Given Hussein's abhorrence of any opposition, there was no evidence that the words of the document would bear any relation to practical reality. At the same time, he made efforts to improve relations with his Arab neighbours. He concluded non-aggression pacts with Saudi Arabia and Bahrain, and joined with the non-oil-producing states of Egypt, Jordan and North Yemen to form an Arab Co-operation Council.

The continued existence of the massive army raised to wage the Iran–Iraq War was another of Hussein's problems. A rapid reduction in its size was a strategic, social and economic impossibility: a sudden influx onto the streets of large numbers of unemployed young men would be a recipe for disaster. Hussein knew only too well that his term of unenlightened government had not made the country any less susceptible to violent upheaval than at the time of the 1958 and 1963 coups. The answer to the problem of the army, he decided, was to use it rather than lose it.

Insight

After the Iran–Iraq War, Hussein had the sense to realize what the American invaders did not in 2003–4: the rapid disbandment of a large army at a time of economic dislocation would lead almost inevitably to civil unrest.

INCREASING ISOLATION

The West, headed by the US, had been prepared to back Iraq during the 1980s as a bulwark against the fiercely anti-Western

Islamism of the Ayatollahs' Iran. Even so, Hussein's dictatorial regime was hardly a natural ally of democratic capitalism, and support for it had been seen very much as the lesser of two evils. Nor was the relationship easy. In 1987, for example, the Pentagon and Washington were forced to exercise considerable restraint when a stray Iraqi Exocet missile hit *USS Stark*, killing 37 of the crew.

Immediately after it had enabled Hussein to claim victory over Iran, the US began to pull back from its close relationship with him. It had not been best pleased by his use of what came to be known as weapons of mass destruction (WMDs) against Iranians and Kurds. Israeli reports that he was attempting to fit nuclear warheads to Soviet-built Scud-B missiles were also worrying. In November 1988, there was a mutual expulsion of diplomats from Washington and Baghdad.

Two years later, the administration of President George Bush Sr took Iraq to task over the misspending of agricultural credits. His former allies were even less impressed when Hussein boasted that he was developing a three-stage rocket capable of carrying a warhead 1,930 km (1,200 miles), bringing the entire Middle East within range. Nevertheless, at the start of 1990, US–Iraq trade was still worth some $3 billion.

The French also had strong commercial links with Iraq, especially in the arms trade. True to their pragmatic and independent approach to world affairs, the administrations of President Mitterrand were not often willing to let political niceties stand in the way of economic advantage. The closeness of the relationship between President Hussein and right-wing Prime Minister Jacques Chirac gave the French media plenty of opportunity to mock the affair between the phonetically united Chirac and Iraq.

On the other hand, Soviet support for Iraq was on the wane. Thousands of Soviet advisors remained in Iraq but their numbers were being reduced all the time. Caught up in the spirit – and economic necessity – of détente, President Gorbachev was eager not to annoy the US. The collapsing Soviet economy obliged him to reduce international aid on every front. By the autumn of 1990, the Soviet Union itself was on the way out and in no position to play a major role in an international debacle developing in the Gulf.

The government of Britain, Iraq's third largest trading partner, was also having second thoughts about backing the regime of a man whom its tabloid newspapers were calling the 'Butcher of Baghdad'. Two issues brought the matter to a head. One was the discovery that British firms had been secretly manufacturing parts for a 'super gun' and illegally exporting them to Iraq. The mysterious assassination of the weapon's Canadian inventor added to public disquiet. The second issue was the arrest and execution on false spying charges of the British journalist Farzad Bazoft. It seems that Saddam Hussein, furious at attacks on him in the British press, personally demanded the death penalty.

THREATENING KUWAIT

Against this background of debt, potential unrest and growing international isolation, in February 1990 President Saddam Hussein attended a meeting of the newly formed Arab Co-operation Council. The price of oil had dropped the previous month, making his country's economic plight yet more precarious. Nevertheless, even when in trouble it was beneath the dignity of a proud man from Tikrit to plead for help. Saddam spoke of himself as the saviour of Sunnis from Shia extremism. He had, he said, borne on his own shoulders the entire weight of defending the Arab world. It was only right, therefore, that he should be rewarded with a cancellation of his war debts and a strict adherence to agreed production quotas in order to push up the price of oil.

The requests fell on deaf ears. The robed aristocracy of the Gulf had no desire to help an aggressive and vulgar parvenu from upcountry Iraq. Hussein was humiliated.

PRESSURE ON KUWAIT

The Iraqi president was seriously handicapped by a lack of objective
and honest advice. The problem was entirely of his own making.
Surrounded by a phalanx of fawners and sycophantic relatives,
he rarely heard the truth and was never offered unpalatable policy
suggestions. Thus isolated within a cocoon of fear, during the
first half of 1990 he searched desperately for a way out of his
troubles.

One obvious solution lay on Iraq's very doorstep: Kuwait.
Hussein's plan was to cajole and frighten the tiny Gulf sheikhdom
into helping him out. It is worth remembering that the state
of Kuwait, like Iraq, had been created by British imperialism.
Although frontiers had appeared on the map, on the ground they
had yet to become an established part of the political scene. As we
saw at the start of the Iran–Iraq War, several boundaries were still
disputed. Indeed, on a number of occasions in the recent past, Iraq
had laid claim to the whole of Kuwait. Until only days before he
gave the command, however, the Iraqi dictator did not intend to
invade. He simply did not think it would be necessary.

Hussein made three claims. Kuwait had 'stolen' Iraqi oil worth
$12 billion from the Rumaila oilfield; it had allowed too much
oil to come on to the world market, forcing down the price; and
it had contemplated seizing territory from the Iraqis while they
had been combating Iranian Islamic fundamentalism. All of these
serious misdemeanours, Hussein announced, could be settled
amicably with a little Kuwaiti generosity. They simply had to
cut their oil production, hand over financial aid and suspend
Iraq's debts.

Kuwait's ruling al-Sabah family was not impressed. Around 100,000 Iraqi troops moved up to the narrow southern dividing the two states. Believing this to be merely the usual Hussein bluff and bluster, the Kuwaiti leadership stood their forces down. A visit from US ambassador April Glaspie failed to convince Hussein that his attitude towards Kuwait was leading him into dangerous waters. Another visit, this time from Egypt's widely respected President Hosni Mubarak on behalf of the Arab League, left the Iraqi leader unchecked but his fellow Arabs believing that he would never dare attack Kuwait.

CRISIS TALKS

On 31 July 1990, the Saudis invited the Iraqis and Kuwaitis for high-level crisis talks. The oil price had recently risen, swelling Iraq's income. Compromise seemed close: Iraq asked for $10 billion, Kuwait offered $9 billion. The two sides were almost there. At this stage, unfortunately, the conversation became personal.

On one side was Hussein's cousin, Ali Hassan al Majid. Known as 'Chemical Ali', this was the man who had supervised the murderous gas attack on the village of Halabja (see page 169). Opposite him was the Crown Prince of Kuwait.

The cultural and social gulf between the two men was much wider than the economic one. Neither was an experienced negotiator at this level. Unwilling to make the final concession necessary for a compromise, their remarks grew acrimonious, then heated. Before long they were shouting at each other. Alarmed, Saudi guards hurried into the room to find them close to blows.

Chemical Ali pleaded that the Iraqis, fellow Arabs, were in dire poverty. Surely Kuwait could not deny alms to the poor? The Crown Prince snorted. If the Iraqis were hard up, he retorted, they should send their women out on to the streets to earn a bit of cash. The insult, it is said, hinted at rumours that Saddam Hussein was of illegitimate birth. The remark was as pointed as it was tactless.

In such a poisonous atmosphere, compromise was impossible. When the Crown Prince's words were reported to Hussein, his fury knew no bounds. On 2 August, 100,000 Iraqi troops and 2,000 tanks entered Kuwait. The invasion had begun.

Operation Desert Shield

Saddam Hussein's attack on Kuwait took the world by surprise. Mubarak's assurances had created a false sense of security. Few observers believed that Hussein would actually do something quite so outrageous or so foolish. He had talked proudly of fighting Iran to defend the Arabs; he had recently proposed an anti-imperialist and anti-Zionist coalition with Kuwait; he had openly touted for leadership of the Arab world. Now, in stark contrast to all he had said, he had perpetrated an act of naked aggression against a virtually defenceless Arab neighbour.

Politicians everywhere, accustomed to endless rhetoric of Arab unity in the face of Israeli aggression, were deeply perplexed. The action seemed so irrational. But Hussein the dictator had become divorced from reason and logic. Cut off from reality, he was incapable of forming a coherent or long-term strategy. He governed instead by cunning and instinct. That is why the invasion of Kuwait was not widely predicted – it was essentially a spur of the moment, irrational act.

THE RAPE OF KUWAIT

In the face of the overwhelming Iraqi onslaught, Kuwait fell in a matter of hours. The Emir's half-brother made a brave but hopeless last stand with some loyal troops, but the rest of the royal family fled to Saudi Arabia in a fleet of sleek Mercedes. The remaining population, native Kuwaitis as well as many thousands of foreign workers, were virtually imprisoned within the emirate.

The al-Sabahs had run Kuwait as a private fiefdom. The administration, headed by the royal family, was unelected. The National Assembly, wielding only very limited powers, had been suspended for the previous four years. It was hardly the sort of place that democrats normally rushed to assist.

Kuwait, however, had oil. It was also a vital Iraqi bridgehead into Saudi Arabia. Between them these two Gulf states controlled some 40 per cent of the world's known oil reserves. If that was not enough, Hussein horrified decent-minded people the world over by the brutal way he treated his new 'province' – he had formally annexed Kuwait as a province of Iraq on 8 August. Foreigners were not allowed to leave but held as hostages. Kuwaitis were subjected to a plague of rape, murder, beatings, and systematic looting. The neat, tidy and well-ordered little state soon deteriorated into an enclave of sordid cruelty. Although their activities provoked ferocious reprisals, it is estimated that the Kuwaiti underground resistance killed some 100 Iraqis.

THE COALITION FORMS

Resistance within Kuwait was the least of Hussein's worries. If he had wondered before how the international community would react to an invasion, he was quickly left in little doubt. Iraq's action was condemned throughout the world. The West's response was led by the British Prime Minister Margaret Thatcher. Nearing the end of her premiership, she was more prone than ever to seeing issues as either black or white. Britain had guaranteed Kuwait's independence 30 years previously, so it had to do its duty. Nevertheless, it could not act without the US. Schoolmistress Thatcher is alleged to have cajoled the more cautious US President Bush Sr with, 'Now, George, don't go wobbly on me!'

Insight

No one knew at this time that Margaret Thatcher's days as British Prime Minister were numbered, although her popularity was falling. She eventually resigned in November 1990, after failing to get substantial support for continued leadership of the Conservative Party.

Bush did not go wobbly. Furthermore, skilful diplomacy enabled him to go to war on the cheap. The US had plenty of material left over from the Cold War era, and the bulk of the eventual cost of the campaign would be met by its Arab allies. Once the Americans had moved, Soviet President Mikhail Gorbachev had little option but to go along with them. With his country in turmoil, the last thing he needed was a confrontation with the world's one remaining superpower.

The majority of Arab nations joined the chorus of condemnation. To King Fahad of Saudi Arabia, who genuinely feared that his kingdom might be next on Hussein's hit-list, it was 'the ugliest aggression in human history'. Syria's President Assad was equally disapproving of his neighbouring Baathists. Egypt's President Mubarak used more cautious language. The most widely respected Arab leader, he had to make sure that the oil producers and West paid a fair price for his backing. They did. When the affair was finally over, generous foreign subsidies had reduced Egypt's international debt by 75 per cent.

Within the region, only Jordan, North Yemen, Sudan, Libya and the PLO registered any approval of Hussein's action. At that time Libya's maverick President Gaddafi would support any anti-American cause. Jordan's King Hussein personally disliked President Hussein but felt obliged to go along with the overwhelmingly pro-Iraqi mood of his people. The political, military and economic clout of Yemen and Sudan were negligible.

As we have seen, the decision of Yasser Arafat to throw in his lot with the Iraqi dictator was one of the most unfortunate he ever made (see page 186). Hussein tried to use it to his advantage by linking his action with events in Israel and the territories it occupied. Ten days after the invasion of Kuwait, he agreed to pull out of the emirate if Israel withdrew from the territories it had occupied in 1967. Such crude bargaining deceived no one, nor was the reputation of the Iraqi leader much enhanced in Arab eyes by equating his actions with those of the Israelis. Later, at war with the United Nations' coalition liberating Kuwait, Hussein again made an unsuccessful effort to bring Israel into the equation.

For years the US had been anxious about the vulnerability of the Saudi oilfields. It already had a plan (codenamed 1002–90) to defend them and was eager to move swiftly lest Hussein continue his southward thrust. First, it had to get permission to build up forces on Arabian soil. The administration of King Fahad was understandably anxious about allowing a massive infidel presence inside the country that guarded Islam's holiest sites. His doubts evaporated into the desert air when he was shown US spy satellite photographs of Iraqi forces massing along Kuwait's southern border. The Saudis needed help – if that meant using infidels, so be it. Thus began Operation Desert Shield.

The ending of the Cold War had freed the United Nations to do what it had been created to do. When faced with a serious and violent breach of the UN Charter, the Security Council was empowered to raise forces to fight under the UN banner. However, as the permanent Council members had a veto over the military option, it had been used only once. In 1950, an American-led UN force had gone to the aid of South Korea when it had been invaded by the communist North. At the time, pro-Western Taiwan represented China, and the Soviet Union was boycotting the Security Council and therefore unable to use its veto. Thereafter, UN military action had been limited to observing and peacekeeping.

In the autumn of 1990, East–West relations were better than they had been for almost half a century. The members of the Security Council unanimously agreed resolutions condemning the Iraqi invasion, calling for immediate withdrawal, and placing an economic embargo on Iraq. On 29 November, a further resolution gave Iraq until 15 January to withdraw or face armed intervention in the name of the UN.

The build-up of forces in the Gulf was the largest military operation of its kind since the Second World War. Munitions, money, troops and ships poured in from all over the world. The bulk – 500,000 of the 800,000 soldiers, for instance – was provided by the US. Japan, limited by its pacifist constitution, provided $10 billion. Ironically, in the light of future events, even the Mujahedin of Afghanistan managed a contingent of 300. One of the few hiccups stemmed from France's refusal, for commercial reasons, to provide the coalition with details of the weapons systems it had sold to Iraq.

If Hussein had planned to invade Saudi Arabia, he should have moved straight away. The longer he left it, the more difficult his task became. By Christmas it was all but impossible. Ranged against him were thousands of the most modern combat aircraft, helicopters, tanks and guns. In the Gulf steamed dozens of warships ranging from vast aircraft carriers to minesweepers and submarines able to launch the latest ship-to-shore missiles.

Despite the massive arsenal at their fingertips, the American officers in overall command of the operation were anxious. The last war the US had fought – against the Vietcong – had vividly demonstrated that technology alone could not guarantee victory. What if the Iraqi armed forces rallied behind their leader as steadfastly as the North Vietnamese had done behind Ho Chi Minh? With the exception of one or two Arab contingents, the coalition soldiers were fighting for an abstract principle. It mattered little to them personally who ruled Kuwait. It is unlikely that their morale would have held up in a protracted and bloody war. Nor would the public back in the US have remained steadfastly behind the war if large numbers of their sons and daughters had been brought home in body bags. A swift and comparatively painless victory was a military and a political necessity.

Iraq's armed forces were considerable in size and battle-hardened after their recent war with Iran. Numerically the army was the fourth largest in the world. It was backed by 6,000 assorted battle tanks, 200 armed helicopters and thousands of anti-aircraft devices. The air force was the sixth largest in the world, boasting some of the latest Russian Mig-29s and French Mirage F1s.

Perhaps more alarming was Iraq's array of unconventional weapons. It did not yet have a nuclear bomb, but it did possess thousands of tons of mustard gas, quantities of the nerve agents Sarin and Tabun, and some biological weapons like botulinum and anthrax. Moreover, on elusive mobile launchers it had 800 Scud missiles capable of delivering a lethal dose into any neighbouring state. In the event, Hussein did not use his weapons of mass destruction, perhaps because he feared that the coalition would respond with WMDs of their own. It is fairly certain that some coalition members did indeed have a range of such weapons at the ready.

Operation Desert Storm

SOFTENING UP

As the UN deadline of 15 January approached, national and international diplomats tried in vain to find a way out. Despite the overwhelming force ranged against him, and numerous UN resolutions demanding his withdrawal, Hussein refused to budge. He seems to have hoped that unwavering resistance to what he called 'imperialist bullying' would endear him to his people and perhaps bring some fellow Arabs to his side. In truth, he had no option. Had he called his forces home, the failure and humiliation would almost certainly have provoked rebellion. Even if he had survived that, he would still have been no nearer sorting out his economic difficulties. It had to be war.

The First Gulf War began on 17 January 1991. It was a war the like of which had never been seen before: more precise, more controlled, more technological, and less randomly destructive than any previously fought. It featured 'stealth' bombers, 'cruise' missiles and 'smart' bombs for the first time. Guided by satellite, laser and radio, bombs and missiles could pinpoint targets as small as a window. The enduring image of the new warfare was provided by a CNN reporter sitting in a hotel room in Baghdad. Looking out of the window, he watched a 5.5 m (18 foot) Tomahawk cruise missile fly down the street, turn right at the traffic lights and proceed on its programmed path towards its target. It might well have been launched from a B-52 bomber that had made the 22,500 km (14,000 mile) round trip from Louisiana.

Determined to make the recapture of Kuwait as straightforward as possible, over a period of five weeks the coalition systematically destroyed the enemy's command and control structure, his air force and airfields, his anti-aircraft defences, his communications, his oil refineries, and his navy. Once they were out of the way, the attack turned to the ground forces. Outgunned and isolated, the Iraqi troops lost all stomach for a fight long before one began. Even the famed Republican Guard cracked under the onslaught.

Soldiers whose previous experience of war had been mowing down waves of lightly armed Iranians found themselves targeted with terrifying accuracy by aircraft that had complete mastery of the skies. Iraq's armed forces might have been large but they were equipped with a hotchpotch of weapons that faver at least a generation behind those of the coalition. In everyday household terms, the technological difference between the two sides was like that between a vinyl record and a CD.

Of course there were civilian casualties – part of what US litotes-speak termed 'collateral damage'. By the end of the war, some 2,500 Iraqi non-combatants had died (315 when an air-raid shelter was mistaken for a command bunker) and a further 6,000 injured. The numbers were dreadfully high, but comparatively fewer than in any previous bombing campaign of that scale. The number killed was half that in the village of Halabja when it was gas-attacked by Hussein's forces one afternoon in 1988.

A degree of mystery surrounds the Iraqi Scud missiles. It seems that for some reason only around 200 were ever fired. Half were directed at Saudi Arabia, where one hit a US army barracks. Three went for Bahrain, and some 40 were targeted at Israel. Two Israelis were killed, about 200 wounded and many buildings damaged. Hard-line Israeli leaders, including Ariel Sharon, demanded that their government persist with its current policy and retaliate immediately with great force. This is precisely what Hussein wanted. Had Israel gone to war with Iraq, Arab members of the coalition would have found themselves fighting alongside an impossible ally. This might well have pulled the coalition apart. As it was, the White House put immense pressure on the government of Prime Minister Shamir not to retaliate, and it did not. Coalition attempts to seek and destroy the Scuds' mobile launchers appear to have been a complete failure.

DESERT SABRE

In overall command of the coalition's land operation – Desert Sabre – was the huge figure of General H. Norman Schwarzkopf. As impressive in intelligence as in bulk, this deceptively sophisticated and sensitive soldier skilfully handled the tricky relations with his partners. The success of his battle plan coupled with a formidable appearance and sometimes brusque manner led to the media dubbing him 'Stormin' Norman'.

Officially, Schwarzkopf's land war lasted 100 hours. One force of mainly US and Arab troops moved on Kuwait City. Advancing behind armoured helicopters that blasted every moving Iraqi target they could find, they swiftly liberated the capital. The battered Iraqis put up scant resistance. There were even rumours of commanders cutting their men's Achilles tendons to prevent them running way.

Meanwhile, a huge force of coalition armour drove into Iraq to the west of Kuwait. Their target was Iraq's armoured reserves, particularly the Republican Guard. When the Guard tried to fight a rearguard action before Basra they were pounded into submission.

Thousands were killed as they tried to escape, and many thousands more surrendered. The road north from Basra – the 'Highway of Death' – became a ribbon of fire and smoke as coalition aircraft and helicopters made every effort to destroy as much enemy material as possible before the war ended. US pilots described the one-sided killing as a 'turkey shoot'. It is estimated that Iraq lost 80 per cent of its tanks and 90 per cent of its artillery.

There was a moment when, with the Iraqis in full retreat and the coalition forces hot on their heels, President Bush was tempted to allow his forces to press on to Baghdad and try to topple Saddam Hussein. President Eisenhower had faced a similar decision during the Korean War, when General MacArthur had wanted to carry the war into China. As Eisenhower had cautiously declined the escalation, so did George Bush. George Bush Jr took over where his father had left off 12 years later, and finished the anti-Hussein mission for him (see Chapter 14).

Repercussions and revolts

LOSSES

The most obvious consequence of the First Gulf War was the liberation of Kuwait. The al-Sabah family returned and over the next decade or so took steps to make their government more accountable to the people (see page 248). Individuals and companies set about rebuilding and repairing the devastated buildings and infrastructure.

For a long time, Kuwait was at the heart of an environmental disaster. The retreating Iraqis had set fire to 700 oil wells and opened the taps so that the largest oil slick in history slid out over the northern waters of the Gulf. The price of the horrific water, land and air pollution may never be accurately ascertained.

Insight

While an estimated 8 million barrels of oil poured into the Gulf, 20 times that amount filled lakes of oil in the Kuwaiti desert and soot from the burning wells polluted the snows of the distant Himalayas.

The loss of human life could be more precisely worked out. Two thousand Kuwaitis had been killed and many more injured. A large number (around 600) had simply disappeared. The coalition had lost 246 lives, 147 of them American and 24 British (some from so-called 'friendly fire'). A number of coalition troops reported suffering from a mysterious 'Gulf War Syndrome', a malaise they said they had contracted either from the prophylactic injections they had been given or from an unknown enemy biological agent.

Iraqi military losses are less easily computed. Some estimates say 100,000 lives were lost. A more accurate figure is perhaps 20,000, with a further 60,000 wounded. Long after the war, there were repeated complaints of the harmful effects on civilians of the depleted uranium used to harden the coalition's armour-piercing shells.

HUSSEIN SURVIVES

Remarkably, Saddam Hussein survived. That he did so was due partly to a mistake by General Schwarzkopf, partly to the reluctance of the US to intervene in the internal affairs of Iraq, and partly to the dictator's sheer bloody mindedness. Schwarzkopf's error occurred during the ceasefire talks he held with Iraqi generals. He stipulated a list of weapons they were no longer to hold, including military aircraft. As most of the bridges across the Tigris and Euphrates were down, replied the Iraqis, might they retain their helicopters to ferry essential supplies? Without thinking through the implications of the request, Schwarzkopf said that they might keep their helicopters.

Shortly afterwards, encouraged by US exhortations to overthrow the Butcher of Baghdad, the Shia of southern Iraq rose in revolt. Two days later the Kurds in the north rose up. In both north and south Hussein's forces – mainly surviving units of the Republican Guard – quashed the rebels with horrific force. Helicopter gunships played a significant part in the massacres. The Americans and British failed even to provide the dissidents with arms. In Basra, captured insurgents were made to swallow petrol before being set alight. Perhaps 20,000 Shia were slaughtered. Entire Kurdish villages were razed and over a million men, women and children fled for their lives into Iran and Turkey.

In March 1991, the coalition delineated an autonomous safe area for the Iraqi Kurds. To defend it, they declared a no-fly zone over wide swathes of the countryside. The following year a similar no-fly zone was declared in the south. For many thousands, these measures were far too late.

Before we hasten to criticize the US and Britain too strongly, it is worth remembering that the United Nations Charter specifically disallows intervention in the internal affairs of sovereign states. Technically speaking, once Kuwait had been liberated, there was no legal basis for taking action within Iraq. The leaders of the coalition knew well that the more they interfered in a Muslim Arab state, the more they would invoke Muslim and Arab hostility. In short, they were damned whatever they did.

Insight

Not until they returned to an unwelcoming Iraq in 2003 did Coalition forces realize just how deep was the sense of betrayal felt by the unsupported rebels of 1991.

The terms of the ceasefire were enshrined in a UN Security Council Resolution (687). This also demanded the elimination of Iraq's WMDs. To verify that this happened, a special UN commission was set up (UNSCOM) to work with the International Atomic Energy Authority. The weapons inspectors' sorry story is dealt with in Chapter 14.

THE UN AND THE SUPERPOWER

The Gulf War marked a massive restoration of the fortunes of the United Nations. Having been hamstrung for decades by East–West rivalry, it seemed now able to play an important role in guiding the affairs of nations. The Gulf operation was followed by a host of observer, protective and enforcing missions in countries such as Bosnia, Somalia, Angola and East Timor. It is worth pointing out that as none of these places boasted vast oil reserves, superpower support for UN action was not always unstinting.

By the middle of 1991, it was clear that a world dominated by two rival superpowers had given way to one of a single superpower. The Gulf War marked the US's emergence as the pre-eminent global power in military as well as economic and political terms.

The war also marked the beginning of a new phase of US involvement in the Middle East. Hitherto, apart from sending peacekeeping forces into Lebanon and the ill-fated rescue mission in Iran (see pages 131 and 159–60), it had been content to pull strings rather than intervene directly. From now on it was firmly and physically allied with the conservative, oil-producing Gulf states. It had fought for them and beside them. Their enemies were now the US's enemies. The road to the terrorist attack of 11 September 2001 began almost exactly ten years earlier on the barren shores of the Gulf.

More immediately, closer US involvement in the Middle East meant hope for Israelis and Palestinians. Taking advantage of its new global authority and the 'peace dividend' brought by the ending of the Cold War, the White House was determined to make a concerted effort at settling once and for all the problems between Israel and the Palestinians.

THINGS TO REMEMBER

1 *By the end of the Iran–Iraq War (1988), Iraq was virtually bankrupt. It owed around $100 billion overseas and faced a huge bill for rebuilding at home.*

2 *The regime of Saddam Hussein, based upon Iraq's Sunni minority, faced continual opposition from the Shia majority in the south and the Kurds in the north of the country.*

3 *By 1989, there was serious international disquiet about Iraq's possession of weapons of mass destruction (WMDs) – nuclear, biological and chemical weapons.*

4 *Eager for money and to divert attention away from domestic difficulties, Saddam Hussein made a number of dubious demands of his small and defenceless neighbour, Kuwait.*

5 *In August 1990, the Iraqi army occupied Kuwait and sacked it.*

6 *Rather than offer resistance, Kuwait's ruling al-Sabah family fled to Saudi Arabia.*

7 *A massive international coalition, headed by the US and backed by the UN, assembled to liberate Kuwait by force, if necessary.*

8 *In the First Gulf War (1991), the large but technologically backward armed forces of Saddam Hussein were annihilated by the hi-tech weaponry of the coalition. Kuwait was liberated but the coalition stopped short of going on to topple Hussein.*

9 *The Shia of southern Iraq rose in revolt at the close of the Gulf War. Unsupported by the coalition, the rising was ruthlessly crushed.*

10 *The First Gulf War marked a new phase in the history of the Middle East, with the US – now the world's only superpower – intervening directly in the region.*

12

The 1990s: Searching for settlement

This chapter will cover:
- *moves made after the First Gulf War to settle the Arab–Israeli conflict*
- *the Oslo Accords and the reactions to them*
- *the difficult progress of the peace process during the mid-1990s*
- *how the peace process finally broke down and a Second Intifada erupted.*

Instability, religion and power

As the twentieth century drew to a close, the Middle East was entering a new and more dangerously unstable phase in its history. The basic ingredients of this instability had long been present: inequality, tyranny, oil, water, race, conflicting faiths, unsure frontiers and outside interference. By the 1990s, these factors overlapped and intertwined in complex patterns that were hard to distinguish, let alone unravel.

Saudi Arabia proved a classic example. The controller of the world's largest oil reserves was fabulously wealthy, yet over its borders to the south and north dwelt some of the poorest people in the region. It was the defender of Islam's holiest sites, but needed the military umbrella of the Christian West to maintain that defence. The staunch ally of many liberal democracies, its own regime was one of the most illiberal and dictatorial on earth. Moreover, although the Saudi royal family professed adherence to the puritanical Wahabite sect, fundamentalists of both Sunni and Shia persuasion condemned it as corrupt and impure.

The principal factor responsible for raising the political temperature within the region was religion, specifically fundamentalist Islam. Before the Iranian Revolution of 1979, most inhabitants of the Middle East felt impotent in the face of Western military and economic power. Governments that wished to succeed invariably aligned themselves with a Western power, communist or democratic-capitalist. After the poor showing of the Muslim Brotherhood in the early struggles with Israel, there seemed no other way of getting on. The Iranians demonstrated this to be a false assumption: Islam could provide a home-grown source of inspiration, a rallying point against outsiders, a reason for pride in one's own culture. Furthermore, it gave power. It enabled the Iranians to defy the mighty United States, an example that spread rapidly among the dispossessed and dissatisfied.

Insight

It is worth remembering at this juncture that the PLO, for long the most radical organization in the Middle East, had been established with a secular constitution and had called for the replacement of Israel by a new, secular two-nationality state.

With this in mind, the moment the First Gulf War ended in 1991, the US administration turned its attention to Israel. The new post-Cold War world order was very much in their favour. Russia would almost certainly co-operate in a peace initiative. The PLO was impoverished and isolated. Israel, still dependent upon US aid, was no longer needed as an anti-communist bastion in the Middle East. In fact, given the US's new alliance with the Gulf states, Israel was becoming something of a liability. At last, the

White House believed, there was a chance of extinguishing a long-burning fire before it did any further damage.

The Declaration of Principles

TOWARDS MADRID

As soon as the First Gulf War ended, US President George Bush Sr announced an initiative to extend the peace of the Gulf across the entire Middle East. Secretary of State Baker, who had been dashing backwards and forwards in a frenzy of preparatory diplomacy, put forward a nine-point plan as the basis for an international conference. Ambitiously, he sought to usher in the new and widespread peace by ending the conflicts between Israel and the Palestinians, Syrians and Jordanians. As far as Palestinians were concerned, Baker suggested a form of interim self-rule that envisaged full independence at some future date. Arafat proudly rejected the proposal.

The Palestinian leader's response was merely a gesture of independence. The war had considerably reduced his influence. The PLO was in serious financial difficulties – staff were leaving and its bureaucracy was becoming even less efficient than previously. Among the international community the Palestinians' reputation had been harmed by their joyful reaction to the Iraqi missile attacks on Israel, while the Israelis' refusal to react to Hussein's unprovoked aggression had won them sympathy and respect (see page 186). Consequently, Arafat was in no position to denounce the US–Soviet talks. That would have been political suicide. Moreover, he was obliged to accept the PLO attending with the Jordanian delegation rather than with that from the occupied territories. The people of the West Bank and Gaza, expecting a negotiating team representing the Palestinian nation, were bitterly disappointed.

Israeli Prime Minister Yitzhak Shamir was equally sceptical about the whole process. His foot-dragging so angered President Bush that he was refused US loan guarantees of $10 billion for Israeli housing projects. At a time when Israel was striving to assimilate around 250,000 Russian Jews, the move was no mere empty gesture. Shamir would attend the conference.

THE MADRID TALKS

A series of conferences was held in Madrid, Spain, to find a comprehensive peace acceptable to all parties. Separate working groups dealt with issues such as water and the environment. Not surprisingly, the talks soon ran into difficulties. Prime Minister Shamir was happy to stall as a way of avoiding concessions: treating the talks as a minor distraction, he actually returned home after barely 24 hours in the Spanish capital. He would not dream of agreeing anything without cast-iron guarantees of Israel's security. Israeli settlements in the occupied territories were essential to this security and they continued to expand throughout the period of negotiation. No act could have been better designed to persuade the Palestinians of Israel's half-hearted approach.

At the same time, the Palestinians were troubled with internal difficulties. The PLO, for instance, would not grant real negotiating power to compatriots attached to the Jordanian delegation. Arafat insisted on trying to control matters from long range, appointing dozens of useless coffee-sipping sycophants to the PLO delegation and not supporting his most able politicians. He was unhappy, too, with the US idea of some vague semi-autonomy for his people. He had not striven all his life to become head of a pseudo-Palestine, he complained.

A few months later, Arafat's position was strengthened by an accident. In April 1992 his plane crashed in the Tunisian desert and for 13 hours, until located by US satellite, he was believed to have been killed. Premature obituaries appeared, some flattering, others less so. His reappearance – seemingly risen from the dead – added considerably to his influence among Palestinians. To many of his supporters, though not to himself, his immortality had been confirmed. Worried by this, the Israelis were soon putting out stories that he really had died in the crash and the man calling himself Yasser Arafat was in fact an agent of Mossad, the Israeli Secret Service. It was not explained how they had found an Arafat look-alike, unless by plastic surgery.

The flagging peace talks had by now been moved to Washington DC. The change of venue made no difference. In an effort to get the Palestinians to walk away from the negotiating table and so bring the whole process to an end, the Israelis deported activists from the occupied territories. The move provoked a fresh wave of Intifada violence. By the summer of 1992 it looked as if the whole Madrid-Washington process would collapse. It was saved by a change of leadership and an inspired Norwegian initiative.

YITZHAK RABIN

In June 1992, the Israeli electorate chose a Knesset that enabled Yitzhak Rabin to head a Labour-led coalition administration. Rabin also took over the defence ministry and made it responsible for the peace talks. He gave the foreign ministry to Shimon Peres. The prime minister's negotiating freedom was hampered by his coalition's reliance on the support of the Shas religious party.

Rabin had campaigned on the ticket of peace. Soon after taking office, he announced a freeze on all new Israeli settlements on the West Bank and in the Gaza Strip. Arafat nodded in approval and President Bush re-activated his government's housing loan guarantees. (Actually, Rabin's offer was not as generous as it sounded: all planned new settlements went ahead and during his administration the settler population rose from 100,000 to 135,000.) The Knesset also relaxed the law on talking to members of the PLO, making it legal for individuals to hold discussions with the organization. So far, so good.

OSLO

Entirely unofficially and without the full knowledge of the US, secret and mostly informal talks began in the Norwegian capital of Oslo. On one side was a Palestinian delegation led by Abu Ala, head of the PLO's economic department, on the other an Israeli delegation led by the academic Yair Hirschfeld. The two parties talked over possibilities. It soon became clear that there was some common ground between them. The great majority of Israelis had no desire to remain in the Gaza Strip, for example, while the Palestinians wanted the territory for themselves. There was an obvious solution here.

Insight

Gaza, the place where the Biblical hero Samson had been held captive, never exercised the same grip over Israeli hearts and minds as the territory to the east of the 1949 ceasefire line. Significantly, the Strip housed few Israeli settlers.

Gradually, step by step, a series of principles was hammered out amid the Oslo snows. When these ideas were shown to the world, they were heralded as a breakthrough. In some ways they were, as we shall see. But behind them lurked one inescapable fact: the Palestinians held precious few trump cards and negotiated from a position of extreme weakness. Their only power was the ability to make a nuisance of themselves and to evoke popular sympathy. Arafat knew this. Painfully aware since his desert experience of his own mortality, he wanted settlement at any price. He had changed. Even a pseudo-Palestine would now suffice, as long as he was its leader. If the talks failed, the destitute PLO would almost certainly break up.

Elsewhere, the formal Washington talks finally collapsed in December 1992 after Israel had deported 415 Palestinian militants. Nine months later, the gloom was dispelled when the fruits of the Oslo talks went on public display.

The US, now headed by the Democrat President Bill Clinton, came in on the 'Declaration of Principles on Palestinian Self-Rule' (better known as the Oslo Accords) late in the day, but in time to ensure that no side could back out and that the agreement was given maximum recognition. The Accords were signed in the

White House on 13 September 1993. Afterwards, with Bill Clinton towering over them like a political godfather, the diminutive Yasser Arafat and Yitzhak Rabin shook hands before the world's media. The reluctance of the latter to extend the hand of friendship was obvious to all.

The Accords were mostly about what would happen in the future. For the present, the key feature was recognition. The PLO recognized Israel's right to exist, denounced terrorism and promised to revise its charter to eliminate references to destroying Israel. In return, the Israelis recognized the PLO as the sole representative of the Palestinian people. The gain for Israel was great, as also it was for Arafat and his creaking organization. For the Palestinian people at large, however, there was nothing in the immediate principles at all.

The Accords talked much of what would happen over the coming five years. There would be interim, limited self-government for Palestinians. Starting in Gaza and the city of Jericho, Palestinian rule would involve only non-strategic matters such as sanitation and education. Then elections would be held for a Palestinian president and council. After that the area of self-rule, and perhaps its scope, would be expanded. Talks on the permanent status of the Palestinians were to begin within three years and a solution agreed within five. In the short term, Palestinian leaders would gain some control over their people but the land would remain Israel's. A Palestinian police force, when assembled, would help to keep Israel secure from extremist threats.

Again, as in the general principles of the Accords, there was almost nothing specific in their more detailed proposals that would be of much benefit to ordinary Palestinians. They knew this too – the PLO executive committee had approved the agreement by only one vote, and even then the ballot had been of questionable veracity. The Israelis had their right to exist recognized, an end to the Intifada, and they kept all the territory they wanted. The Palestinians had only promises. No specific frontiers had been mentioned, nor had the question of refugees. There was to be no exchange of prisoners. Israeli settlements in the occupied territories could continue apace. Most significant of all, no mention whatsoever was made of a Palestinian nation.

The Palestinians of the occupied territories remained a stateless people. Many of them saw the whole Oslo business as a charade and a betrayal. Israel, they were now certain, would never let them have a country of their own. This attitude hardened in many minds over the years to come, making further progress towards peace very difficult.

Struggling for peace

Many hoped that the Oslo Accords would be the start of a long but ultimately successful peace process. Sadly, it was not to be. Almost 50 years of hatred, mistrust and bloodshed could not so easily be set aside. There was some progress, to be sure, but for each two steps forward there was at least one-and-a-half backward. Well into the next century, the divisions between Palestinians and Israelis remained almost as bitter as they had been at the beginning. Moreover, by appearing so grand yet giving so little, the Oslo Accords divided Palestinians still further between pragmatists, willing to accept Oslo as a starting point, and absolutists, who saw the whole process as a charade. In other words, by further widening Palestinian divisions, Oslo made a lasting settlement less likely.

ONWARD FROM OSLO

The majority of Israelis welcomed the Oslo Accords in the hope that they would usher in a new era of stability and security. The plan to pull out of the overcrowded and unpleasant Gaza Strip, in particular, was widely popular. Likud and the right, however, insisted on denouncing the agreement as a betrayal of a sacred trust. They argued that Rabin had given in to the barbaric violence of the Intifada and the bombs of militant Islamists.

As if to prove wrong those who accused him of weakness, Rabin maintained the traditional Israeli policy of reacting to violence with extreme force. A fortnight after the Washington ceremony, there were disturbances in the Gaza Strip. Israeli security forces rumbled in, demolishing 17 houses; 16 suspects were arrested and two summarily executed. The new era of peace and co-operation had not got off to an auspicious start.

Hamas resumed its bombings. When asked to do something about them, Arafat said he wished to incorporate Hamas members within the peaceful PLO, not fight them openly. The Israelis were unimpressed. Hamas leaders were identified by Israeli agents, singled out and killed by a variety of means. Some were blown up, others shot or poisoned.

One incident above all from this period exemplified the depth of blind and irrational hatred that divided the hardliners on both sides. On 25 February 1994, a 35-year-old doctor named Baruch Goldstein donned Israeli army uniform and crept into the Ibrahimi Mosque in Hebron. It was the time of dawn prayers. Originally from New York, Goldstein had moved to Israel for religious reasons: he belonged to the extreme Kahane Chai movement that believed 'Greater Israel' should be cleansed of all Arabs. He chose to start his spring cleaning at the Ibrahimi Mosque, a religious building shared by Jews and Muslims. It contained the tombs of such ancient Jewish luminaries as Abraham and Jacob.

Goldstein was carrying an M16 automatic rifle. Carefully and deliberately he began to fire on the worshippers. Israeli guards stationed nearby either did not hear what was going on or chose to ignore it. Before Goldstein was stopped, 21 Palestinian worshippers lay dead and a further 300 had been wounded. The assassin was killed by enraged survivors.

This wicked act of bigotry almost brought the peace process to a complete halt. The volatile population of the occupied territories burned Yasser Arafat in effigy for keeping negotiations open.

He knew that he had no option: if the process stopped, the Islamists would take control and his career would be over.

Following bombings near Afula and in Tel Aviv that killed 14 Israelis and wounded more than 80, in May Arafat and Rabin signed a follow-up agreement to the Oslo Accords. Dealing largely with Jericho and the Gaza Strip, the paper took the peace process a bit further. The withdrawal of Israeli forces from certain areas was arranged in detail and plans for a Palestinian police force were drawn up. Two months later, Arafat returned to the occupied territories for the first time in 27 years. Hundreds of thousands of supporters set aside their recent misgivings and turned out to greet him. It was not so much the man they were lauding as the hope of freedom and nationhood that he seemed to symbolize.

OSLO TWO

The next year, Arafat, Rabin and Peres (all recently awarded the Nobel Peace Prize) ratified the Oslo Two agreement that moved the peace process on another step. Palestinian elections were planned, arrangements made for the release of some Palestinian prisoners, and a phased Israeli withdrawal from certain zones in the West Bank was detailed. This would leave the area divided into three types of zone: those under Palestinian civilian rule (no more than 20 per cent), those that still had an Israeli military presence, and those that remained wholly Israeli. The new road network would enable the Israeli military to move swiftly between zones should the need arise.

Insight
Whatever territory was officially deemed to be under Palestinian control, a thick network of military roads, each interrupted with armed checkpoints, ensured that real control over the West Bank remained firmly in Israeli hands.

The Knesset passed Oslo Two by one vote. Israeli disillusionment with the peace process was growing. With many on the far right of the Israeli political and religious spectrum still labelling Rabin a traitor for betraying the Jewish homeland and giving in to violence, the scene was set for another act of Israeli extremism. On 4 November 1995, seeking to rekindle support for his cause, the Israeli prime minister attended a peace rally in Tel Aviv. As he was leaving, the Jewish religious fanatic Yigal Amir shot him dead. The world mourned the death of the second Middle East statesman assassinated for seeking peace.

A broader peace

The original American peace plan, put forward by President Bush Sr and Secretary of State Baker, had looked for a comprehensive settlement to include Jordan and Syria. On and off talks with both countries had been conducted since the end of the First Gulf War. Although 20,000 Syrian troops had fought in the US-led coalition, it was Jordan that joined the peace process.

JORDAN

King Hussein of Jordan had long been torn between a personal regard for the West and the fiercely pro-Palestinian feelings of his people, not to mention those of the hundreds of thousands of Palestinian refugees within Jordan's borders. During the First Gulf War, for instance, he had been obliged to repress his personal instincts and offer tacit support to Saddam Hussein. Israel's accord with the PLO, therefore, finally gave him an opportunity to do what he had hoped to be able to do for a long time: end the state of belligerence between his kingdom and Israel.

Prime Minister Rabin and King Hussein, who got on well together, held a series of secret meetings in the early part of 1994. A peace treaty was announced in Washington DC in July and formally signed at the Wadi Araba border post in the Arava Desert at the end of October. President Clinton was witness to both actions, and US backing underpinned the whole process. The first comprehensive peace treaty between Israel and an Arab neighbour since Camp David brought benefits to both parties.

Jordan was released of $700 million of debt to the US and $92 million to Britain. It also received generous aid, including military hardware. The following year, seeking to mollify the Palestinians, most of whom had disapproved of his initiative, Hussein signed accords with the PLO in which he pledged support for their drive for independent statehood. This enabled the Jordanian king to act as a broker between Israel and the Palestinians, something he did with patience and skill before his death from cancer in 1999. He was succeeded by his son, the 37-year-old Abdullah. Although the new king pledged himself to follow his father's policies of moderation and mediation, he found this middle road difficult to negotiate (see page 241).

Israel's motive for peace with Jordan had been largely strategic. The treaty removed the threat of a three-pronged Arab attack from Syria, Iraq and Jordan. It also opened the way for other nations to recognize Israel. Within a few months, diplomatic relations had been established with a number of countries, including Morocco and Tunisia. The Arab boycott of Israel was lifted, freeing major international companies to trade there.

SYRIA

Talks with Syria did not go so well. They were dogged by two problems. First, Syria's President Assad insisted that any lasting peace had to be based upon a return to the pre-1967 war frontiers. As this would mean Syria having control of the strategically vital Golan Heights, a region whose rainfall also provided Israel with essential water, Assad's demands were unacceptable to Israeli negotiators.

Secondly, Syria continued to shelter Hezbollah guerrillas. Frequent clashes between the group and Israeli security forces soured peace talks. In 1994, for example, Israeli planes bombed a Hezbollah camp within Syria, killing 40. The following month, Hezbollah bombed a Jewish community centre in Buenos Aires. Almost 100 civilians were slain.

Vain attempts to reach a Syrian–Israeli understanding continued
through the 1990s. Assad died of cancer in 2000 and was replaced
by his son, Bashar Assad (see pages 244–6). The change of regime
had no immediate impact on Syrian–Israeli relations.

The peace process crumbles

Rabin's assassination brought Shimon Peres back to the Israeli
premiership as a wave of pro-peace, anti-fundamentalist sentiment
swept the country. Troop withdrawals from the occupied territories
continued so that by early 1996 most Palestinians were under
some form of self-rule. Thus far, though, the arrangement was only
temporary and there was still no sign of a Palestinian state.

VIOLENCE RETURNS

In accordance with the Oslo agreements, elections for the
Palestinian Legislative Council and a Palestinian president were
held in January 1996. Yasser Arafat won the presidency with an
overwhelming 88 per cent of the votes cast. His Fatah Party won
control of the Legislative Council by winning 60 of its 88 seats.
Abu Ala, the Oslo negotiator, was chosen as speaker.

At this point, the peace process all but came to a halt. The Israeli
security forces were being as ruthless as ever. In January their
agents killed Yahya Ayyash, a Palestinian militant known as the
'engineer' for his bomb-making skills. Hamas and Islamic Jihad,
both of whom remained pledged to destroy the state of Israel,
responded with a prolonged campaign of terror that left over

50 Israelis dead. The Israelis countered with their customary harshness, sealing off Palestinian communities, conducting brutal searches and arresting suspects. In the north, Hezbollah stepped up its campaign across the Syrian border.

Despite support from President Clinton, who attended an international conference on terrorism in Egypt and promised Peres massive aid in his fight against Islamic fundamentalists, the Labour prime minister was defeated at the polls in May 1996. The elections were the first in which the prime minister was chosen separately from the Knesset. The victor by one per cent was Benjamin Netanyahu, a 46-year-old Likud hardliner.

BENJAMIN NETANYAHU

Netanyahu, recently Israel's ambassador at the UN, had campaigned on the slogan 'Peace with security'. Primary emphasis was on the latter. A member of an élite special operations unit in his youth, he had confronted terrorists face-to-face. He had also fought in the 1973 war and lost a brother in the successful Israeli commando raid on Entebbe that had freed a hi-jacked airliner and its passengers (see page 137). Although not born when Israel had been founded, he had been imbued with the fighting siege mentality of his older right-wing compatriots. If the Palestinians picked up so much as a whiff of Israeli weakness, he believed, the cause of the promised land would be lost.

In the September following Netanyahu's elections, his tough security policy produced a massive flare-up in Palestinian violence. The prime minister personally authorized the opening of an ancient tunnel near the northern end of Jerusalem's Western wall. The 2,000-year-old passage passed near the al-Aqsa mosque and led into Muslim-controlled East Jerusalem. Although of great archaeological interest, its physical position made it of even greater religious significance.

Muslim worshippers saw the opening of the tunnel as a direct threat to the mosque. Crowds gathered, stones were thrown, shooting started. The mayhem saw Israeli soldiers and Palestinian police, who only days previously had been on patrol together, firing at each other. By the time order had been restored, 15 soldiers and 60 Palestinians had been killed. The future of the peace process hung in the balance.

BREAKDOWN

Netanyahu had never approved of the Oslo Accords. Nevertheless, for practical reasons he did not want the peace process to fall apart completely. He was under pressure from President Clinton, and he feared the economic dislocation that prolonged violence inevitably brought. At the start of 1997, he signed an agreement by which the Israelis left the city of Hebron. This completed the handover to Palestinian authorities of the key West Bank towns named in the Accords.

The outbreak of goodwill did not last. Netanyahu had once said that 'Jewish sovereignty and Jewish power are the only deterrents and the only guarantees against the slaughter of the Jews'. He had little difficulty, therefore, in submitting to right-wing pressure to allow more settlements on land captured in 1967, and not to agree further withdrawal from the West Bank. As a consequence, a new Jewish settlement was announced at Har Homa (Jabal Abu Ghneim) in East Jerusalem. This was followed by a decision to hand over to Palestinian local government only another nine per cent of the West Bank instead of the 30 per cent expected from the wording of previous agreements.

The details of what followed are all too painfully familiar. A fresh wave of Islamist bombings provoked the usual reprisals. Arafat released Hamas members he had previously detained and refused further co-operation with Israel over security. Outsiders, particularly the Americans, tried in vain to bring Israeli and Palestinian leaders together. Positions on each side became more entrenched, with the Israeli prime minister actually declaring that his country would always remain in possession of the entire West Bank. The troubles led to a deterioration in Israel's relations with countries within the Middle East and further afield. There was fighting on the borders with Lebanon and Syria, and a tragic shooting of seven Israeli schoolgirls by a Jordanian border guard.

WYE RIVER

In 1998, relying heavily on his country's economic clout and position as the world's only superpower, President Clinton finally forced Netanyahu and Arafat to attend talks. They met at Wye Plantation, Maryland. King Hussein, in the US for cancer treatment, turned up to assist the president in his taxing task. The 27 hours of tough negotiating produced a deal known as the Wye River Memorandum.

Confirmed and signed later in Washington, the Memorandum was intended to pick up the peace process where it had broken off a year-and-a-half before. The old Oslo promises were restored, guaranteeing a safe passage from the West Bank to Gaza, for example, and establishing mutual anti-terrorist measures. Clinton's new thinking included linking staged Israeli withdrawal to specific Palestinian moves against Hamas and Islamic Jihad. This anti-terrorist activity would be monitored by the CIA. The agreement envisaged a phased Israeli withdrawal from the West Bank that would eventually leave the Palestinian Authority (still not a state) in control of about 40 per cent of the land there.

Insight

The proposed 'safe passage' between the West Bank and Gaza is just one example of the sort of small but vital detail on which Israeli–Palestinian negotiations can become bogged down. The Israelis envisage an easily controlled and secure railway link; the Palestinians want a straightforward highway.

Moderates everywhere warmly welcomed the agreement. The Palestinian Authority accepted it and, as the Memorandum stipulated, took steps to curb Palestinian extremists. It also deleted clauses in the Palestinian National Charter that called for Israel's destruction.

The bulk of Israelis welcomed the Memorandum, too. It was agreed by the cabinet and the Knesset. By the end of the year, though, to keep the support of the right, Netanyahu was backtracking fast. He imposed new conditions for further Israeli withdrawal, to all intents and purposes rejecting the agreements he had made earlier in the year. Confused and annoyed, the Knesset voted to dissolve itself and hold new elections. Netanyahu's premiership was over.

The Second Intifada

The Israeli elections of 1999 produced a more fractured Knesset than ever before, reflecting the deep divisions within Israeli society. The premiership went to Labour's Ehud Barak, the most decorated soldier in his country's history. Yet the old warrior with an MSc from Stanford, California, was no blinkered warlord. He had played a key role in negotiating the treaty with Jordan (see pages 218–19) and had campaigned with a One Israel coalition on a promise to bring peace to the Middle East. He was certainly not the first and would not be the last to find that such a promise was much easier to make than to keep.

TALKS RE-OPEN

True to his manifesto, Barak held talks with Yasser Arafat. The latter, finding it difficult to control the increasingly popular extremists within the Palestinian movement, set the bar high. Undaunted, Barak agreed to find a binding peace deal by September 2000 and to withdraw from more of the West Bank.

At the same time, Barak re-opened talks with Syria and withdrew all Israeli forces from southern Lebanon. President Clinton was eager to find a permanent solution to the Israeli–Palestinian problem before his term of office came to an end. In the summer of 2000, he made one last effort. Using a tactic that had succeeded in the past, he invited Israeli and Palestinian negotiating teams, each headed by their elected leader, to Camp David. For 15 days electric golf buggies buzzed negotiators and mediators between the complex of luxurious cabins. This time it was the Israelis who were prepared to give and the Palestinians who dug in their heels. Arafat was terrified of offering his people an agreement that might seem like a climbdown. The Islamists, gaining in power every month, were waiting to denounce him.

Clinton cajoled and shouted. At one point, he actually yelled at Arafat for refusing even to look at a map on which the Israelis had drawn proposed new boundaries. On more than one occasion, both sides threatened to leave. The central sticking point – the issue known to Palestinians as 'bones in the throat' – was the ownership of holy places.

'The problem is,' commented Secretary of State Madeleine Albright in despair, 'they both want the same thing'. On the issue of East Jerusalem, neither side dared give way because of the reaction back home, although Barak had suggested that Israel might find a way of sharing the precious sites with Muslims. In the end, Clinton reconciled himself to the fact that on this issue even his legendary charm had failed. Barak returned home in sombre mood. His Palestinian counterpart was welcomed back in the occupied territories as a conquering hero: Arafat had proved his strength by daring to say 'no' to the Israelis and the Americans.

Insight

The collapse of the 2000 talks is highly controversial. Several sources, including well-placed US diplomats, claimed subsequently that Arafat had rejected a deal giving him control over Gaza and more than 90 per cent of the West Bank, as well as a share of Jerusalem. The Palestinians insisted that they had been offered merely a 'Balkanized' West Bank.

ENTER SHARON

At this point, with the peace process stalling again, one of Israel's most controversial and experienced politicians took steps to see that it finally crashed. In September 2000, Ariel Sharon visited

East Jerusalem's al-Aqsa mosque. A visit to this controversial site by the man widely believed to have been responsible for the Sabra and Shatila massacres and other atrocities was bound to provoke hostility, and it did.

The day after Sharon's visit, a Friday, the leaders of the Muslim community incited anger among their flock. After prayers, stones were thrown at Israeli soldiers. The military responded with tear gas, then with rubber bullets. When the rioting continued, a commanding officer over-reacted: Israeli snipers appeared, firing down on the crowd in an attempt to pick off the ringleaders. Many Palestinians were killed.

The next day armed Palestinian paramilitaries went into action. The wave of Palestinian rage rose, fuelled by the image of an innocent 12-year-old boy cowering beside his father while a gunfight raged around them. Suddenly the boy fell forward, dead. He had been shot several times by Israeli soldiers supposedly targeting the gunmen behind him. The pictures were shown on television in every country in the world. The Second or al-Aqsa Intifada began shortly afterwards. Within a year, the death toll stood at 37 Israelis and 315 Palestinians, 66 of whom were children.

Barak, the man who had based his reputation on being able to bring peace, had failed. A joint plea for a ceasefire from himself and Arafat was ignored. As the violence escalated, Sharon's criticism of the Labour prime minister became more vitriolic.

With the peace process in tatters, Ehud Barak resigned in December 2000. The following February, Ariel Sharon was elected prime minister of Israel. If the outlook for the region was bleak, terrifying events in New York would soon make it bleaker still.

The prospects for the new century were ominous indeed.

THINGS TO REMEMBER

1 *Following the end of the Cold War and the remarkable show of international unity in the First Gulf War, President George Bush Sr initiated a general drive for peace across the Middle East.*

2 *The formal peace talks, held first in Madrid, Spain, and then in Washington DC, quickly became bogged down.*

3 *The peace initiative was reflected in Israel, where in 1992 Yitzhak Rabin came to power at the head of a Labour coalition pledged to make peace with Israel's neighbours and the Palestinians.*

4 *The diplomatic deadlock was broken by secret, informal talks held in Oslo, Norway, which led to the signing of the breakthrough Oslo Accords in September 1993.*

5 *The Oslo Accords led to the formation of an elected Palestinian Authority headed by a president (Yasser Arafat) and limited Palestinian self-rule in certain parts of the occupied territories, but not to the creation of a Palestinian state or even the promise of one in the future.*

6 *In 1996 Yitzhak Rabin, the Israeli signatory of the Oslo Accords, was shot dead by a Zionist fanatic.*

7 *Jordan signed a formal peace treaty with Israel in 1994 but negotiations with Syria continued to stumble over the issue of the Golan Heights.*

8 *In 1996, as Israeli–Palestinian violence mounted once more, the right-of-centre Benjamin Netanyahu became Israel's Prime Minister.*

9 *At the very end of his presidency, US President Bill Clinton tried everything in his power to move the Oslo agreement forward to its next stage. In the end, Arafat rejected what he termed an offer of a 'Balkanized' West Bank.*

10 *In 2000, disillusioned and increasingly under the influence of uncompromising Islamists, the Palestinian people of the occupied territories rose up in a Second Intifada.*

13

Decision time: 9/11 and
the Arab world

This chapter will cover:
- *the Middle East at the start of the new millennium*
- *the events of 11 September 2001 and the US's War on Terror*
- *Egypt, Jordan, Lebanon and Syria in the first decade of the twenty-first century*
- *Saudi Arabia and the smaller states of the Arabian peninsula in the first decade of the twenty-first century.*

The Middle East in 2001

The traumatic and far-reaching changes that had swept the Middle East in the second half of the twentieth century may be outlined under the followings headings:

▶ *Massive new wealth from oil and gas*
▶ *Withdrawal of the old colonial powers*
▶ *Foundation and growth of the state of Israel*
▶ *Emergence of militant Islam.*

Together these developments ensured that the Middle East had moved to the very centre of global politics: analysed, argued over, bargained for, feared and wooed.

OIL

The key to the region's increased importance was oil. Output had been significant in 1945 – enough so for President F. D. Roosevelt to have had a personal meeting with King Abdul Aziz of Saudi Arabia – but it still accounted for considerably less than ten per cent of global consumption. Fifty years later, this had risen to around 50 per cent.

The influence of Middle Eastern oil producers, who by 2000 had the theoretical power to bring the industrial world to a halt, was likely to strengthen in the future. Their reserves were being used up less quickly than those in other regions: it was estimated that by 2020 they would account for 83 per cent of the world's entire stock of crude oil. Stocks of natural gas were similarly impressive.

Oil revenues funded spectacular economic growth. Around the Gulf, new cities soared into the cloudless skies; highways laced across once impenetrable desert; families whose ancestors had dwelt in tents now lived in air-conditioned villas equipped with every convenience modern technology could provide.

GROWING PAINS

The region's dramatic economic advance brought as many problems as benefits. The painful contrast between a country like Kuwait, where the annual national income per person averaged around $18,000 in 2000, and Yemen, where the equivalent figure was less than $600, made the rhetoric of Arab and Islamic unity somewhat hollow. Moreover, as the Gulf Wars of 1990–1 and 2003–7 showed, the possession of oil wealth made the Middle East more, not less susceptible to superpower intervention.

Increased wealth was partly offset by astonishing demographic growth. The annual rate of increase rose to almost three per cent, lifting the region's population from just over 100 million in 1945 to more than triple that 55 years later. This was accompanied by massive migration into the towns, where more than half the population of the Middle East now lived. Riyadh, to take but one example, expanded from an oasis settlement of traditional mud-brick dwellings to an ultra-modern capital of broad highways and skyscrapers housing some 4.7 million citizens. At the other extreme was Cairo. The 16.5 million inhabitants of the 'mother of the world' dwelt in a chaotic and almost ungovernable metropolis that sprawled over 214 sq km (83 sq miles).

SOCIAL CHALLENGE

Education, the new media and increased travel opportunities rapidly transformed Middle Eastern society. Huge numbers of schools were constructed and staffed, and most states developed university systems of their own. Of particular significance was the rapid expansion of education for girls and young women. The region's overall illiteracy rate fell from around 75 per cent to less than 40 per cent.

Part of TV's impact came from its ability to portray in simple images the lifestyles of other cultures, especially American, thereby feeding aspirational dreams. The development of satellite TV and the internet – both less easily controlled than traditional broadcasts – linked Middle Eastern homes to global society in a reciprocal exchange of viewpoints and priorities. Such was the influence of the relatively objective reporting of the Qatar-based Arabic TV station Aljazeera, that in 2005 it was reported that President Bush had considered launching an air strike against it.

Closer links to the rest of the world forced the people of the Middle East to reflect upon their identity. They eagerly sought the conveniences, luxuries and freedoms of the capitalist West, yet were afraid of surrendering their distinctive identity. The result was a sort of social schizophrenia in which individuals and indeed whole societies were torn between past and present, puritanism and consumerism, hatred and love of the US. Traditions of dress and social arrangement, especially the subjugation of women, were often clung to with an irrational intensity that produced a tense and often conflicting blend of traditional Islam and consumerism – the Dior beneath the burka.

> **Insight**
>
> Rarely has an article of clothing been so contentious as the
> burka, an all-covering outer garment worn by some Muslim
> women to protect their bodies from prying eyes. Despised
> by liberals claiming it to be simply a pre-Islamic tribal relic,
> the burka is seen by some as an important feature of the
> Muslim faith.

NEW NATIONALISM

The withdrawal of the Western mandate powers – Britain and
France – bequeathed the difficult task of consolidating into true
nation states the countries they had created. Egypt, Syria and
Iran, each with distinctive cultures, traditions and histories,
adopted Western-style nationalism relatively readily. Elsewhere,
central governments struggled with the traditional allegiances of
tribe and clan.

Saudi Arabia, Oman and Jordan did better than most, consolidating
around their royal families. Elsewhere, nation-building generally
proved a painful process as, especially in rural areas, millions still
placed local, religious or blood loyalties above those of the state.

ISRAEL

The creation and expansion of the State of Israel was closely
related to developing nationalisms. Regionally, Israel's appearance
initially fostered a sense of Arab solidarity as its neighbours sought –
some more wholeheartedly than others – to destroy the parvenu
nation. However, when it was clear to most that Israel could not
be eliminated, enmity arose between Arab governments prepared
to change course (Egypt and Jordan) and between the disillusioned
Palestinians and their erstwhile supporters.

The presence of Israel created a distinct Palestinian nation.
Gradually, prompted and guided by Yasser Arafat, Palestinians
came to think of themselves in the same terms as the Jews had
done before the creation of Israel, as a people seeking to establish

themselves as a nation in their traditional homeland. Solving the so-called 'Jewish problem' had simply led to its replacement by an equally thorny 'Palestinian problem'.

Israel's presence further increased superpower involvement in the Middle East. This was partly due to the Cold War, when East and West competed for influence in every regional confrontation. The small but influential Jewish vote in the US also played a part, as did the West's feelings of guilt about the Nazi Holocaust and its desire to support a state with a democratic representative government against unelected dictators and monarchs. After the end of the Cold War, some commentators held the president of the US to be the most powerful figure in Israeli politics.

MILITANT ISLAM

The last quarter of the twentieth century left a daunting and wholly unexpected legacy. As late as 1975, commentators were describing their century as one of 'secular creeds': communism, capitalism, democracy, fascism, nationalism and so forth. Religion, it was claimed, was in terminal worldwide decline. Then, with the Iranian Revolution (1979) acting as a catalyst, Islam rapidly re-emerged as a major socio-political force throughout the Middle East and beyond.

Shia Iran played a crucial role in the Islamic resurgence. Here the power of the imam (priest) was traditionally greater than in other Islamic cultures, enabling religious leaders to assume a political role. Also significant was the approval in some radical Shia circles of dying for one's faith, no matter how hopeless the circumstances in worldly terms. This led to a number of idealistic young men and women willing to become suicide-bomber 'martyrs'. In terms of its global impact, the later resurgence of militant Sunni fundamentalism in the form of Al-Qaeda was equally important.

The significance of the Islamic revival is hard to overestimate. It gave focus and purpose to those in the Middle East who had long harboured misgivings about the overweening West. Islamist 'victories' – measured in deaths and destruction – restored a sense of racial and religious pride. Here, at last, was a movement around which the downtrodden and exploited of the earth could gather. As it was based in the impenetrable human heart, against radical Islam neither air strikes nor tanks could prevail. Where communism had failed, Muslim's adherents claimed, Islam would triumph and usher in a new world order.

9/11 and America's War on Terror

11 SEPTEMBER 2001

On 11 September 2001, the Middle East came to New York when Islamic militants hi-jacked four aircraft on domestic flights from east-coast airports and turned them into gigantic flying bombs. At about 8.45 a.m. the first plane smashed into the North Tower of the World Trade Center, New York, killing all aboard and hundreds working in the tower or in the vicinity.

About 15 minutes later, a second plane buried itself within the South Tower, causing similar structural damage and loss of life. Seventy-five minutes after impact, the north tower collapsed in a billowing cloud of dust and smoke. The second tower came down some 30 minutes later. Before the buildings crumbled entirely, many of those trapped on the upper floors had flung themselves out of windows. All fell to their death.

Meanwhile, the hi-jackers had launched a third plane into the south-west side of the Pentagon, the headquarters of the US Department of Defense. Phone calls alerted passengers on the fourth aircraft to what was happening and they turned on their captors. The plane plummeted into the Pennsylvania countryside and there were no survivors. Some say it had been en route for the White House.

The final death toll of the 9/11 attacks was around 3,000, making it the most devastating terrorist strike the world had ever seen and by far the worst in US history. Many Americans likened it to the Japanese attack on Pearl Harbor, which had brought their country into the Second World War.

AL-QAEDA

The link between the attacks of 11 September and the Middle East was a 44-year-old Saudi Islamist named Osama Bin Laden. Thirteen years earlier, Bin Laden had set up Al-Qaeda, meaning 'the Base', and all those responsible for the 11 September attacks were connected to this movement. Initially described as an organization, like a business or a warband, Al-Qaeda came to be seen as something less concrete: an idea, a set of shared ideals to be implemented at any cost. Madeleine Albright, a former US ambassador to the UN, described it as 'an ideological virus'.

··

Insight

Osama Bin Laden took positive steps to ensure that his line would endure after his eventual death: himself the only son of his father's tenth wife, he was rumoured to have married four wives and fathered around 20–25 children.

··

After assisting the Afghans against the invading Soviet army, Bin Laden had established Al-Qaeda in 1988 to pursue holy war (jihad) elsewhere. Disillusioned with the perceived immoral corruption of the godless West and horrified when the Saudi government welcomed non-Muslim soldiers to help drive Saddam Hussein from Kuwait, in 1991 Bin Laden set up terrorist training camps in Sudan. His supposed aim was to halt the advance of the West and restore the Caliphate (single government for the entire Muslim world; see page 9).

Islamist terrorist attacks were nothing new. In 1988, for example, Libyan-backed assassins had blown up a Pan Am jet airliner over Lockerbie, Scotland. Al-Qaeda simply brought a new level of intensity to the killing. The movement was linked to a first attempt to destroy New York's World Trade Center (1993), to the deaths of 18 US servicemen in Somalia the same year, to further US military deaths in Saudi Arabia in 1996, and to the loss of over

220 lives when the US embassies in Dar es Salaam (Tanzania) and Nairobi (Kenya) were bombed simultaneously.

In the later 1990s, US President Clinton had responded by launching missile strikes against targets in Afghanistan, where Bin Laden was once again in hiding. The UN imposed sanctions on the Afghan Taliban regime and demanded that they surrender their notorious guest. Refusal led to further sanctions. In October 2000, less than a year before the 9/11 attacks, Al-Qaeda-inspired suicide bombers rammed *USS Cole* in Aden, Yemen, killing 17 American sailors.

THE US GOES TO WAR

The 11 September attacks galvanized the US administration into immediate and drastic action. Within days, Congress had voted $40 billion to fund the American response and by October the US government was blaming Al-Qaeda directly and specifically for Islamist outrages. Shortly afterwards, the US and Britain launched heavy air strikes against the Taliban regime in Afghanistan. Afghan opposition groups (the Northern Alliance) were backed with money, material and personnel. By the end of the year, spied on by satellite, blasted from the air, and harassed at every turn on the ground, the Taliban had been overthrown. However, neither its leader, Mullah Omar, nor Bin Laden had been taken.

In his State of the Union Address on 29 January 2002, President George Bush Jr declared, 'Our nation is at war ... a war on terror'. Later came an announcement that the world was threatened by an 'axis of evil' comprising Iran, Iraq and North Korea. This list was then expanded to include Libya, Syria and Cuba. As four of the six 'evil' states were in the Middle East, the region was directly in the firing line of the world's only superpower. Furthermore, President Bush singled out Hamas, Hezbollah and Islamic Jihad as belonging to a 'terrorist underworld'. As all three were dedicated to Israel's elimination, the Israel-Palestine confrontation became part of the US's new war.

The Middle East's premiers were virtually unanimous in their condemnation of the 9/11 outrage. The most predictable reaction came from Israel, itself subject to Islamist attacks for many years. To some Israelis, hoping the outrage would further strengthen Israeli–US links, 9/11 even brought a sense of macabre relief. This may have been at the back of Prime Minister Ariel Sharon's mind when he declared that 9/11 would be 'a turning point in the war against international terror'.

A genuinely shocked Yasser Arafat expressed horror at the attacks on the US and condemned them utterly. Hamas, on the other hand, simply announced that it had no interest in action outside 'Palestine'. The governments of Egypt, Jordan, Saudi Arabia, Yemen and other states in the region (except Iraq – see page 254) all made public declarations of support for the American people. Many expressed themselves in Islamic terms, reminding the world that Muslims were prohibited from harming the weak and defenceless.

Three of the four Muslim states featured in President Bush's 'axis of evil' – Libya, Iran and Syria – had echoed the general chorus of disapproval. Iraq's Saddam Hussein was the lone voice of dissent, announcing that, 'the American cowboys are reaping the fruit of their crimes against humanity'. It was a remark he probably came to regret. There was a hint of reserve in some of the remarks of other axis members, too. President Khatami of Iran, for example, spoke of the 'international duty to try to undermine terrorism'. Although 'undermine' may not be a perfect translation of his words, it makes clear his reluctance to speak of a 'war' against terror. The problem, Khatami implied, was not simply a matter of evil people behaving wickedly but of a deeper, socio-political malaise that, like poverty and disease, needed to be tackled from the roots upwards.

In the Middle East, popular reaction to the attacks was mixed. The majority denounced them, although welcomed rumours – still prevalent today – that explained the whole business as a Jewish conspiracy, perhaps even with American help, to inspire hatred of the Arab and Muslim worlds. There was also in some hearts a sneaking admiration at the way Bin Laden and his tiny movement had managed to inflict such massive damage and injury on so powerful an enemy. The Islamist minority welcomed 9/11 as a blow against Islam's arch enemy.

INVESTIGATIONS, ACTION AND ARRESTS

As well as launching its Afghanistan operation, the US expanded the CIA and boosted its funding, set up a Department of Homeland Security, deployed troops to Yemen to back government forces attacking an Al-Qaeda stronghold there, and, later, launched missiles against the Yemeni group held responsible for the bomb attack on the *USS Cole* (see page 236). For a while the US had worldwide backing, with a number of governments offering various degrees of practical support. The UN, too, backed the US and the Security Council established a Counter Terrorism Committee of its own.

Investigations revealed that the 9/11 attacks, organized in Germany and funded with Gulf money, had been planned since 1996. Around the globe, from Indonesia to Spain, questionable bank accounts were frozen and suspects detained. Notable arrests included Khalid Sheikh Mohammed, a senior figure in Al-Qaeda, and Ali al-Ghamdi, the mastermind behind Saudi bombings. Several of those apprehended early on were later released when no specific evidence against them could be found. The US military was less scrupulous: hundreds of prisoners taken during the Afghan conflict were held as prisoners of war in harsh conditions at Camp X-Ray on the US base of Guantanamo Bay, Cuba.

'AXIS OF EVIL'

The United States's arrests and military strikes were all very well, but they did not break the Al-Qaeda movement. At the end of 2001, a British citizen professing allegiance to Bin Laden was arrested after trying to blow up a Miami-bound flight with explosives hidden in his shoes. The next year, Al-Qaeda was believed to have been behind bomb outrages in Tunisia, Bali (Indonesia), Yemen and Mombasa (Kenya). A US citizen was also arrested for planning to detonate a 'dirty bomb', and Muslim rebels from the Russian province of Chechnya killed over 100 hostages in a Moscow theatre.

Despite huge efforts to track him down, Osama Bin Laden remained at large and taunted his pursuers with video messages urging supporters to continue their jihad. These tapes, often shown through Aljazeera TV, referred to the West's anti-terrorist action as an anti-Muslim 'crusade' and its participants as 'the infidel'. Some young and disaffected Muslims found such vocabulary inspirational, ensuring Al-Qaeda a ready supply of recruits.

By the time the first anniversary of 11 September came round, the Bush administration was clearly frustrated by the elusive nature of its enemy. After Yemen and Afghanistan, opportunities for overt shows of strength had dried up. Even with satellite surveillance and laser-guided weapons, it was proving difficult to bomb a 'mentality'. Aware that the public wanted action showing the war on terrorism was being won, the White House re-focused on the 'axis of evil'.

North Korea, Cuba, Syria, Libya, Iran and Iraq did not appear equally dangerous. Cuba, though communist, posed little danger. North Korea, it was hoped, could be dissuaded by non-military pressure from developing nuclear weapons. For the moment, Syria and Libya were discounted, the former because of its traditional wariness of Muslim extremism and the latter because President Gaddafi hated Bin Laden and was probably afraid of him.

Iran, the birthplace of modern Islamism, had done most to promote international terrorism and its government refused to hand over the Al-Qaeda suspects it claimed to have arrested. However, any possible attack on Iran would face the double danger of inhospitable terrain and a guarantee of suicidally ferocious Shia resistance. Moreover, President Khatami's elected government appeared to be trying to moderate his country's fundamentalism. No, US advisors concluded,

Iran was not a suitable target for direct US intervention. Right next door lay a much more realistic alternative: Iraq (see Chapter 14).

A new millennium: 1. Egypt, Jordan, Lebanon and Syria

EGYPT

In the years immediately following the 9/11 attacks, the situation in Egypt remained relatively calm under the regime of the astute President Hosni Mubarak. One of the longest-serving heads of state in the Arab world, Mubarak was re-elected for a fifth six-year term in 2005. For the first time, opposition candidates were allowed to stand. However, as the Egyptian constitution outlawed religious parties, the main opposition grouping – the Muslim Brotherhood – was unable to field a candidate.

The Brotherhood got round the ban in the December elections to the lower house of the Egyptian parliament by standing as independents, and won 20 per cent of the seats. However, Mubarak's National Democratic Party maintained its grip on power. The turnout was a dismal 23 per cent.

During 2007–8, Egypt entered a period of mounting unrest fuelled by a number of issues. The world economic crisis provided a gloomy background in a country with few natural resources and heavily dependent on remittances from Egyptians working abroad. Egypt's soaring population suffered from unemployment and severe economic hardship: by 2010 around 20 per cent of the population of 82,999,000 (2009) were officially classed as living in poverty. The number of strikes and protest walkouts, some politically motivated, rose.

The nature of the regime was another source of unrest. Although the political climate in Egypt was more open than in many Middle Eastern states, there were harsh laws – instituted during the state of emergency that followed Sadat's assassination (1981) and reinforced in 2007 – restricting free expression. In 2008, the independent Egyptian Organization for Human Rights reported that over the previous seven years there had been 226 cases of torture and 93 suspicious deaths in police custody.

Despite the ruthlessness of the security apparatus, terrorist incidents still occurred. In July 2005, the Red Sea resort of Sharm al-Sheikh was targeted, leaving almost 90 dead. The following April over 20 were killed at Dahab on the Gulf of Aqaba, and three years later one man was killed and 24 were injured by an explosion in a district of Cairo popular with tourists.

Year on year uncertainty mounted over who would succeed the ailing president, who celebrated his eightieth birthday in 2008. Some said that his banker son Gamal was being groomed for the task. Lieutenant General Omar Suleiman, the country's intelligence supremo, was another possible candidate, as were opposition politician Ayman Nour and the former head of the International Atomic Energy Authority Dr Mohamed Mostafa ElBaradei, a winner of the Nobel Peace Prize. However, as it was illegal for the media to even discuss the president's heath, the situation remained at best murky.

JORDAN

Ruling Jordan proved no easier for King Abdullah II than it had been for his father. Without oil, short of water, and home to an estimated 1.7 million Palestinian refugees, the country inherited by the 39-year-old monarch in 1999 had few natural advantages. British- and US-educated Abdullah, a collector of antique weapons and a car-racing enthusiast, sought to maintain his father's balancing act of friendship with the West and simultaneous support for the Palestinian cause. His position was reflected by his family circumstances: his mother (Toni) was British-born while he himself was married to a Palestinian.

Like Egypt, the only other Arab country to talk openly with Israel, Jordan's government attracted admiration and hostility in equal measure. Western support came in the form of massive aid (Jordan was one of only four states to have a free trade agreement with the US) and approval of the king's efforts to develop a constitutional monarchy. In the spirit of a grand-sounding National Agenda reform plan, women were allocated a quota of MPs and the country's first female ministers were appointed in 2003.

This was all very well, but prime ministers rarely served for long, and the king apparently vacillated when it came to reducing his own power. In December 2009, for instance, he dissolved parliament half way through its term and appointed a new premier in the hope of speeding up the process of economic reform. Meanwhile, reports of human rights abuses, notably trafficking, detentions and torture, continued to blot the country's record.

Such behaviour was far from unusual in the region. The regime's defenders argued that it was an unfortunate necessity to protect against Palestinian and Islamist extremism. This manifested itself most forcibly in episodes such as Aqaba-launched missile attacks on US warships (August 2005), the suicide bombing of luxury Amman hotels (November 2005) and the shooting of a tourist in 2006. Perhaps as many as one million Iraqi refugees flooded across the border after the US invasion (2003) and subsequent insurgency, putting a huge burden on Jordan's already strained resources.

LEBANON

Lebanon, which had come perilously close to becoming a failed state towards the end of the twentieth century, entered the new millennium with a degree of reserved optimism. Following a US-brokered deal, in 2000 Israel withdrew from its 'security zone' in the south; the following year, Syrian peacekeepers pulled out of Beirut and withdrew to the east of the country.

Under the second premiership (2000–4) of Sunni billionaire Rafiq Hariri, the country made some economic and political headway. Although the prime minister's tycoon-style and blatant corruption annoyed many, his commitment to religious and political toleration was widely recognized. So was his charitable generosity: he is said to have educated several thousand students at his personal expense.

Only just below the surface, however, serious trouble still lurked. There were rows with Israel over shared water supplies, and periodic bomb blasts served as bloody reminders of past horrors. A major crisis erupted in the autumn of 2004 when the UN Security Council demanded that all foreign troops – that is, Syrian – leave Lebanon. Following his resignation in 2004, Prime Minister Hariri fell victim to a massive bomb explosion early the following year. The assassination, in which Syria was heavily implicated, sparked the nationalist 'Cedar Revolution'. The upshot was a government led by the Hariri ally, Fouad Siniora, and the final withdrawal of all Syrian troops. The Syrian regime of President Bashar Assad (see below), not noted for its grace in defeat, took revenge by picking off prominent Lebanese opponents in a series of car bomb attacks.

Insight

In October 2005, investigations into responsibility for the Hariri assassination took a fresh twist when Syria's media suddenly announced that Ghazi Kanaan, the interior minister who had for years managed his country's affairs in Lebanon, had committed suicide. Rumours abounded.

SUMMER WAR

Meanwhile, the Shia party Hezbollah – along with its militant wing Islamic Resistance – had been gaining popularity. Although the US had condemned Hezbollah as a terrorist organization, Siniora included two of its leaders in his cabinet. Backed by Syria and Iran, Hezbollah was fiercely anti-Israeli and, in the summer of 2006, the party brought Lebanon close to breaking point once again. When Islamic Resistance kidnapped two of its soldiers, Israel responded with the 'Summer War' against Hezbollah, blockading Lebanon and launching massive air strikes intended to set the country back 20 years.

Islamic Resistance retaliated with surprising vigour, sending thousands of rockets into northern Israel that killed some 43 civilians. Lebanese casualties were far higher: about 1,100 civilians slain, many more injured and almost a million forced from their homes. Days of continuous air raids smashed roads, bridges, power stations and other vital structures. A ceasefire brokered by the UN in mid-August pledged a large force of international peacekeepers in the south of the country.

The Summer War did indeed set the Lebanese economy back years. It also launched a long period of instability during which, at one stage, the country was without a head of state for six months. Eventually, Christian army commander Michel Suleiman was sworn in as president in 2008 and the Sunni Muslim Siniora was reappointed prime minister.

The elections of June 2009 brought fresh impasse as the country's four principal political groupings – Amal (pro-Syrian, Shia), Free Patriotic Movement (Christian but linked to Hezbollah), Hezbollah (Shia, pro-Syrian with Islamist links), and March 14 Alliance (pro-Western, anti-Syrian) – competed for influence. The deadlock was finally broken at the end of the year when Saad Hariri (son of Rafik), leader of the March 14 Alliance, established a government of national unity. A recovering economy, which had stood up remarkably well during the 2008–9 recession, and full diplomatic relations with Syria for the first time since independence, suggested that by 2010 Lebanon might be entering a more hopeful phase in its history.

SYRIA

In 2000, following the death of his father, the sometime ophthalmology student Bashar Assad was elected unopposed as president of Syria. His accession heralded a brief liberal spring. Political prisoners were released, press censorship was relaxed and open political discussion tolerated. The withdrawal of Syrian troops from Beirut and the visit to Damascus by Pope John Paul II in May 2001 symbolized the new openness. Unfortunately, it did not last. By September, outspoken MPs were being detained and free speech curbed.

The about-turn may have been prompted by the re-emergence of the Muslim Brotherhood, which had once attempted to assassinate Bashar's father. Others say the crackdown was instigated by the oligarchy of elderly and conservative Baathists, including the vice-president and minister of defence, the true bastions of power within Syria. The new president, unable or unwilling to exert his authority, fell back on the pillars of support that had underpinned his father's rule: the army, the Baath Party and the small but influential group of Alawite Shia.

Insight

Aljazeera, among others, reported that Syria's President Bashar Assad relied heavily on his intelligent sister, the pharmacist Dr Buishra Assad, and her husband, General Assef Shawqat, head of military intelligence.

INTERNATIONAL ISOLATION

Largely because of its continued support for terrorist groups, Syria had few friends in the international community. It fell within the US's 'axis of evil' and President Bush was strongly critical of the Assad regime for allowing militants to slip across its border into Iraq during the bloody insurgency there (see page 260). Israel made air strikes on Syrian targets in 2003 and 2007, the latter hitting a supposed half-finished nuclear facility. The Arab world was wary of their troublesome neighbour, too. International and local pressure forced Syria to withdraw its forces from Lebanon in 2005 (see above), and several prominent heads of state stayed away from the 2008 Arab League summit held in Damascus.

Syria's sluggish economy was not helped by disproportionate military expenditure and the government's slowness in dismantling the old Soviet-style state control. By 2006, despite exploitation of its oil and gas reserves, Syria's income per capita was barely one-quarter that of neighbouring Lebanon.

Insight

It has been rumoured that, in an act of extreme duplicity, the Bush administration secretly took terrorist suspects to Syria where they were tortured into revealing details of their organizations and plans.

By 2010, Syria remained one of the harshest regimes in the Middle East. Censorship of all forms of media was widespread; imprisonment without trial, torture and unexplained assassinations (sometimes by car bomb) remained features of everyday life. Repression of the Kurdish and Assyrian minorities was commonplace. Yet here, as elsewhere in the region, there were signs of hope.

In 2006, Syria and Iraq established diplomatic relations for the first time in decades. The EU made overtures towards a better understanding in 2007, and even US diplomats began talking with their Syrian counterparts. In 2008, France's president took matters a step further, leading to a significant summit between Syria, France, Turkey and Qatar. With Turkey as a mediator, there were even efforts to reach an agreement with Israel over the Golan Heights. At home, the opening of a Damascus stock exchange (2009) signalled a further freeing up of the Syrian economy. None of this was exactly revolutionary, but it did suggest that there might possibly be light ahead.

A new millennium: 2. Saudi Arabia and the Gulf

Nowhere were the difficult decisions facing the people and governments of the Middle East at the dawn of the twenty-first century more apparent than in the states of the Arabian peninsula. Where did they belong in the catalogue of nations? Many had the wealth of the developed countries but the political institutions of the developing world. Equally tricky was the clash between their material development and their socio-religious heritage. Sensitivity, skill and no little good fortune were needed if they were successfully to overcome these challenges.

SAUDI ARABIA

In the opening decade of the new millennium, the family regime that ruled the incongruous fiefdom of Saudi Arabia faced three distinct threats. The first was from Islamic extremism, both from

Shia Iran across the Gulf and the home-grown variety under the umbrella of Al-Qaeda. The second and quite contrary threat was posed by liberal-minded Saudis seeking to open up the government and remove its more oppressive laws, notably those placing extraordinary restrictions on women. Finally, there was the longer-term difficulty of keeping the country viable in a post-oil world. The background to these pressing issues was mounting hostility, both at home and abroad, towards the corruption and conspicuous improvidence of many members of the ruling royal family, personified in the character of the chain-smoking King Fahad who, following a stroke in 1995, was little more than a figurehead for the last ten years of his life.

In 2003, a strongly supported reform petition appeared and a public demonstration took place in the capital, Riyadh. It was swiftly broken up by police. The government responded by increasing the scope of the appointed Consultative Council and establishing elected municipal governments (2005). With political parties outlawed and women denied the vote, it was really just a gesture, especially when, in 2009, the upcoming elections were 'postponed' for 'evaluation'. As a sop, the ultra-cautious King Abdullah appointed US-educated Nora bint Abdullah al-Fayez to head the Department for Female Students – the kingdom's first woman minister. Meanwhile, the kingdom's dreadful record on human rights continued to attract the bitterest criticism.

After the 9/11 fundamentalist attacks, extremists targeted Saudis as well as foreign residents. Headline-catching events included the arrest and torture of British nationals, massive suicide bombings in 2003 and 2004, and the filmed and broadcast beheading of an American hostage. 2006 saw a failed attack on an oil installation and gunfights with Al-Qaeda. Further arrests and secret trials of Al-Qaeda supporters took place in 2009. In the south, Saudi forces tried to enforce a 10 km (6 mile) buffer zone along the border with Yemen to keep out Shia Houthi rebels (see page 81). The 75 km (47 mile) and 885 km (550 mile) 'security fences' along Saudi Arabia's borders with Yemen and Iraq brought into question Arab criticism of Israel's barrier along its border with the West Bank (see page 277).

While investing vast sums in the infrastructure of the country, Saudi Arabia was less successful than some oil-rich states in diversifying its economy. Part of the explanation was cultural: for years the country's enterprise sector had been reliant upon foreign workers. Reactions to international concern about carbon-related pollution included a multi-million dollar research project to make oil a 'greener' fuel, powerful lobbying against those hostile to fossil fuels (prominent at the 2009 Copenhagen Climate Change Summit), and steps to develop solar energy in the country's sun-soaked deserts.

KUWAIT AND THE GULF STATES

Of all the Gulf states, **Kuwait** was the one most subject to Western influence. This came from the presence of thousands of foreign troops and other military personnel on its soil, first in the War of Liberation (1990–1) and then in the US-led invasion and occupation of Iraq (2003 onwards). This external influence combined with the oil-rich emirate's tradition of comparative tolerance to produce a number of liberalizing reforms.

Having established the Gulf's first elected parliament, in 2005 Kuwait gave women full political rights. Four years later, it elected its first women MPs. In the same year, the courts ruled that women might apply for passports in their own right and were not obliged to wear Islamic head-dress. Even so, a more representative form of government inevitably brought problems. In 2003 and 2008, for example, Islamist candidates fared well. The Sabahs were criticized openly, too, and in 2009 the emir dissolved parliament to prevent it questioning Sheikh Nasser Mohammad al-Sabah, the prime minister and a royal family member, about allegations of corruption.

The **Bahrain archipelago,** a firm ally of the US and base of its fifth Fleet, became a constitutional monarchy in 2002. Although the Sunni Al-Khalifah family retained much power, the country continued to develop along liberal lines. It built up a flourishing tourist trade, allowed considerable freedom to the media and granted female emancipation. A remarkable example of Bahrain's new tolerance occurred in 2008 when Houda Nonoo, a Jewish woman, was appointed ambassador to the US. Nevertheless, tensions remained between the Shia majority and the Al-Khalifahs, and between Westernizers and Islamists.

Staggeringly high revenues from oil and gas gave those fortunate enough to live in twenty-first-century **Qatar** the world's second highest per capita income ($74,000). This, together with freedom of the press and TV and a burgeoning democracy, made the emirate a miniature haven of luxury for its inhabitants. Guided by the Al Thani family, Qatar stuck closely to its alliance with the US and therefore attracted some Islamic fundamentalist violence. By and large, though, it remained one of the most settled and harmonious states in the region. Its tolerant attitude, reflected in its official acceptance of the Roman catholic church (2008), made it an obvious home for Aljazeera, the leading Arab news agency.

The six states of the nearby **United Arab Emirates** (UAE), guided for many years by the Abu Dhabi sheiks, Zayed and his son Khalifa (UAE president from 2004 onwards), rivalled Qatar in wealth and toleration. Paradoxically, the UAE was slow to introduce democracy. Only in 2006 was the first advisory Federal National Council elected on a limited franchise of 6,689 souls, of whom 1,189 were women.

The UAE's vigorous economic liberalization and expansion ran into serious difficulties in 2009, notably in Dubai. The government-owned conglomerate Dubai World defaulted on its debt repayments, requiring a $10 billion bailout from super-rich Abu Dhabi. Nothing daunted, 2010 saw the opening of Dubai's Sheikh Khalifa al-Nahyan Building, the tallest in the world. For all its espousal of Western luxury, however, the UAE was still a strict Muslim state. As a reminder of this, in 2008 it jailed a British couple for having post-party sex on the beach.

YEMEN AND OMAN

The recently united **Republic of Yemen**, blessed with far less mineral wealth than its Arabian neighbours and the region's poorest state, struggled into the twenty-first century under the leadership of President Ali Abdallah Saleh. Nominally elected in 1999 (the chief opposition group was not permitted to field a candidate), Saleh maintained power through personal loyalty and the support of a powerful, US-backed army. The principal opposition came from Shia dissidents in the north (the Houthi; see page 81), Al-Qaeda and Common Forum, a coalition of religious and socialist groups demanding more representative government.

Already with a reputation as a safe haven for Islamist terrorists, in 2009 Yemen was believed to have received an influx of militants following the crackdown on Al-Qaeda in Afghanistan and Pakistan. The rumours were given some credence when a Yemeni branch of Al-Qaeda claimed responsibility for the planned attack on a Delta Airlines flight from Nigeria to Detroit on Christmas day 2009. Following a ceasefire with the Houthi early in 2010, Saleh's supporters both at home and abroad hoped he would be able to give his full attention to rooting out remaining Al-Qaeda cells.

Unlike in Yemen, the tourist trade flourished in twenty-first-century **Oman**. This was an indication of Sultan Qaboos Bin Said's success in bringing law, order and a modern infrastructure to his small but strategically important country. Although Oman allowed citizen representation through an elected, two-chamber Consultative Council chosen on a full adult franchise, real political power remained in the hands of the sultan. He maintained his state's traditionally strong links with Britain (which was believed to have used Oman as a base for operations in Afghanistan) and cultivated close relations with the US. Understandably, therefore, he willingly joined the anti-fundamentalist campaign, arresting dozens of suspects in 2005.

THINGS TO REMEMBER

1 *With its oil reserves estimated to account for over 80 per cent of the global total by 2020, the Middle East was central to the world's economic and political development in the new millennium.*

2 *Middle Eastern society often found it difficult to balance the appeal of Western culture with maintenance of regional traditions.*

3 *The population of the Middle East tripled between 1945 and 2000.*

4 *After the 9/11 attacks on the USA, Iran, Iraq, Libya and Syria were among the six states listed on America's 'axis of evil'.*

5 *Despite serious economic difficulties and much political opposition, Egypt's ageing President Mubarak remained in power well into the twenty-first century.*

6 *King Abdullah II of Jordan's progress towards the establishment of a constitutional monarchy in his troubled country was slower than many had anticipated.*

7 *Lebanon's return to prosperity and stability after long years of civil war was stalled by bitter political wrangling and a disastrous 'Summer War' with Israel in 2006.*

8 *The repressive and terrorist-supporting regime of Syria's President Hafiz Assad was maintained into the twenty-first century by his less impressive son, Bashar Assad.*

9 *Enormously wealthy and increasingly influential on the world stage, Saudi Arabia made painfully slow progress towards improving its record on human rights and representative government.*

10 *While the Gulf states of Kuwait, Bahrain, Qatar, the UAE and Oman all prospered and took steps to make government more accountable to the people, poverty-stricken Yemen was beset by terrorism and regional separatism.*

14

Tragedy and intransigence: Iraq
and Iran in the new millennium

This chapter will cover:
- *The US-led invasion of Iraq, 2003*
- *Resistance to the invasion and Iraq's insurgency*
- *Iraq's new constitution and government*
- *Iran during the first decade of the twenty-first century*
- *beleaguered Iraq.*

By the time the US condemned it as part of an axis of evil, Saddam
Hussein's Iraq was in a sorry state. A UN oil-for-food programme
had limited the country's income and not all the money intended
for food and medicine was spent on such necessities. The United
Nations Children's Fund (UNICEF) estimated Iraq's child poverty
to have doubled during the 1990s.

All along, Hussein had been playing a game of cat and mouse with
the UN Special Commission's inspectors charged with seeking
and destroying his stock of illegal weapons of mass destruction
(WMDs). After years of resistance, obfuscation and obstruction,
in 1998 the team gave up and withdrew. Britain and the US
responded with Operation Desert Fox, a bombing campaign to
'degrade' Hussein's WMD capacity, although how many remained
by this stage is uncertain. Hussein's rejection of a second UN
weapons inspection service, Unmovic, prompted fresh Anglo-US air
strikes in 2001. These drew a largely hostile international reaction.

Meanwhile, Hussein maintained his iron rule. Although the dictatorial prime-minister-cum-president had never been popular, his position was probably strengthened rather than weakened by the USAF and RAF attacks as they enabled him to justify his crushingly tight security and allowed him to demand patriotic support to combat 'imperialist' aggression. Backing came most readily from the Sunni minority. Iraqi Shia, whose spiritual leader was assassinated in 1999, did as they were bidden largely because they had little option: memories of the bloodletting after their unsuccessful 1991 rebellion were still raw.

MOTIVES AND REASONS

Britain and the US always regretted not having toppled Hussein's regime in 1991. They had other motives for attacking Iraq, too. President Bush, keen to avenge Hussein's attempted assassination of his father, had not been impressed by the Iraqi dictator's 'cowboys' remark about the 9/11 attacks (see page 237). He may also have coveted control over the Iraqi oil fields. Furthermore, the US hoped that a show of overwhelming military force might overawe their other enemies in the region and further afield.

None of the aforementioned motives for attacking Iraq were even whispered in public. Instead, the US president presented two further reasons why Hussein had to go. The first was the most dubious: that the Iraqi regime somehow had links with Al-Qaeda. No concrete evidence for this was ever forthcoming, and it is now patently obvious that though Hussein relished the sight of the collapsing Twin Towers, he had no time for the religious fanatics who brought them down. This left President Bush and his faithful

British ally, Labour Prime Minister Tony Blair, one further card to play: Iraq's supposed retention, contrary to the express demands of the UN, of WMDs.

President and prime minister declared that Hussein's retention of WMDs was sufficient reason for what they called 'regime change' in Iraq. Most of the rest of the world disagreed. They argued on two grounds: first, that Hussein's possession of WMDs was not proven and second, that pre-emptive action against another state because of what it might do was illegal in international law, especially without UN approval. The forceful removal of the Taliban had been expressly sanctioned by the UN Security Council. It was a moot point whether that body's resolutions specifically permitted military action against Iraq on the question of WMDs.

By 2002, the US and Britain seemed prepared to defy international opinion and take unilateral action against Iraq. At this point, Saddam Hussein, having refused to accept UN weapons inspectors for the past four years, agreed to let them return. Delighted, the Security Council passed Resolution 1414 saying that he would face 'serious consequences' if he did not co-operate with their work. In December, Hussein produced a monster 12,000-page document detailing the status of his weapons programme. A couple of months later, to the further embarrassment of Bush and Blair, leading weapons inspector Hans Blix announced that Iraq was co-operating with the UN team's work. Saying that he had not been 'watching the breaking of toothpicks' (BBC News, 16 January 2003), he cited as evidence the destruction of 40 Iraqi missiles. More significantly, he confirmed that he had found no evidence of remaining WMDs.

The Security Council was divided between doves and hawks. The latter comprised the US and Britain, who both said that Hussein still had WMDs and was merely playing for time. To clarify their legal stance, the British government also asked for a new resolution stating clearly that the 'serious consequences' of Resolution 1414 meant war. France, which had serious economic interests in Iraq, headed the opponents of regime change. Their position was that Hussein's wickedness was by no means unique in the world, and he should not be forcibly removed unless and until it was proved that he still possessed WMDs and was ready to use them.

In all probability, the Bush administration had set its heart on an invasion of Iraq many months before. The troops, missiles, ships and aircraft were all in position, and the battle plans prepared. That is not to say that Bush and Blair lied about Iraq's possession of WMDs – both almost certainly believed they were there. In the end, though, the illegal presence of the weapons was simply the most politically acceptable of a multitude of reasons for removing a man they believed was a real threat to world peace.

THE IRAQ WAR

In some ways the Iraq War (also known as the Second Gulf War) turned out as everyone had prophesied; in others it proved surprising and, to the invading coalition, even slightly embarrassing. The most predictable aspect of the conflict was its outcome. The invading US-British Coalition, backed by some 30 other states, including Albania, Australia, Denmark, Japan, Spain, and Uzbekistan, launched its attack on Iraq on 20 March 2003. Baghdad fell in mid-April and on 1 May President Bush, upright and proud on the deck of *USS Abraham Lincoln*, declared that the Coalition had won their victory and the campaign was over.

Also predictable was the precision of the Anglo-American assault with 'smart' bombs and missiles that destroyed Iraq's command and control structure even more swiftly than in 1991. The US also unleashed a new 'shock and awe' tactic based upon overwhelming firepower and 9.5-ton bombs (grimly nicknamed MOABs – the 'Mother Of All Bombs') that had the destructive power of a small nuclear device. The air attack was followed by armoured brigades tearing at great speed through the desert towards Baghdad. Equipped with the latest sighting equipment, US tanks destroyed their Iraqi counterparts even before they came into view. Although no Arab government openly declared its support for the invasion, the Coalition attacked from bases in Kuwait and other stations around the Gulf.

What most observers had not predicted was the extent of Iraqi resistance. Hussein's commanders knew there was little point in tackling the Coalition head on. Instead, specially trained Iraqi units, some known as 'Saddam Brigades', let the enemy roar by before emerging to attack them unawares from the flank and rear. This happened first in the Gulf port of Umm Qasr where 50 Iraqi soldiers held at bay the entire might of the US for six whole days – a feat of remarkable, even heroic resistance. The consequence of such rearguard actions – and debilitating sandstorms – was that a campaign optimistically predicted to be over in a fortnight dragged on for six painful weeks.

The attitude of ordinary Iraqis also took the Coalition by surprise. The invaders expected streets lined with cheering crowds greeting them as liberators. Instead, although there was some celebration and pulling down of grotesque statues of the dreaded dictator, the most common reaction to the Anglo-American soldiers was one of stolid, even sullen, indifference.

To wise observers, the lukewarm reception afforded the Coalition came as no surprise. Britain, after all, had been Iraq's imperial master and, together with its American ally, it had been blasting the country with bombs and starving its people with sanctions for the past 12 years. Nor would Muslims readily see an 'infidel' as a saviour. Had the Coalition forgotten how it had abandoned the rebels of 1991? Surely, too, it realized that Hussein's propaganda had been preparing Iraqis to reject the seemingly arrogant and overfed invader whose invasion had been heralded by a bloody bombardment of their homeland?

The war aroused enormous opposition right around the world. In dozens of cities, from London to Sydney, millions of men, women and children turned out in the streets to protest against what they saw as illegal bullying by an over-confident superpower and its ex-imperialist lapdog. The campaign also took an unexpectedly long time to achieve one of its prime objectives – the killing or capture of Saddam Hussein.

The initial plan was to take out the dictator right at the start of the conflict with a surgical strike on a base where he was believed to have been operating. The intelligence was wrong and the dictator escaped. Most of the other leading members of the regime were killed or captured relatively swiftly. Uday and Qusay, Hussein's detested sons, were killed in a shoot-out with US troops in July. But their fugitive father, with a huge bounty on his head, remained at large until December. Eventually, grey-haired, bearded and gaunt, the 'Butcher of Baghdad' was found hiding in a crude spider-hole beneath a farmhouse south of his home town of Tikrit. He had been sheltered not out of pity, admiration or fear but out of something the Coalition found difficult to comprehend: clan and tribal loyalty.

Insight

Previously always spruce in his public appearances, with neat, carefully dyed black hair, the Saddam Hussein dragged from his hiding place was shockingly transformed into a gaunt and grey-haired tramp.

Insurgency and democracy

COALITION AIMS

At the outset of its campaign, the Coalition gave itself three aims: the removal of Hussein, the rooting out and destruction of remaining WMDs, and the establishment of true democracy. The first of these was now achieved and, in October 2005, the ex-dictator was put on public trial in a heavily guarded Baghdad courtroom. Charged with killing 148 Shia in the village of Dujail in 1982, the defendant refused to accept the validity of the court. Interrupting, ranting, swearing, throwing himself about, pleading illness, and going on hunger strike, he made as much of a nuisance of himself as he could during his year-long trial. Three of the defence lawyers were killed by anti-Baathist elements. In the end, sure he was going to be condemned to death, the incorrigible ex-president demanded to be shot rather than hanged. His wish was not granted and he was executed on 30 December 2006.

Iraq's WMDs were nowhere to be found. As the UN inspectors had rightly surmised before the occupation, they did not exist. They had been destroyed in the early 1990s in response to international pressure. Their non-existence was formally declared in October 2004. Finally admitting his error, President Bush declared in December 2005, 'Much of the intelligence turned out to be wrong.' Nevertheless, he still justified the invasion on the less specific grounds that 'the American people and the world is better off because he [Hussein] is no longer in power' (BBC, 14 December 2005). There was little point now in pointing out, as UN Secretary General Kofi Annan had done in 2004, that such woolly justification for war was unacceptable in international law.

By this time Iraqi democracy was proving almost as elusive as the infamous WMDs. The problems were four-fold. First, in a state scarred by deep and overlapping ethnic, political and religious divisions, consensus was hard to find. Since its creation in 1921, Iraq had been dominated by a Sunni minority that comprised around 20 per cent of the population. The majority Shia group (perhaps 60 per cent of the population with their own holy places, such as Najaf and Karbala) saw the ousting of Hussein as an opportunity for settling old scores and asserting their authority. Fellow Shia in Iran were quite prepared to offer support. The large Kurdish population in the north, itself riven with hostile factions but eager for independence, made the situation still more complex.

Second, Iraq had never before experienced true democracy. The necessary traditions of freedom of expression, toleration and the rule of law could not simply be transplanted from Washington DC to Baghdad and expected to root and flower overnight. They needed time – a commodity the Coalition was short of.

Third, many Iraqis disliked the idea of a form of government being imposed on them from without. They were allowed to vote whether to accept it or not, but resented the fact that a foreign power – and an 'infidel' one at that – had brought the situation about.

Fourth, the more fundamentalist Muslims did not share the West's love of popular democracy and free-market economics. Both, they said, permitted licence, not liberty, and paved the way to selfishness and sin by pandering to people's baser instincts.

THE COALITION AND ITS OPPONENTS

The occupation force of around 170,000 troops was divided between 150,000 Americans, 8,000 British, 3,600 South Koreans, 1,700 Poles, 400 Australians and token contingents from Spain, Italy and elsewhere. The UN, eager to help with the reconstruction of Iraq, withdrew when its Baghdad headquarters was bombed in August 2003. More than a year later, it still had only 59 staff in the country. The British were based largely in the southern Shia capital of Basra. With years of peacekeeping experience, they had some initial success in being accepted by the local population and took relatively few casualties. Elsewhere, the Americans were having a much tougher time.

Not only did the US opt to handle the major confrontations, but its soldiers' heavy-handed tactics sometimes made them appear aloof and bullying. For example, US Marines were seriously criticized for the unnecessary killing of civilians while sweeping houses for opponents. The Coalition also scored spectacular own goals when revelations came to light of serious mistreatment of Iraqi prisoners and detainees. Although the offenders were duly questioned and dealt with, the damage done to the Coalition's image was incalculable. Its mission, after all, had been to liberate Iraqis from such inhumane behaviour.

The occupying forces chose the catch-all term 'insurgents' to describe their multifarious opponents. Some were the remnants of Hussein's old Baath Party, others simply disaffected youths. Still more were inspired by a heady mix of religion and nationalism. Foremost among these was the Mahdi Army of the fiery and unpredictable Shia cleric Moqtada Sadr. From the summer of 2004 onwards, his army was powerful enough to play a significant role in the way events panned out.

Although the extent of their involvement was difficult to pin down, Syria and Iran also lent support to the Coalition's opponents. Some sources said that ten per cent of all insurgent fighters were foreigners. The British faced Iranian armour-piercing weaponry, and US Secretary of State Condoleezza Rice (appointed November 2004) was sure of Syrian backing for at least some of the opposition. Taking advantage of the chaos, thousands of Al-Qaeda fighters infiltrated Iraq to side with the Sunni against Shia and Westerners alike.

VIOLENCE ESCALATES

At first the insurgents employed sniper fire, roadside bombs, car bombs, mortar attacks – whatever weapon or tactic might prove the most effective – to strike at Coalition forces. Occasionally, as when they were fighting for the Sunni city of Falluja in 2004, the US military engaged in large-scale action. By now, though, suicide bombers had made their appearance and what the Coalition had feared most was starting to happen: the anti-Western movement had splintered into a multi-factional conflict that was coming to look perilously like civil war.

At the risk of over-simplifying, the bulk of the violence took the form of Shia extremists (Iran-backed) v. Sunni; Sunni extremists (Al-Qaeda-backed) v. Shia; all militant opposition (including Baathists of the old regime) v. Iraq's new non-sectarian government; Kurdish extremists v. Arabs; Turkish forces v. Kurds; and all insurgent groups taking pot shots at Coalition forces when the opportunity arose. There were also attacks on the country's vital oil pipelines and other industrial plant. Zalmay Khalilzad, the US ambassador in Baghdad, admitted in March 2006 that the toppling of Saddam Hussein had opened a 'Pandora's Box' of anarchic turmoil.

As individual incidents are far too numerous to list, examples must suffice. In August 2003, 125 people were killed, including Ayatollah Mohammed Baqr al-Hakim, when a car bomb exploded in the Shia city of Najaf. In March the following year 140 died when suicide bombers struck Shia festival-goers in Karbala and Baghdad. The new US-backed government was the target in September 2004 when a large bomb went off near Baghdad's central police station, killing and injuring dozens.

The situation deteriorated sharply in 2005 and 2006: 114 were slain by a car bomb in south Baghdad in February 2005, the worst single incident since the start of the insurgency; 67 separate attacks were recorded in April 2005 alone and in August civilian and military casualties were averaging 60 a day. By the following summer, the UN estimated that this figure had risen to over 100 a day – and that was just civilians. Only occasionally was the Coalition able to claim any notable success. Once such incident occurred in June 2006 when Abu Musab al-Zarqawi, the Al-Qaeda leader in Iraq, was killed in an air strike. The previous September he had demanded extermination of all Shia as bedfellows of the Western 'crusaders'.

DISILLUSIONMENT

As well as costing hundreds of American lives, Iraq was hitting American pockets: by early 2006, taxpayers were forking out some $4.7 billion a month to sustain the operation. In August, the total bill had reached an astounding $311,088,969,000. By then, over 50 per cent of Americans believed that their country should never have gone into Iraq in the first place and about two-thirds of them felt President Bush had handled the situation badly.

If Americans were disenchanted, the Iraqis were close to despair. Unemployment stood at around 50 per cent in 2006 and inflation was running at a savings-destroying 70 per cent. The economy, potentially one of the most buoyant in the world at a time of soaring oil prices, was at best stagnant. Education and health services had collapsed in many areas; corruption, smuggling and other malpractices were widespread, and life expectancy had fallen to 57 for men and 60 for women. In 2004, around 70 per cent of Iraqis had viewed the future with optimism; by 2005 this had fallen to 50 per cent, and under 40 per cent a year after that. Small wonder, then, that an estimated 2.2 million Iraqis had fled abroad.

A SPREADING CONFLICT

Coalition action in Iraq fuelled Islamist extremism elsewhere. By 2004, Al-Qaeda was estimated to have 18,000 operatives at large in 60 countries. No country that had supported the Coalition was safe. In May 2003, bomb attacks rocked the Saudi Arabian capital, Riyadh. Four days later, 45 died when Western and Jewish targets were hit in Casablanca, Morocco. In December it was the turn of Turkey, where two synagogues, the British consulate and a British bank were blown up.

2004 saw further shooting in Riyadh and a bomb attack on the Madrid rail network that left 191 commuters dead and more than 1,800 injured. The following year, London became the terrorists' target when, on 7 July, four suicide bombers blew up underground trains and a bus, killing dozens and injuring hundreds. Al-Qaeda bombs later smashed two hotels in Amman, Jordan, killing 56. Many more planned terrorist attacks were foiled before they took place. In 2006, for instance, security forces uncovered a plot to bring down aircraft with liquid explosives carried in hand luggage. Rather than making the world safer, it seemed, the removal of Saddam Hussein had served only to make it markedly more dangerous.

CREATING A CONSTITUTION

Despite mounting unrest, the Coalition and its supporters pressed ahead with giving Iraq a genuinely democratic system of government. The plan was for a provisional government to assume power at the end of June 2004, for elections to a provisional assembly six months later, and for this assembly to agree a constitution to be put to the people. The UN accepted the arrangement and on 30 June 2004 a Provisional Authority under the leadership of long-term exile Ayad Allawi took over nominal rule of the country. This formally ended the occupation. The Authority could, in theory, ask all foreign troops to leave, but as it was dependent upon their presence until Iraq's own security forces were recruited and trained, this remained a purely academic option.

In January 2005 some 8 million Iraqis elected a Transitional National Assembly, although the majority of Sunnis (98 per cent in some areas) refused to vote. Undaunted, the Assembly elected a Kurdish president (Jalal Talibani) and two deputies, one Shia and the other Sunni. These in turn chose an interim prime minister, the Shia Ibrahim Jaafari. A Constitutional Committee then drew up a constitution for an Islamic federal democracy. On 15 October, despite rejection in two Sunni provinces, it was approved by the electorate.

Insight

The long arm of Saddam: Born Ibrahim al-Eshaiker, after fleeing Iraq in 1980 to work for opponents of the Baathist regime, Ibrahim al-Jaafari had to change his name in order to protect those of his family whom he had left behind.

The last step was taken in December 2005 when, amid tight security, nation-wide elections – described by Al-Qaeda as a 'satanic plot' – were held for the country's first 275-seat National Assembly. The turnout was over 70 per cent, with most Sunnis now joining in. Chosen for four years, the Assembly comprised 230 seats allocated according to the population of each of Iraq's 18 provinces. The remaining 45 seats were distributed among parties whose support was spread over more than one province. Remarkably for an Islamic nation, one-third of each party's candidates had to be women.

The Shia-led United Iraqi Alliance (UIA) won the most seats, but no overall majority. Three months of wrangling followed before a coalition administration was finally brought together. This was achieved only after the re-elected Jalal Talabani had put forward a Shia compromise candidate, Jawad al-Maliki. In April 2006, he was accepted as Iraq's prime minister.

Towards settlement

THE SURGE

By the end of 2006, many commentators believed that the Coalition's mission in Iraq was going nowhere as violence mounted and the country slid towards disintegration. As evidence of how bad things had become, the UN reported that 34,000 Iraqi civilians had been killed in 2006 in civil violence of one kind or another. US President George Bush and his advisors decided that as withdrawal, implying defeat, was unacceptable, the only way forward was to make a greater effort to win the battle against the insurgency.

The result was the US administration's New Way Forward, popularly known as the 'Surge'. It involved a clampdown on security by deploying 20,000 more US troops and extending the tour of duty of those already in Iraq. The new forces were concentrated in Baghdad and in the deeply troubled province of Al Anbar, to the west of Baghdad. The largest of Iraq's provinces, Al Anbar's Sunni population was widely infiltrated by Al-Qaeda sympathizers who were able to slip across the long, sparsely populated borders with Syria, Jordan and Saudi Arabia.

At first, the Surge seemed to have the opposite effect to that intended. The 130 deaths caused by a bomb in a Baghdad market in February 2007 was the heaviest loss of life in a single incident since the early days of the insurgency. Nor did it mark the peak of atrocity: two months later 200 men, women and children were slain in a single day. May saw 300 members of the Iraqi security forces killed, and the number of violent attacks of all kinds reach a staggering 1,400 each week. US service deaths rose, too, from near 100 in January 2007 to close on 120 by July. Then, quite rapidly, the tide began to turn.

By the new year, weekly attacks had fallen to fewer than 600; Iraqi military deaths per month averaged 70, while those for the US forces were around 10. Thereafter, for some 18 months, the scale and number of attacks continued to decline, although they never ceased entirely. The British handed over control of Basra in July 2007 and withdrew entirely two years later. By 2008, the US was also giving control of provinces to the Iraqis. In September, in a move of great significance, the Americans felt confident enough to pass security operations in the Sunni stronghold of Al Anbar to the country's Shia-led government. The following year, President Obama's new Democrat administration announced a plan to pull the majority of US forces out of Iraq by mid-2010, followed by a total withdrawal by the end of the following year.

OUTLOOK UNCERTAIN

The US Surge played a key role in ending Iraq's civil turmoil. Other factors were at work, too. The re-modelled Iraqi army had grown more effective with each month that passed: in 2008, it proved strong enough to take on and overcome Moqtada Sadr's Shia-based Mahdi Army in its Basra stronghold. The willingness of the Coalition to work with Sunni tribal leaders, notably in Al Anbar, was another factor helping to restore law and order. The new Iraqi government was settling down, too, and, under the astute leadership of Prime Minister al-Maliki, it and the constitution under which it operated were slowly winning the hearts and minds of the people. Exhausted by years of killing and occupation, ordinary Iraqis had become increasingly unwilling to tolerate all forms of extremism. The vast majority of them wanted nothing more than to get on with their normal lives in peace.

Insight

One of the most infamous incidents of the entire US occupation of Iraq involved civilian security guards working for the Blackwater Worldwide security organization. On 16 September 2007, while escorting a US State Department convoy, the guards shot dead 17 innocent Iraqi civilians in an orgy of unprovoked slaughter.

By 2010, however, lasting peace and stability were still a long way off. The relationship between Kurdistan and the rest of the country remained strained and there was periodic fighting along the Kurds' border with Turkey. Further south there was tension along the Iranian border, too. At the end of 2009, terrorist attacks were also on the increase once again. The Islamic State of Iraq, a group linked to Al-Qaeda, claimed over 350 lives in bomb outrages.

Perhaps more serious because they demonstrated the fragility of Iraqi democracy, sectarian disagreements caused the elections due at the end of 2009 to be delayed until March 2010. The eventual outcome of the vote, which left the secular Al-Iraqya group with two more parliamentary seats than al-Maliki's shaky State of Law Coalition, led to further deadlock as the country's elected representatives were unable to agree over the make-up of the necessary coalition administration. What lay ahead, therefore, no one dared predict with any degree of certainty.

Twenty-first-century Iran

MODERATE MOVES

Iran was in a state of flux at the beginning of the new millennium. With around half of the country's 69 million inhabitants under the age of 25, discontent with the rule of the conservative old men who had overthrown the shah and led the country during the immensely costly war with Iraq was all but inevitable (see page 167). Ayatollah Khamenei, who in 1989 had replaced the trailblazing Ayatollah Khomeini as Iran's Supreme Leader, was almost as rigid in outlook as his predecessor had been.

In the 1990s, technological developments such as satellite television and the internet gave the country's young population almost uncontrollable access to a more liberal world. This fuelled the tension between them and the strict Islamic revolutionaries. The man who sought to bridge this gap was the moderate cleric, sometime newspaper editor and minister of culture, Mohammed Khatami. Elected president by an overwhelming majority (70 per cent) in 1997, he relaxed censorship and encouraged a more liberal interpretation of Islamic law. The new mood was captured in the massive pro-democracy protests at Tehran University in 1999. The anti-liberal establishment responded by making thousands of arrests.

The Iranian constitution reserved supreme authority to Shia religious leaders, but it did embrace a considerable degree of popular participation. In 2000, the people's will made itself felt in a way that dismayed conservatives: Khatami supporters and liberals won 170 of the 290 seats in the Majlis (parliamentary assembly), leaving the hardliners with a mere 44 seats. The liberal swing was maintained with Khatami's re-election the following year.

Lest it be thought that Iran was returning to the pro-Western days of the Shah, it is worth remembering that it continued to fund Islamic extremist groups like Hezbollah. Furthermore, whatever Khatami and his young supporters might have wanted, the final say in all matters still rested with elderly and conservative clerics supported by the judiciary. These occupied the so-called Assembly of Experts, charged with appointing the country's Supreme Leader and the Guardian Council. Able to veto legislation and bar candidates from standing for election, this body of six theologians had effective control of Iran's development. By labelling them 'anti-Islamic', it vetoed liberal reforms on many occasions.

NUCLEAR POWER

The difficulties faced by Iran's moderates at home were matched by hostility abroad. Broadly speaking, this had two sources. The first stemmed from the country's nuclear power programme, the second from its association with Islamic terrorism.

In the autumn of 2002, Iran began to build its first nuclear reactor at Bushehr. Even before this, rumours were circulating about the country's plans to produce uranium suitable for use in a nuclear weapon. Alarmed, the International Atomic Energy Authority (IAEA) sent an inspection team to see what was going on. Although not given all the access they wanted, the inspectors realized that Iran had not been open about its nuclear activities. At a meeting with three European foreign ministers in 2003, the Iranians duly agreed to stop producing enriched uranium. At the end of 2003, they signed a protocol to this effect.

Barely two months later, Iran was again accused of dabbling in dangerous nuclear activity, this time using technology bought from Pakistan. The IAEA and the US once more insisted that Iran cease such activities. Further negotiation led to a provisional halt in nuclear experimentation. The EU remained suspicious, however, and in 2004 threatened trade and economic sanctions if Iran ignored the IAEA and resumed its weapons programme. At this point the government in Tehran changed and the whole issue assumed a much greater importance.

ABOUT TURN

President Bush's condemnation of Iran as part of his 'axis of evil' in January 2002 had caused outrage among Iranians of every class and persuasion. The moderates felt particularly depressed; in their struggle to liberalize the country they needed American support, not hostility. Massive anti-clerical protests in the summer of 2003 confirmed Khatami's popularity among the urban young and middle classes, although by now events in neighbouring Iraq were beginning to prise open an alarming gap between them and their potential American allies.

The extent to which Iran interfered, officially or unofficially, in the affairs of Iraq during the insurgency was unclear. Certainly the establishment was eager to assist fellow Shia in their efforts to throw off years of Sunni domination. Although direct help was difficult to prove, the US and Britain were sure that the Shia insurgents received support, official or unofficial, from within Iran (see page 260).

The worsening relations between the West and Iran played into the hands of the country's conservatives. The presence of Western troops just across the border, killing Muslims in the name of liberal democracy, also set back the moderate cause. Moreover,

Khatami's backing in the countryside and among the poor had also been wearing thin because his much vaunted reform programme had failed to provide the promised jobs and improved wages. As a result, in February 2004, greatly assisted by the disqualification of thousands of moderate candidates, the conservatives took back the Majlis. The next year, to the surprise of almost everyone, Tehran's ultra-conservative mayor, Mahmoud Ahmadinejad, triumphed in the presidential election.

MAHMOUD AHMADINEJAD

The West found Iran's new president hard to fathom. His revolutionary credentials were impeccable: he had played a key part in setting up the student union that had seized the US embassy in 1979 (see page 159); he claimed to have the interests of the poor and needy close to his heart; and he was undoubtedly a devout Muslim. At the same time, he was Iran's first non-clerical president for almost a quarter of a century, and his 2009 cabinet was the first since the foundation of the Islamic Republic to include women.

Ahmadinejad's nationalist and anti-Western rhetoric was highly inflammatory, whether he was talking of Iran's 'inalienable right' to produce nuclear material or saying that the State of Israel should be wiped off the map. Several commentators believed, however, that his bark was worse than his bite as his words were intended more to boost his support at home than as statements of actual policy. Similarly, his cat-and-mouse tactics over Iran's nuclear programme (see below) might well have been to raise his country's profile on the world stage and ensure that it got the best possible terms for not going ahead with the production of nuclear material.

There were others who claimed that real power within Iran did not rest with Ahmadinejad anyway, but with the less accountable Islamic coterie of the Supreme Leader, Assembly of Experts, Council of Guardians and Council for Discernment of Expediency – and, increasingly, the Revolutionary Guard. Established in 1979, the 125,000-strong Guard had become much more than an élite fighting force. From the 1990s onwards, it had been gathering a vast and deeply corrupt business empire that included construction projects, hotels, airlines and telecoms. This sinister development led US Secretary of State Hillary Clinton to warn in 2010 that Iran was in danger of becoming a military dictatorship.

TERROR THREAT

A few months after Ahmadinejad's election, Iran was once again at odds with the IAEA when its work on uranium conversion was condemned for breaking the internationally accepted nuclear Non-Proliferation Treaty. The confrontation continued to the end of the decade. The UN Security Council became seriously involved in 2006 and from 2007 onwards Iran was subject to penalizing industrial, travel and economic sanctions, although China and India were reluctant to throw their weight behind these measures.

Insight

By 2010, 189 states, including Iran, had signed the 1970 Treaty on the Non-Proliferation of Nuclear Weapons. Four states who had not signed up (India, Pakistan, North Korea and Israel) were known or believed to possess nuclear weapons.

Hard facts were difficult to come by, as Iran made inspection difficult and insisted that it was developing nuclear fuel for domestic purposes only. Moreover, Ahmadinejad pointed out, there was no need for anyone to worry about Iran misusing its nuclear fuel programme, because Supreme Leader Ayatollah Khamenei had issued a fatwa (religious condemnation) against nuclear weapons. The IAEA begged to differ, saying in 2010 that Iran was indeed seeking to make a nuclear weapon.

The discovery of a secret nuclear site at Qom in 2009 hardly helped the Iranian case. Nor did its development of new rockets, such as the medium-long range Sajjil-2 capable of reaching Israel and Eastern Europe. However, the international community's real worry stemmed less from official Iranian action than from its links with terrorist groups like Hezbollah. The ultimate nightmare was that a nuclear weapon might find its way into the hands of fanatics prepared to embrace death, including suicide, for what they saw as a righteous cause. Would extremists of this persuasion view a nuclear holocaust in quite the same way as the rest of the world?

AHMADINEJAD'S RE-ELECTION

Ahmadinejad's presidency boasted few successes. His state-led and largely unsuccessful efforts to help Iran's growing number of poor alienated the business community. Conservative clerics worried about his mystical religious beliefs. Reformers and moderates of all persuasions took strong exception to the rigorous censorship and increasing human rights abuses taking place under his leadership. Amnesty International, for example, announced that executions in Iran rose from 177 in 2006 to 350 in 2008, eight of them of prisoners under 18.

The right-wing clampdown manifested itself in the 2008 Majlis elections in which, after many opposition candidates had yet again been barred from standing, conservatives won over 60 per cent of the seats. The presidential election of June 2009 produced a far greater scandal when Ahmadinejad was declared winner with 24 million votes. In 2005, he had polled 17 million. Furious crowds took to the streets to protest against what they claimed was blatant vote-rigging. During the worst public disorder since 1979, some 30 people died and an unknown number – probably over 1,000 – were arrested. Two of those detained were executed early the following year. Further riots took place in December 2009 after the death of the popular cleric Grand Ayatollah Hoseyn Ali Montazeri.

In the face of increasing international isolation for its obdurate stance over nuclear development and shaken at home by political dissent and serious economic difficulties, by 2010 the outlook for Iran was at best uncertain.

THINGS TO REMEMBER

1 *The reasons why the US wished to impose a 'regime change' on the Baathist regime of Saddam Hussein were more complex than a simple wish to remove its weapons of mass destruction.*

2 *A US-led coalition that included Britain, Spain, Australia and Japan invaded Iraq on 20 March 2003.*

3 *Although Saddam Hussein and his supporters were overcome relatively swiftly, the invasion force was not widely welcomed and Iraq swiftly descended into chaos.*

4 *The 'insurgency' in Iraq developed into a complex sectarian, political, regional and nationalist bloodletting in which thousands of Iraqis were killed and millions fled abroad.*

5 *Al-Qaeda spread Islamist terrorism from Iraq to wreck havoc in Saudi Arabia, Morocco, Madrid, London and other cities.*

6 *In 2004–5, the Iraqi republic produced a new constitution whose citizens elected their first 270-seat National Assembly.*

7 *The situation in Iraq finally began to settle down when the US launched a massive security surge in 2007.*

8 *Between 1997 and 2000, moderate reformers came to power in Iran and began to relax some of the republic's illiberal practices.*

9 *The Iranian conservatives returned to power with the election of President Mahmoud Ahmadinejad in 2005. His government was condemned around the world for not complying with international protocol regarding the manufacture of nuclear material.*

10 *The re-election of Ahmadinejad in 2009, widely believed to have been the result of a rigged election, led to violent anti-government protests.*

15

Israel–Palestine in the new century

This chapter will cover:
* *the situation in Israel–Palestine at the start of the new millennium*
* *the death of Arafat and the incapacity of Sharon*
* *the Hamas–Fatah split and Lebanon's Summer War*
* *the ongoing search for peace.*

New century, old problems

AFTER OSLO

By the start of the new millennium the population of Israel had risen to over 6 million, approximately double the number of Palestinians living within what were known as the Emerging Palestinian Autonomous Areas (2.4 million in the West Bank and 1.2 million in the Gaza Strip). Israel also retained possession of East Jerusalem and the Golan Heights. Jerusalem was Israel's official capital, although few states recognized it as such. Successful peace negotiations meant that Syria was the only Arab state technically still at war with Israel.

The peace process between Palestinians and Israelis that had begun with the Oslo Accords and continued with the Wye River Memorandum (see pages 212–24) was stalled. Quite how little the Israelis had been prepared to give way is borne out by crude figures.

Of the 5,900 sq km (2,270 sq miles) of the West Bank, only 342 sq km (130 sq miles) were under the direct rule of President Yasser Arafat and the Palestinian Authority. A further 2,189 sq km (845 sq miles) were under joint Israeli-Palestinian administration. The rest (well over half) remained in the hands of Israelis, of whom scarcely 200,000 lived there. Within the Gaza Strip, territory which the Israelis had no great desire to hang on to, the picture was different. Of the enclave's 363 sq km (140 sq miles), 236 sq km (91 sq miles) were administered by the Palestinian Authority. The Strip's Israeli population was a mere 7,000.

The Israeli prime minister, 72-year-old Ariel Sharon, had been elected in February 2001 on the slogan 'security and true peace'. With only 19 of his own right-wing Likud Party in the Knesset (the Israeli parliament), he had been obliged to form a coalition government that included members of the Labour Party. For example, Sharon's old Labour rival, Shimon Peres, took the position of foreign minister in this 'Government of National Unity'.

The ferocity of the Second Intifada had taken the Israeli authorities by surprise. Employing bombs and suicide attacks rather than stones and insults, it was on a different scale from the first. Radical groups like the PFLP, Hamas, and Islamic Jihad competed with Arafat's own terrorist-style unofficial militia, Fatah Tanzim, to cause the most damage and loss of life. The violence had destroyed Prime Minister Barak's peace policy and led to the election of Prime Minister Sharon.

Insight

Between 1996 and 2001, Israel's prime ministers were directly elected. Netanyahu (1996), Barak (1999) and Sharon (2001) were chosen in this manner before the country reverted to the previous system in which the president chose a commanding Knesset politician for the post of prime minister.

THE SECOND INTIFADA AND 9/11

Sharon's political record, besmirched by tales of provocation, corruption and deliberate slaughter, was hardly one to inspire hopes of a compromise, and few were surprised at the dismay with which the Palestinians greeted the hardliner's election. Hamas, the uncompromising Palestinian group that emerged out of the First Intifada, launched into the first of what it said would be ten suicide bombings by Islamic 'martyrs'. True to its word, an attack on Israeli civilians in the seaside town of Nelanya was followed by further bloody bombings across the country. Hamas received vocal and, many believed, financial and military backing from Iran, perhaps via Syria.

The Israelis responded to the Hamas onslaught with 'targeted killings' of those believed to be urging and planning the suicide missions. It also isolated Palestinian communities thought to have had links with the killers. As part of these operations, Yasser Arafat was confined to his West Bank HQ in Ramallah. Reprisals sparked more suicide attacks, and so the cycle of killing continued in the new millennium much as it had in the old. A well-meaning attempt by ex-US senator George Mitchell to find a peace plan came to nothing. On 1 June 2001, a particularly bloody suicide bombing, blowing up 20 young Israelis at a Tel Aviv disco, served only to cement prejudices.

Insight

Whereas the First Intifada had been very much an instinctive rebellion of stone-throwers, the Second was an altogether more organized, more Islamist and more murderous affair.

Sharon had little faith in peace talks. Instead, his aim was 'unilateral disengagement'. This involved replacing Arafat and the Palestinian National Authority with more moderate alternatives, taking out the leading militants by armed strike, and defending Israel with insurmountable physical barriers. As even moderate Palestinians would not enter talks until they knew where such negotiations might lead, both sides continued to perpetrate acts of unspeakable violence against each other.

The effect on the situation of the 11 September attacks on New York was two-fold. Initially they simply reinforced US support for the Israelis, whom it now viewed as fellow victims of Islamic terrorism. In the longer term, it led the US and other Western governments to realize that a comprehensive Middle East peace settlement – essential if global terrorism were to be undermined – had to rest on a solution to the long-standing Israeli–Palestinian conflict. From that realization sprouted small shoots of hope.

ARAFAT ISOLATED

The Second Intifada caused many more Israeli deaths than the First: by late July 2002, some 800 of them had died compared with almost 1,800 Palestinians. As well as small-scale 'decapitations', Israel launched larger-scale counter-Intifada operations in 2002. Each involved attacking Palestinian militants in Gaza with heavy armour and jet aircraft. Homes and other buildings were smashed, hundreds arrested and suspicious characters were shot on sight. Talk of a civilian massacre was later disproved.

Three other incidents caught the attention of the world's media. One was the siege of militants holed up in the Church of the Nativity, Bethlehem; the second was the destruction of nearly all Arafat's compound in Ramallah; the third was an Israeli air attack on positions inside Syria that were said to be used as guerrilla training camps. Hardship within the occupied territories mounted week by week. Unemployment rose to 50 per cent and GDP dropped to half its 1999 level.

By now Arafat's reputation outside Palestinian circles had taken a dreadful battering. In May 2001, the IDF seized arms allegedly being shipped to the PFLP on board the *Santarini*. As the Palestinian National Authority (PNA) was apparently going to bring the weapons ashore, this was a blow to Arafat's public declaration that the PNA had no links with armed action against Israel. Seven months later, a cache of weapons, including rockets, mortars and missiles, was supposedly found on a vessel actually owned by the PNA, which also employed the crew. The arms were bound for the Al-Aqsa Martyrs Brigades.

Finally, when the Israelis overran Arafat's compound they carried off papers that purported to prove that Arafat's government was deeply corrupt and had directly provided militants with money for weapons and bomb-belts. Of course, these three incidents could have been clever Israeli fabrications. In the event, though, they were sufficient for Sharon to condemn Arafat as 'irrelevant' to the peace process and for President Bush to reject him in favour of an alternative Palestinian leader 'not compromised by terror'.

THE SECURITY FENCE

By the spring of 2002, Sharon was implementing the second part of his 'unilateral disengagement' strategy: a 'security fence' separating Israel from the West Bank. Based on the principle behind existing fortifications around Gaza, for most of its length the eventual fence was a battlefield-style barrier of cleared land and barbed wire. Whatever its effectiveness – and the Israelis said it led to a considerable reduction in cross-border attacks – the image the fence sent out to the rest of the world was aggressively negative. Barriers were associated with repression, specifically with communist Eastern Europe during the Cold War. The barrier also ran into legal problems. The decision by the International Court of Justice (July 2004) that the fence was illegal was ignored by the Israeli government, but it did re-route parts of it in accordance with a ruling from its own Supreme Court.

The obvious path for the barrier was along the 'green line' established between Israel and Jordan at the time of the 1949 ceasefire. Sharon, however, wanted as many Israeli settlements as possible behind the fence, including several built on land occupied in 1967. Thus places like East Jerusalem, Ariel, Oranit, and Maale Adumim found themselves on the Israeli side of the fence, while some Palestinian towns like Marda were virtually surrounded by it. Disagreement over the barrier was one of reasons why Labour left Sharon's Unity government in November 2002, leading to the administration's collapse.

Peace plans and disengagement

THE ROADMAP

Seeking to resolve the debilitating conflict that had destabilized the Middle East for so long, in February 2002, Crown Prince Abdullah of Saudi Arabia had proposed that if Israel withdrew to its pre-1967 frontiers, the Saudis would do all they could to ensure that it received full recognition from the Arab world. The plan was officially endorsed at the next month's Arab summit. Although Sharon rejected the proposal out of hand, the US reserved judgement.

In fact, the Bush administration was working on a peace plan of its own. The 'Roadmap to Peace' adopted the earlier step-by-step approach, but with a definite goal – a two-state solution – and precise waymarks along the route. The Map was formally launched the following year with the full backing of a powerful 'Quartet' of powers: the US, the EU, Russia and the UN. In theory, at least, it was irreproachable.

Seeking to end Israel's political chaos, Sharon defeated Netanyahu for leadership of Likud. Elections to the sixteenth Knesset, held in January 2003, returned him to power at the head of a conservative coalition based around Likud's 40 seats. By now, the Bush administration was pressing Yasser Arafat, whom they had completely given up on, to appoint a prime minister. Legally speaking, he should have done this years earlier. Eventually, in March 2003, the Palestinian premier gave the post to a long-standing PLO member and colleague, Mahmoud Abbas (also known as Abu Mazen).

AQABA

Now there was a leading Palestinian whom they felt they could trust, in April the Quartet put forward the Roadmap. Phase one involved (i) the Palestinians ending all violence, confiscating illegal weapons and establishing true democracy; (ii) Arab states ceasing to support 'terrorist' groups like Hamas; (iii) Israel building no more settlements on occupied land and abandoning those built since September 2000. Phase two would lead to the establishment of an independent and democratic Palestine. Phase three would finalize frontiers, sort out the status of Jerusalem, and determine the right of return for Palestinian refugees. The target date for completion was December 2005: laudable, certainly, but in no way realistic.

Sharon and Abbas duly met at a US-brokered summit in Aqaba – the US was already the Quartet's driving force. Having agreed the outline of the Roadmap, the Israeli prime minister accepted the concept of a sovereign Palestine, and Abbas called for an end to the Second Intifada. Harmony lasted just days. The slaying of Israeli soldiers and a failed assassination attempt on Hamas leader Abdulaziz al-Rantissi prefaced further suicide attacks and targeted assassinations. Impotent to control the extremists within his movement and despairing at Arafat's unreliability, Abbas resigned in September and was replaced by Ahmed Queia (also known as Abu Ala), a PLO financial expert.

DISENGAGEMENT

With immediate hope of compromise gone, Sharon decided to press ahead with his disengagement strategy. The plan, borrowed from Labour, was to withdraw from Gaza and parts of the West Bank and rest secure behind impenetrable barriers. To an astounded international community, in November 2003 Sharon announced that Israel was to begin its withdrawal, starting with Gaza, in six months' time. It was no peace plan, but it did demonstrate a willingness on the part of one of Israel's most fervent patriots to abandon at least some of the fruits of the 1967 war. Although President Bush welcomed the move, Sharon's coalition partners were not impressed.

Meanwhile, the tit-for-tat killings and reprisals continued unabated. Occasional suicide and rocket attacks took place, while Israeli security forces harassed ordinary Palestinians in both the occupied territories. In March 2004, gunships killed the wheelchair-bound paraplegic Sheikh Yassin, Hamas' founder and spiritual leader, as he was being led from a Gaza mosque. Hamas said the act had 'opened the Gates of Hell'. A month later, Israeli assassins finally got Abdulaziz al-Rantissi, the head of Hamas in Gaza, leaving only one of Hamas' original founders still alive. In such circumstances, finding his task as impossible as Abbas had done, Prime Minister Ahmed Queia proffered his resignation. Arafat rejected it out of hand. With his faction-ridden Fatah close to open conflict with Hamas, the seriously ill Palestinian president needed all the support he could get.

When Likud walked out in April 2004, Sharon's coalition fell apart and he was left heading a minority government. Palestinians were divided over how to react. Pragmatists saw Sharon's policy as a step towards compromise. The militants, on the other hand, saw Israeli withdrawal from Gaza as evidence that their violence worked. Such differences stoked Palestinian inter-communal violence, especially between Fatah and Hamas within Gaza itself. And all the while, militants kept up their drizzle of home-made Qassam rockets into Israel, provoking a number of violent reprisals on the territory Israel was about to leave.

THE DEATH OF ARAFAT

The year ended with the death of Yasser Arafat. Imprisoned within his Ramallah compound for the better part of two-and-a-half years, his health had seriously declined. Finally, when he was found to be suffering from a mysterious blood disorder, his wife insisted on flying him to Paris for treatment. Following a massive stroke, he died there on 11 November 2004. To this day, a good many Palestinians insist he had been poisoned by Mossad.

Insight

When Arafat's widow Suha refused permission for an autopsy to determine the cause of her husband's death, she left the way open for a flood of accusations and theories. Suggested causes of death ranged from food poisoning to deliberate poisoning, an unknown infection and AIDS.

Arafat's funeral, held in Cairo for security reasons, attracted heads of state from all over the world, although no official Israeli representative attended. Sharon having vetoed use of Jerusalem's Al-Aqsa mosque, the body was buried in Ramallah amid extraordinary scenes of hysterical chaos. As the mob fired guns in air thick with screaming, shouting and wailing, the old warrior was laid to rest as he had lived – in passionate disorder.

Almost everything written about Arafat is in some way true. A fine guerrilla leader and an able orator, he understood the Palestinians and their cause better than anyone. By turns amusing, charismatic, brave, inspiring and determined, he also had deep, serious weaknesses. Disorganized, autocratic, corrupt, tactless, unsophisticated and cursed with a furious temper, he was a poor diplomat and a hopeless administrator. More than anyone else, he created the modern Palestinian nation and made the world recognize it. At the same time, his failings were crucial in preventing it from becoming a state.

SHARM AL-SHEIKH AND THE TAHEDIYEH

Now Arafat was out of the way, pragmatists on both sides of the divide hoped international mediation would finally find a way of ending the 56-year feud. They were sadly mistaken. For all his faults, Arafat had given the Palestinian cause focus. Now he was gone, cracks expanded rapidly into wide fissures. Within a year, peacemakers faced not two irreconcilable parties, but three.

Mahmoud Abbas took over as chairman of the PLO on 11 November 2004 and two months later, with 61 per cent of the vote, he was elected president of the Palestinian National Authority. Over in Israel, Sharon formed a National Unity Government from members of Likud, Labour and the left-wing Zionist party Meimad. In February, the two leaders met with President Mubarak of Egypt and Jordan's King Abdullah II in the Egyptian resort of Sharm al-Sheikh.

Benefiting from a constructive and cordial atmosphere, progress was made through the Roadmap agenda. The Intifada was declared over, ceasefires and prisoner exchanges were announced, and Sharon promised to withdraw the IDF from certain Palestinian towns. Although Islamic Jihad did its best to spoil the party by launching a suicide bombing in Tel Aviv, the Knesset and Israeli cabinet endorsed the plan to abandon all Israeli settlements in Gaza and a further four in the West Bank.

Palestinian groups meeting in Cairo responded with a *tahediyeh* (a 'slowing down', usually interpreted as a ceasefire) that suspended attacks on Israel. Optimism rose still higher when the IDF pulled out of Jericho and Abbas held a meeting with President Bush at which the Palestinians were offered $50 million in aid if the *tahediyeh* became permanent. That was as far as it went. Sharon was coming under increasing criticism from the right and Abbas was sorely troubled by the widening rift between Fatah and Hamas. When the two met with US Secretary of State Condoleezza Rice, neither was prepared to make any significant concessions. Smooth words failed to hide the summit's failure.

OUT OF GAZA

The killing of five Israelis by an Islamic Jihad suicide bomber ended the *tahediyeh* a few weeks after the sterile summit, ushering in a new period of violence. The Israelis reoccupied troublesome Palestinian areas and resumed targeted killings of notable *fedayeen*. Hamas stepped up the rain of rockets across the Gaza border, making a mockery of the 'security fence' philosophy. Israel said the rockets were smuggled across the newly opened Rafa crossing between Gaza and Egypt. Even more worrying, after 20 Gazans had died when a car load of Qassam rockets exploded accidentally and Hamas had outdone Fatah in local elections, by the end of 2005 the two major Palestinian factions were close to all-out armed conflict.

Still backed by the IDF, Sharon had pressed on with the Gaza withdrawal. Although there was some violent Israeli opposition, the operation passed off relatively smoothly and by 11 September the last Israeli had quit the Strip. Sharon cashed in on the inevitable international goodwill to call before the UN in New York for peace and wider recognition of Palestinian rights. Progress, therefore, had been made. Nevertheless, Gaza alone could not make a Palestinian state. And, with each day that passed, the Israeli presence in the West Bank and in East Jerusalem was becoming more and more deeply entrenched.

Olmert, Abbas and Hamas

EXIT SHARON, ENTER HAMAS

In November 2005, cross-border violence in one form or another continuing unabated, Sharon's new coalition broke up. The prime minister responded with a dramatic move: abandoning Likud, he founded a new liberal, centrist political party called Kadima ('Forward' or 'Onward'). He was joined by ex-mayor of Jerusalem Ehud Olmert, Minister of Justice Tzipi Livni, Labour leader Shimon Perez and many other Israeli politicians. Peace with the Palestinians was the key plank in the Kadima platform.

There were several reasons for this somewhat surprising development. Some said that the apparent change of heart by the Israeli 'Bulldog' was mere rhetoric. Others suggested he was motivated by a wish to go down in history as a great statesman, Sharon the Peacemaker. More pragmatic explanations included the rising cost of the ongoing conflict, both in financial and human terms. The Second Intifada had claimed 1,000 Israeli lives, unemployment was over 10 per cent and poverty was rising. The US, which was pumping some $3 billion annually into Israel, was also pressing for some good news to relieve the uninterrupted gloom coming out of Iraq.

Whatever Sharon's motives had been, he never got time to set them down in his memoirs. On 4 January 2006, he was laid low by massive brain haemorrhages and never recovered consciousness. In elections held three weeks later, Hamas won 74 seats out of

the 133 in the Palestinian National Assembly. It had promised
an end to Fatah corruption and endless, ineffective talk. In their
place, it offered a fresh start and real help for all people. But it also
promised never to surrender one square millimetre of Palestinian
territory to Israel, whose existence it did not even formally
recognize. What hope the peace process now?

DESCENT INTO CHAOS

Sharon's demise and the surge of support for Hamas ended the period
of optimism triggered by Arafat's death. Years of suffering followed
as Palestinian divisions widened and Israel's disproportionate
responses to attacks remained as brutal as ever. In Gaza, the worst
affected area, life became almost unbearable.

Israel refused to recognize the new Hamas-led Palestinian
administration. It would not talk to Prime Minister Ismail Haniya and
suspended all revenues previously payable to the PNA. The US, the EU
and other states stopped their aid to a regime that openly supported
acts condemned as 'terrorist'. The PNA was saved from total collapse
only by funds smuggled in from Russia and Iran, and later by EU
money brought in via non-governmental organizations (NGOs). Even
then, a high proportion of the funding was siphoned off by corrupt
officials before it reached those for whom it was intended.

Relations between President Abbas of Fatah, who sought talks and
a compromise deal with Israel, and the Hamas-led government of
the PNA, which advocated an Islamic armed struggle against Israel,
were steadily deteriorating. Each side had its armed forces. Fatah
controlled the official PNA security apparatus and turned a blind
eye to other supportive militant groups. Hamas had an 'Executive
Force' that operated apart from its military wing, the Izz ad-Din
al-Qassam Brigades. By mid-2006 violent conflict – kidnappings,
shoot-outs, assassinations and so forth – between Fatah and the
Islamists was commonplace. In Gaza, where Fatah was under
most pressure, it was almost endemic. As a consequence, Abbas
was unable to stop the steady bombardment of Israel by Qassam
rockets. Some 1,000 were launched in the first half of 2006 alone.

The sole hopeful sign came, interestingly, in the form of a document produced jointly by Palestinian prisoners detained in Israel. The National Conciliation Document of the Prisoners recognized Israel and backed President Abbas to create a Palestinian state in the West Bank and Gaza. Sadly, as it did not conform to the criteria of the Roadmap, the Document received little international support.

Insight

In the remarkable Palestinian National Conciliation Document of the Prisoners (May 2006), ex-Fatah leader Marwan Barghouti joined with members of Hamas, the PFLP, Islamic Jihad and the DFLP to agree a coalition government that could negotiate for an independent Palestine.

OLMERT

Leadership of the Kadima Party was now in the hands of Ehud Olmert. With an election due, his party fleshed out its unilateral disengagement policy. It was soon clear that Kadima's proposal for withdrawal from the West Bank was much less extensive than many had anticipated. Essentially, years of putting the 'facts on the ground' had meant 400,000 Israelis now lived in the occupied territories. As no government could contemplate removing such a number, Kadima proposed maintaining an Israeli presence in Hebron and in the Jordan Valley, and including major settlements, like Gush Etzion and Maale Adumim within Israel. This left a potential Palestinian state comprising just 22 per cent of the territory allocated to it by the UN in 1948.

The new party's manifesto was sufficiently attractive for Olmert to return at the head of a new coalition headed by Kadima and Labour. Observers of the March 2006 election suggested that a low turnout (63 per cent) and scattered voting patterns reflected a disenchanted and fragmented society. Maybe, but this did not stop Olmert taking firm action to try stopping the rocket rain from Gaza. (Hezbollah was said to be rewarding each launch with US $1,000.) In June 2006, following the kidnapping of an Israeli soldier by Islamists, the IDF launched Operation Summer Rains. Although the massive air and land attack on Gaza killed a number of militants, it brought fresh misery to thousands of civilians and neither rescued the Israeli soldier nor stopped the rockets.

THE SUMMER WAR

After the IDF withdrew from southern Lebanon in 2000, the peace along Israel's northern border had been punctuated by nothing more serious than the occasional artillery shell and small rocket. All the while, though, the Iranian-backed Shia of Hezbollah had been building up their forces – especially stockpiles of anti-tank weapons and short-range rockets – in southern Lebanon. In July 2006, perhaps to draw attention away from Iran's row with the international community over its nuclear plans (see page 270), Hezbollah stepped up its cross-border activity.

When three Israeli soldiers were killed and two more captured, Olmert's government ordered a full-scale attack on Hezbollah. It was preceded by air and artillery strikes designed to 'set Lebanon back' 20 years. TV audiences around the world were regaled with shocking images of civilian losses and the apparently wanton destruction of essential facilities such as roads, bridges and power-plants. Hezbollah guerrillas, positioned in areas of high-density civilian population in the border region, were well prepared, and for the first time the IDF failed to sweep all before it. It lost men, tanks and heavy armour as it tried to wipe out pockets of Hezbollah resistance. All the while, rockets continued to fall on the Israeli cities of Haifa, Tiberias and Safed. Hezbollah even scored at sea, hitting an Israeli cruiser with an Iranian-made C-802 missile.

When a UN ceasefire took effect in mid-August, 1,000 Lebanese and 120 Israelis lay dead. For all the destruction it had wrought, Israel had failed to recapture its missing soldiers. More significantly, Hezbollah claimed victory and its stock within the Arab world, especially within Lebanon, rose markedly. Elsewhere, Israel was widely blamed for starting the conflict and pursuing it with unnecessary force and brutality. At home, the Olmert government was attacked from left and right for its handling of the war. Rallies demanded the prime minister's resignation. Already under suspicion of corruption, he was further criticized both by cabinet colleagues and in an internal report into the ill-fated Summer War.

Insight

The prime corruption charge against Ehud Olmert (April 2010) was that, when mayor of Jerusalem, he accepted massive bribes (over US $500,000) to accelerate residential development within the city.

THE HAMAS COUP

Olmert and Abbas attempted to restore their fortunes by resurrecting the peace process. A summit in late 2006 was followed the next year by one with President Mubarak of Egypt and a second with US Secretary of State Condoleezza Rice. As neither the US nor Israel was prepared to include Hamas, little progress was made. Hamas itself was more interested in consolidating its position in Gaza where, by early 2007, the situation was worse than ever. Over the previous year, 270 Israeli air raids had smashed the main power station and brought widespread destruction and loss of life. That, together with the collapse of effective government and the severance of international aid, had driven about 80 per cent of the population into poverty.

Hamas struck in June, launching a bloody but ultimately successful coup in which it seized control of the Strip at the expense of Fatah. European observers monitoring the Rafah crossing with Egypt were dismissed and thousands of weapons, provided by the US and others to enable the PNA to tackle the Islamists, came into Hamas' hands. The post-coup administration of Gaza was hardly an improvement on what it had replaced. The Hamas commanders in Damascus squabbled for power with the local leaders of such groups as the Izz ad-Din al-Qassam Brigades, Islamic Jihad and Popular Resistance Committees. Despite, or because of, swingeing international sanctions against Gaza, rocket attacks on Israel intensified.

There were now in effect two Palestines-in-waiting: one in the West Bank, recognized by the international community, and a second in Gaza. In the former, a short-lived Unity Government having failed, Abbas appointed the moderate economist Salam Fayyad as his prime minister. There were now two men in the office as the previous incumbent, Ismail Haniya, refused to quit. To all but the most intractable optimists, the Israel-Palestine problem looked as far from solution as it had ever been.

More jaw, more war

ANNAPOLIS

Gaza and Lebanon were by no means Israel's only security concerns. A far more serious threat, it appears, was materializing in Syria. The details remain obscure, but in September 2007 Israeli jets violated Syrian airspace – apparently with US approval – to destroy a mysterious rectangular building located in remote desert. President Assad's government said it had contained a stockpile of conventional rockets. His enemies claimed it was an embryonic nuclear facility under construction with the help of North Korea.

For all his reduced authority, Abbas pressed ahead with the peace process. First, he single-handedly changed the Palestinian Legislative Assembly's electoral system to proportional representation. While he said this was to make the parliament more representative, his critics grumbled that it merely helped Fatah. Second, in November 2007, he met with Secretary of State Rice and Prime Minister Olmert at the US Naval Academy in Annapolis, Maryland. The trio were joined by President Bush and representatives from the Quartet, Arab states and other influential nations, including China.

Annapolis achieved no breakthrough, but it was the first such meeting at which all parties agreed a common two-state solution based upon the 1949 armistice position. Abbas suggested six areas for future discussion: borders, Jerusalem, refugees and the 'right of return', Israeli settlements in the West Bank, the distribution of water resources, and security. On his side, Olmert conceded that part of Jerusalem ought eventually to become a Palestinian capital. Compromise concessions such as this drew furious criticism from hardliners on both sides, but the delegates left Annapolis with a clear idea of the road ahead. Indeed, as news filtered through of promising Turkish mediation over discussions about the Israel–Syrian border, there was even talk of a brighter future ahead.

TRUCE

The optimistic mood gathered momentum in the summer of 2008, despite the year not starting well on the Gaza front. During the customary round of rocket attack and reprisal, in January Israel severed Gaza's fuel supplies. Desperate, Hamas blew up the Rafah crossing. Before Egypt could re-seal the border, thousands of Gazans had poured into Egypt to stock up on much needed supplies. After that, the deadly tit-for-tat warfare resumed with fresh vigour.

Then, in June 2008, Hamas surprisingly announced an Egypt-brokered *tahediyeh*. The rockets slowed to a shower (launched by groups beyond their control, said Hamas), prisoners were exchanged and the blockade of Gaza was provisionally lifted. As it controlled the rebuilt Rafah crossing, Gaza's only reliable access point to the outside world, Egypt is believed to have pressured Hamas into the ceasefire.

The new mood of optimism did not save Prime Minister Olmert. His government pleased hardliners by allowing 1,300 new housing units in East Jerusalem, and it fostered the Fatah–Hamas divide by letting Fatah supporters enter Israel from Gaza and by supplying arms to the PNA. Nevertheless, the mounting allegations of corruption forced him to announce that he would serve only to the February 2009 elections. He remained in office until that date because his Kadima replacement, Foreign Minister Tzipi Livni, was unable to form a coalition.

Remarkably, the mood of international optimism regarding the Israel-Palestine problem was maintained almost to the end of the year. Fresh faces helped. The French President, Nicholas Sarkozy, sought to use his country's long-standing links with Syria to bring that country in from the cold. In November 2008, Barack Obama, another peacemaker, was elected to the White House and a further meeting of the Quartet in Sharm al-Sheikh reiterated the way ahead established at Annapolis.

THE GAZA WAR

As so often, the situation was too good to last. And it didn't. Cross-border attacks from Gaza had been escalating throughout the autumn. Israel was hit by around 340 explosive devices between 4 November and 18 December 2008. Some of these were the larger, Russian-made Grad or 'Katyusha' rockets. Somewhat superfluously, Hamas declared that the *tahediyeh*, already a dead letter, would officially end in mid-December. The Israeli cabinet met and decided that, as there was no point in trying to reason with Hamas, the alternative was their only option. They had to smash it.

The IDF went in eight days after the *tahediyeh* ended. Operation Cast Lead started with air attacks followed by a massive ground operation involving heavy armour as well as infantry. The estimated 20,000 armed Gazans were totally outgunned and resorted to still more rocket attacks and tough street fighting. Large numbers of civilian casualties were inevitable in such a crowded, largely urban environment. Hamas reports, denied by Israel, said 700 civilians, including 400 children, were killed. When it withdrew in early January, the IDF reckoned it had slain some 725 Hamas fighters at the cost of ten Israeli soldiers and three civilians. A UN report of September 2009 said both sides had been guilty of war crimes.

After the war, Hamas stopped its cross-border rocket bombardment.
Despite this, Israel had once again lost the propaganda war as graphic
images of civilian misery and the appalling destruction of homes,
mosques and schools flashed around the world. In vain did the Israeli
government claim that the suffering was self-inflicted because Hamas
had placed its fighters among civilians. In the longer run, though,
the war might have made the wretched, starved and battered civilian
population of Gaza more likely to accept a compromise peace: Hamas
had probably never commanded more than around 20 per cent of
their support (Aljazeera TV, quoting opinion polls of January 2010).

In the short term, however, little changed. The 1.4 million
inhabitants of Gaza, including over 1 million registered refugees,
remained blockaded in hardship and poverty. With the security at the
Rafah crossing extended underground to counter tunnelling, it was
increasingly hard to bring in even the basic necessities of life. Disease
and malnutrition were rife, the region's infrastructure was ruinous,
its people desperate, its government arbitrary and disorganized. By
2010, it was hard to imagine a worse place to live in the entire world.

ABBAS AND NETANYAHU

President Abbas' term of office officially ended in 2009. Fearing
chaos if he stood down, he remained in office and negotiated for
Palestinian National Assembly and presidential elections to be held
simultaneously in June 2010. He said he would not stand himself
unless Israel honoured its pledges to further the peace process by
stopping construction in East Jerusalem and the West Bank.
Hamas rejected all talk of elections, saying it would punish Gazans
who participated.

Although Kadima gained one more Knesset seat than Likud in the Israeli elections of February 2009, Tzipi Livni was again unable to form a coalition. President Peres then invited Likud leader Benjamin Netanyahu to try his hand at forming a government, something he eventually managed to do with the support of right-wingers and Labour. Once his Government of National Unity was in power, Netanyahu showed himself more prepared to talk peace than he had indicated during his election campaign. In September 2009, he agreed with Presidents Obama and Abbas that talks on the Roadmap should be resumed shortly. Nothing happened, and he annoyed both the PNA and the White House by sanctioning yet more construction in occupied territory. He placed a further block on the path to a two-state solution by supporting a law that obliged the government to hold a referendum on the issue before any existing settlements in the occupied territories could be abandoned.

During the first months of 2010, preparations for peace talks were again mooted. With Hamas remaining outside the process and Israel proving intransigent over settlement construction, the prospects were not good. Nevertheless, the fighting had died down, the Roadmap and the Annapolis route were still available, and there were moderates on both sides desperate to move things forward. There was even talk of the West Bank unilaterally declaring itself a Palestinian state.

Perhaps these signs were hopeful? Yet Israelis and Palestinians and well-meaning mediators had been charged with hope so many times before, and on each occasion their dreams had faded into nightmares. One day it will be different. When that time will come, though, only history will eventually tell.

THINGS TO REMEMBER

1 *By 2000, the population of Israel (6 million) was approximately double that of the Palestinians living in the occupied territories of Gaza and the West Bank.*

2 *In the early years of the new millennium, the alleged discovery of arms dealing and secret support for terrorism destroyed Yasser Arafat's credibility as a peacemaker in the eyes of the West.*

3 *In 2002, Israel began building a 'security fence' between itself and the West Bank. Its path, cutting into occupied territory to protect Israeli settlements, caused anger and hardship.*

4 *A 'Quartet' comprising the US, the UN, the EU and Russia presented a Roadmap along which it was hoped that Israel and the Palestinians could progress towards a peaceful settlement.*

5 *As part of Prime Minister Sharon's disengagement strategy, Israel pulled out of its settlements in Gaza in 2004.*

6 *President Yasser Arafat died in a Paris hospital on 11 November 2004 and was buried in Ramallah on the West Bank. Mahmoud Abbas, a Fatah stalwart willing to compromise with Israel, replaced him as president of the Palestinian National Authority.*

7 *Early in 2006, Prime Minister Ariel Sharon, founder of the new Kadima Party, was totally incapacitated by two massive brain haemorrhages.*

8 *Israel's new prime minister, Kadima leader Ehud Olmert, engaged his country in a highly destructive and ultimately unsuccessful Summer War against Hezbollah in Lebanon (2006).*

9 *In 2007, feuding between the Islamist Hamas, which rejected compromise with Israel, and Fatah, which was willing to negotiate for a Palestinian state, came to a head when Hamas seized control of Gaza.*

10 *Negotiations at Annapolis, Maryland, USA (2007), produced a set of concrete proposals that inched the peace process forward but did not stop Hamas–Israeli conflict for long.*

Glossary

Al-Aqsa Martyrs Brigades Extremist offshoot of Fatah.

Alawis (also Alawites) Religious sect claiming affinity to Shia Islam.

Arab One who speaks Arabic.

Arab League Organization of Arab states formed to promote cultural, economic and political co-operation.

Arab Legion British-trained (Trans) Jordanian army.

Ashkenazim Jews of European origin (specifically from Poland and Germany).

Ayatollah Shia religious leader.

Caliphate Empire comprising the entire Muslim world.

DFLP Democratic Front for the Liberation of Palestine.

Druze Religious offshoot of Islam with separate leaders and emphases.

Fatah Yasser Arafat's Palestinian guerrilla organization that developed into the largest Palestinian political party.

fedayeen Palestinian guerrillas.

Gaza Small strip of territory beside the Mediterranean Sea with Gaza City at its heart.

Greater Israel Israel extending across both banks of the River Jordan.

Gulf, the Persian or Arabian Gulf.

Haganah Jewish guerrilla organization of the pre-Israel era.

Hamas Palestinian organization fiercely opposed to Israel.

Hezbollah Iranian-backed organization fiercely opposed to Israel.

IAEA International Atomic Energy Authority.

IDF Israel Defence Force.

Intifada Palestinian uprising against Israel.

Irgun Jewish guerrilla (terrorist) organization of the pre-Israel era.

Islamic Jihad Anti-Israeli guerrilla (terrorist) organization.

Islamist Shorthand, catch-all phrase used in the West to describe militant Islamic groups dedicated to combating the West and promoting Islam by force.

Jihad Muslim holy war.

Kadima Israeli political party of the centre-right founded in 2005.

Knesset Israeli parliament.

Likud Israeli right-wing political party.

LNM Lebanese National Movement, largely Shia organization to help Lebanon's Muslim majority.

Maronite Lebanese Christian group.

Mizrahim Jews of Middle Eastern or Central and Southern Asian descent (but see Sephardim).

Mossad Israel's secret service (officially the Institute for Intelligence and Special Operations).

NATO North Atlantic Treaty Organization.

occupied territories Lands on the West Bank of the River Jordan, and around Jerusalem and Gaza City, conquered by Israel in 1967.

OPEC Organization of Petroleum Exporting Countries.

Ottoman Empire Former Turkish Empire.

Persia Iran.

PFLP Popular Front for the Liberation of Palestine.

Phalange Right-wing Lebanese Christian paramilitaries.

PLA Palestine Liberation Army.

PLO Palestine Liberation Organization.

PNA Palestinian National Authority.

PNC Palestine National Council.

Qassam rockets Home-made Palestinian missiles.

Rafah Crossing point between Egypt and Gaza.

Roadmap Israel-Palestine peace process drawn up by the US in 2003.

Sephardim Jews of eastern origin, specifically those of Spanish, Portuguese or North African origin, but used here more loosely, as is customary, for all those not of Ashkenazi origin (see Mizrahim).

shah Hereditary ruler of Iran/Persia.

sheikh Arab chief.

Shia Minority branch of Islam centred around Iran.

Sinai Largely desert peninsula between Israel and Egypt.

Sunni Majority branch of Islam.

tahediyeh Ceasefire.

Transjordan Original name for the state of Jordan.

UAE United Arab Emirates.

UAR United Arab Republic.

West Bank Land on the west bank of the River Jordan captured by Israel in 1967.

WMDs Weapons of mass destruction.

Zionism Movement for the establishment and maintenance of a Jewish state.

Taking it further

Objective history of the Middle East in recent years is rare, if not impossible: researchers are advised to consult as many sources as possible. Here are a few starting points:

Books

Abrahamian, E., *A History of Modern Iran* (Cambridge University Press, Cambridge, UK 2008)

Aburish, S. K., *Arafat: From Defender to Dictator* (Bloomsbury, London, 1999)

Alavi, N., *We are Iran* (Portobello Books, London, 2005)

al-Rasheed, M., *A History of Saudi Arabia* (Cambridge University Press, Cambridge, UK, 2002)

Etherington, M., *Revolt on the Tigris* (Cornell University Press, Ithaca, New York, 2005)

Fisk, R., *Pity the Nation: Lebanon at War* (André Deutsch, London, 1990)

Franklin, D., *A Peace to End All Peace* (Orion, London, 2003)

Hinchcliffe, P. and Milton-Edwards, B., *Conflicts in the Middle East since 1945* (Routledge, London, 2007)

Keay, J., *Sowing the Wind: Seeds of Conflict in the Middle East* (John Murray, London, 2003)

Keddie, N. R., *Modern Iran: Roots and Results of Revolution* (Yale University Press, New Haven, Connecticut, 2003)

Laqueur, W. and Rubin, B. (eds), *The Israel-Arab Reader* (Penguin, London, 2001)

Lewis, B., *The Middle East, 2000 Years of History* (Phoenix Press, London, 2000)

Ross, D., *The Missing Peace* (Farrar, Straus & Giroux, New York, 2004)

Ross, S., *Understand the Israeli-Palestinian Conflict* (Hodder Education, London, 2010)

Schulze, K. E., *The Arab–Israeli Conflict* (Longman, Harlow, 2008)

Shindler, C., *A History of Modern Israel* (Cambridge University Press, Cambridge, UK, 2008)

Shlaim, A., *The Iron Wall: Israel and the Arab World* (Penguin, London, 2001)

Tripp, C., *A History of Iraq* (Cambridge University Press, Cambridge, 2007)

Tyler, P., *A World of Trouble: America in the Middle East* (Portobello Books, London, 2009)

Websites

Israeli government website:
http://www.israel.org/mfa

History in the news:
http://www.albany.edu/history/middle-east

Modern history sourcebook:
http://www.fordham.edu/halsall/mod/modsbook54.html

Arab Gateway:
http://www.addameer.org/september2000/front.html

BBC:
http://news.bbc.co.uk/1/hi/world/middle_east/default.stm

CNN:
http://edition.cnn.com/WORLD/meast/archive

Pars Times (Iran):
http://www.parstimes.com/Iran_history.html

Arab world:
http://www.arab.net

Aljazeera:
www.aljazeera.com

Disclaimer

The publisher has used its best endeavours to ensure that the URLs for external websites referred to in this book are correct and active at the time of going to press. However, the publisher has no responsibility for the websites and can make no guarantee that the site will remain live or that the content is, or will remain, appropriate.

Index